Business Background Investigations

Tools and Techniques for Solution Driven Due Diligence

By Cynthia Hetherington

PO Box 27869
Tempe, AZ 85285
800.929.3811
www.brbpub.com

Business Background Investigations
Tools and Techniques for Solution Driven Due Diligence

©2010 By Cynthia Hetherington and BRB Publications, Inc.

First Edition, 2nd printing

ISBN: 978-1-889150-49-9

Written by: Cynthia Hetherington
Edited by: Kim Ensenberger and Michael L. Sankey
Cover Design by: Robin Fox & Associates

Cataloging-in-Publication Data
(Provided by Quality Books, Inc.)

Hetherington, Cynthia.
    Business background investigations : tools and
techniques for solution driven due diligence / by
Cynthia Hetherington. -- 1st ed.
    p. cm.
    Includes bibliographical references and index.
    ISBN-13: 978-1-889150-49-9
    ISBN-10: 1-889150-49-5

    1. Business enterprises--Evaluation--Handbooks,
manuals, etc. 2. Business enterprises--Information
resources--Handbooks, manuals, etc. 3. Business--
Research--Methodology--Handbooks, manuals, etc.
I. Title.

HD30.4.H48 2007   338.7
                  QBI07-600234

Acknowledgements

First and foremost, this book is dedicated to my family for their open minds, encouraging spirit and fathomless patience.

I would not be the professional I espouse to be without the mentors I have learned so much from. I would like to thank William Vincent, William Majeski, Dr. William Tafoya, Michael Geraghty, Ann Sparanese, Kathleen Lehmann, Lucille Bertram, Vincent and Pamela Amico, Jimmie Mesis, and the fine members of the Association of Independent Information Professionals as well as the National Association of Legal Investigators. From these professionals I have learned about business, research and investigations.

It is impossible to comprehend the amount of time and effort that goes into writing a book until you have produced one. Michael Sankey, CEO of BRB Publications, Inc., and Kim Ensenberger have spent hour after hour turning my "talky style" and Jersey'ism's into pearls of wisdom. There would be no *Business Background Investigations* book without their tireless editing pen. Nor would this text exist without Mark Sankey, who started me down the path from a lecturer to an author.

In closing, I wish to recognize the over 6,000 lecture audience members, consisting of business and industry professionals, federal, state and local law enforcement, researchers, security and private investigators that encouraged me to write after years of lecturing. I have often learned more from them then I felt I brought to the podium. I hope this work makes us even. :)

You have all made this book possible.

Cynthia Hetherington

Table of Contents

Business Background Investigations

Chapter 1 Introduction to Business Investigations 11

The Necessary Skill Set; The Information Edge; Who Uses Business Investigations; Types of Business Investigations; Information Retrieval Language; Selling Information; Key Chapter Points

Chapter 2 Learning to CRAWL 21

Communicate; Research; Analyze; Write; Listen; I Can hear You, But I Don't Know What You Are Saying; Key Chapter Points

Chapter 3 Research & Analysis Fundamentals 33

Research Basics; Collecting and Tracking Information; Know the Market or Industry; Using Industry Journals; Using Government Agency Resources; The Basics on Analysis; SWOT Analysis; Value Chain and Supply Chain Analysis; CARA Analysis Key Chapter Points

Chapter 4 Discovering & Dissecting Company Information 49

Identify the Type of Business Entity; Researching Publicly Owned Companies; Understanding Private Ownership and Investors; Identifying Small Companies; Identifying the Large Company Structure; How to Locate the Company Headquarters; Parent Companies, Subsidiaries, Divisions and Affliates; Franchises; Non-profit and Charitable Entities; Identifying and Researching Key Location Concerns; Recommended Online Database Services; Other Sources of Note; Key Chapter Points

Section 3: Putting It all Together 211

Section 4: The Appendix 239

The Index 281

Section 1

Setting the Foundation

This section examines important elements needed to prepare an investigator when performing a business background investigation.

The first two chapters present a hard look at the required skill set and essential fundamentals needed by an investigator to be competent.

The last chapter is an in-depth examination of how to perform strategically-directed research and analysis. Research and analysis are the necessary tools for gathering information and discerning the correct conclusions.

Chapter 1

Introduction to Business Investigations

An investment in knowledge always pays the best interest.
—Benjamin Franklin

Business investigations examine the backgrounds of businesses and the principals who run them. *Business Background Investigations* is applicable to all professionals who are involved in investigations, helping them and their clients, insurance and risk managers, attorneys, and security practitioners. Regardless if the investigator is a military analyst looking for terrorist assets, or a Wall Street general counsel looking for a hedge fund, learning the tactics to research businesses will help in solving investigations.

The Necessary Skill Set

My goal in writing this book is to give you the insight and education to perform quality business investigations. You will learn analysis techniques, how to solve research challenges, and be introduced to hundreds of Web sites and online resources. However, beyond reading, writing, and looking up a Web page, there are other skills necessary when conducting business investigations.

The business investigator[1] must understand various businesses, principals, industries, economics, finances, and risks. This is not to say that expert knowledge is required in each area, but a basic knowledge in these areas within the corporate world is necessary so that valuable information is not missed when investigating. The challenge comes when researching specific businesses, as you work to understand the specific type of industry that your target company is involved in. For example, one day you might be investigating a computer software developer with locations in India, Israel, and California. You will need to learn about and become familiar with the computer software industry, the players in the business, and become familiar with the language of computer technology. In addition, the legal issues for Israel and India, and the

---

[1] Also known as a corporate investigator.

implications of having businesses located in those countries, may come into play during the investigation.

There are four key areas that are indispensable to a business investigator.

1. A **sense of imagination and determination** is necessary. This is especially true when investigating cases involving crimes, fraud, or deception. An investigator's dogged determination is the catalyst to keep pushing through the mounds of information that need to be uncovered. An investigation is not for the lazy, but is for the individual who is easily consumed in picking apart minutiae, one fact at a time.

   Tracking lead after lead can be mentally exhausting, especially when cases go from days to weeks, and months to beyond. But when a fact makes itself apparent, and you realize that the marathon research you have been doing to get there was the sole reason for finding that key piece, you feel like you have won the lottery. That is the moment when you can hear "Yahoo!" coming out of my office.

2. Another necessary skill, which can sometimes be a struggle, is **proficiency with a computer**. Knowing word processing, spreadsheets, Web browsers, email, and anti-virus software are the basics to be an able online investigator. Everyone eventually learns these basic skills. But good investigators must take a step beyond. Your work will benefit greatly if you learn how the Web works, how email is transmitted, and information is stored. The important consideration here is that most of today's corporate crimes in some way involve a computer.

3. What else what makes some business investigators better than others? Good investigators **speak the language**. Understanding the business community and the industries you may be associating with will help you win over clients, as well as give you a better knowledge base to perform business background investigations.

4. Perhaps the biggest necessary skill is to know how to gain **the information edge**.

Information Edge

The differences between everyday investigators and business investigators are evident by the tools used to find the needed information in order to properly investigate a case. Every investigator will likely tell you that he or she conducts business or corporate investigations. Unfortunately, saying you are conducting a business investigation is not the same as actually executing an investigation. Those who dedicate themselves to this avenue of research provide themselves with the proper sources, education, and understanding of the market they serve.

A fundamental understanding of how businesses are organized is necessary for all investigators, no matter if they are due diligence researchers, computer-crime forensic examiners, or arson investigators[2]. Business investigators need to know the difference between a Limited Liability Partnership, a Limited Liability Corporation, and a Sub-Chapter S Corporation. They need to

---

[2] Check out a sampling of the different types of investigators from the New Jersey Licensed Private Investigators Association, Inc. Web site at www.njlpia.com/codes.shtml.

know how to read a balance sheet, how to find the trade associations connected to business operations, and how to use a company's annual report as an investigation tool.

They will find that public companies may have volumes of data ready for the taking, but to obtain specific information may require going offline. The search for private company and foreign company information requires knowledge of the specific industry or country. Most importantly, business investigators realize their limits with databases and online sources, and know when to bring in the interviewers, conduct on-site inspections, and explore other traditional investigative tactics.

Author Tip ➡ I have worked with my own arsenal of databases that exceeds 2,500 services and may even be double that amount. I have spent plenty of time (as I would encourage the reader to do) sitting and learning about these sources so that I could understand what I was paying for and the limitations. Even a free service like www.freeerisa.com has details to learning the extent of information and the value offered.

I cannot stress enough the importance in always taking the time to review the source. You must know if you are getting first-hand information, public records, private sources, or just obtaining an aggregated pool of data that is put into a fancy report.

But, you do not need to subscribe to thousands of databases to be a smart and successful business investigator. The databases that I feel are necessary to conduct investigations intelligently are highlighted throughout this book. However, you will need to know the services you are using intimately to answer the on-the-spot questions from your clients about your reports. Knowledge of where information comes from and how to obtain the most current sources possible are also necessary.

Every time I lecture, the question arises: "How do you keep up with the newest Web sites and sources?" My answer is always the same: "Keep your nose in the news, read the journals, buy books on research, venture into industries you are not immediately tied to, join associations, and communicate." When I teach and share my sources, I always get two in return.

Finally, business investigators must maintain an information edge as they run their own businesses. For example, an arson investigator is a professional who is hired to assess how a fire occurred and spread throughout a building. He is paid for his analysis of what occurred, for presenting the evidence, testifying in court, and writing reports or depositions. But an arson investigator also should be an expert in this unique field so that he can examine a building and offer suggestions to prevent fires.

The edge in knowledge is to *know*. Know more about the tools you use, know more about the products coming out on the market, know your client's needs and know your limitations!

Who Uses Business Investigations?

Consider the following everyday scenarios—

- To find new clients you research a prospective list of attorneys in a geographical area.
- You are interested in a new product, but it is expensive and you want to check its ratings.
- You are committing to a long-term relationship with an adult-care facility, and want to check its ratings for a parent.
- You are interviewing for a new job.

The Interview

In the 1990s, I was invited to interview with a technology company that was known for its news transmissions from satellites to Web sites. I was particularly interested in the opportunity to work in a think-tank environment, where programmers invented the intelligent components that eventually led to the software programs used by most search engines and news transmission services today. This was the time of the "dot.com" bubble, and I knew going in that working for a company like this was risky because of its reliance on venture capital money versus actual revenue to support its costs.

Prior to my interview, I studied as much as possible about the company. From the president down to the mid-level programmers, I knew what types of software they were interested in, the company's financial statements, all of their business locations, and how their growth and opportunity were presented. More importantly to win the job, I researched the chief technology officer (CTO) and the vice president, both of whom would be interviewing me. I found their biographies outlining their business histories, the projects and companies they had worked for, their college degrees, and a few key pieces about their interests.

During the interview, I mentioned that I used a particular technology that had never quite taken off in the market. It was something that the CTO had been involved with years ago, and he was impressed with my disclosure. He laughed and told me I was probably one of five people who ever bought it. It showed him that I was interested enough in his company to take the time to educate myself about it. Not only was I offered the position on the spot, but also at $10,000 more than I anticipated.

I enjoy sharing that fun story because it really explains that business investigations are not only for discovering fraudulent practices. A business investigation encompasses much more, like understanding all the intricate pieces of a company, how the products move across the market, who the players are, and where you fit into the equation.

Question: So who are possible clients of business investigators?

Answer: The reality is that just about any business that is dealing with a problem, a new product, a possible new investor, a merger or acquisition or hiring a new key employee is a candidate of a business investigation.

Big users of business investigations are Wall Street related investors. These business professionals move millions of dollars daily, shifting assets from one company to the next. The decisions made by these people are not happenstance, but carefully considered occurrences based on financial health, reputation, stability, growth, projection, history and a number of other factors. Business investigators play a strong roll in helping these investors capture everything available **that could be known** on the companies and individuals under consideration.

Perhaps the best way to understand who may be possible clients for a business investigator is to review the types of investigations that may need to be performed.

Types of Business Investigations

As you will learn throughout this book, there are several approaches to take in business background investigations, and all depend on what type of investigation is being requested.

Over time, I have learned that clients often will ask for what they think I can find, and not for what they really want. There is a difference. When taking on an assignment, be sure to ask the client what is expected in the investigative report. Each possible answer will guide the investigator in a different direction; the approach will not be the same for every case.

A typical phone call from a client goes something like this: "I would like to know more about ABC Company." The investigator's follow-up questions should be, "What do you want to know about ABC Company? Is it a **competitor**, a **potential acquisition**, or a **defaulted company**?"

The client's answer to that question should trigger a response from the investigator that clearly identifies how the investigator should handle the investigation, using an information edge.

Below are examples of how I begin an investigation for each of these client needs.

Competitor Investigation

I begin an investigation by drawing an outline of the company, with an emphasis on supply chain vendors, clients, and revenue streams. In addition, I look for new trends in the market to formulate where it is heading in the next six months to a year. Finally, I analyze this information and write a SWOT[3] analysis, emphasizing the company's position in the market compared to similar companies. My report offers recommendations for continued monitoring of this company to avert any surprises.

Potential Acquisition

Recognizing that reputation is as important as finance in business, I search various media, including the Internet, to insure that the company has not come under fire for any malpractices or misdeeds, and that its principals have not been accused of criminal misconduct like fraud or collusion. From there, I examine the company's financial health to see if it is ripe for an acquisition. Perhaps it is on its last leg of venture capital investment, and is desperate for a new company to purchase it. Finally, looking at the company's marketing strategy, Web site, and industry reviews, I learn about its products and services,

---

[3] SWOT is an analysis methodology term. The acronym comes from Strengths, Weaknesses, Opportunities, and Threats. How to use SWOT is covered in Chapter 3.

and assess, through analysis, how it compares to its competition in the market. Perhaps this is a technology company with some cutting-edge software. But, the management is incompetent and cannot market its product effectively. If I see positive reviews of the software, but notice that the product is not selling as much as its competition, then that indicates to me that management does not understand the product it is selling. Perhaps the company has incredibly brilliant software developers, but its marketing is targeting the wrong industry. This could be a sign the company is struggling, and is just waiting for a more competent competitor to acquire it.

Defaulted Company

If I understand the intended goal, the company may owe the client some money. It has defaulted on its payments, and now the client is looking to sue for compensation, or collect on a judgment. My task is to track the assets. Assets could have been moved into the personal funds of the shareholders. I identify all the responsible parties, then examine these principals, including their wealth, homes, other business interests, families, associates, and intangible assets like trademarks and patents.

Other Issues

Each type of investigation has a different starting and ending point. Once the type of investigation is established, you will know if you need to conduct a due diligence investigation on a person or a company, or a competitive intelligence analysis on several emerging companies coming to market. Perhaps the investigation is really about finding out who is funding the latest project for a competing company.

Many investigative resources will be repeatedly used, whether it is an acquisition, asset or due diligence investigation. However, when you get into the minutiae of an investigation that is specifically acquisition, asset, or due diligence, you will find that you must tap into other resources that are specific to what you need.

For example, many business investigations involve compliance issues. Companies are required by various compliance rules, such as SOX[4] and Foreign Corrupt Practices Act (FCPA)[5] to hire outside vendors to remain unbiased in reporting information. The conflict-of-interest issue is avoided because compliance laws, like SOX, do not permit an accounting firm to conduct due diligence for the same client being audited. As a result, many of these corporate clients look for independent investigators to conduct impartial, business investigations. The marketplace is certainly open to those investigators with the right resources and the necessary skill set.

Information Retrieval Language

There are many terms used throughout this book. Some terms refer to investigative resources, others refer to reporting detailed results to clients. There are still other terms that are part of the

---

[4] The Sarbanes-Oxley Act of 2002 is often referred to as SOX. This is covered in a later chapter.
[5] Foreign Corrupt Practices Act requires companies to have reasonable assurance that they are not working with known corrupt companies or persons. http://www.usdoj.gov/criminal/fraud/fcpa/

information world that investigators reside within. I like to say that an investigator "makes business with information." The concept or point here is that understanding what kind of investigator you are, and what role you play in business investigations, will help you become a better investigator.

The following are some terms and definitions that will help you better understand the information gathering process used in business investigations.

Information Aggregators

Information aggregators collect and resell data. They collate information from multiple sources of public records. Companies like Dun & Bradstreet (D&B), Experian, ChoicePoint, Westlaw, and LexisNexis have made enterprises of themselves by aggregating disparate public records from across the country and putting them into readable and usable reports. On the Internet, they offer easy-to-use search interfaces, and are considered the go-to sources for business investigators, regardless of the type of investigation. These services have something for everybody. But, an aggregator cannot collect data from every U.S. county and city, and it is not comprehensive enough to be a complete turnkey service offering. This is a benefit to investigators because if there was one completely comprehensive tool offered, there would be no need to hire an investigator.

The two types of reports that are created by aggregators are **business reports** and **comprehensive reports**. For the sake of clarity in this book, I will define them as follows, but with the understanding that vendors of all types use both titles to describe their services.

- Business reports are generated by services like D&B and Experian, and focus on company information. These aggregators get their data from public records, vendor-supplied information, self-reporting, government filings, and limited research.

- Comprehensive reports are generated by companies like ChoicePoint and Accurint, and focus on individuals. This type of report also is created from aggregated data that is collected from public records.

Visit the services of each company just mentioned. Each will explain its record-collection techniques[6] and the coverage, scope, and limitations of its databases.

Data Mining

Data mining is researching specific data and analyzing it for trends. Data mining occurs when a company, like Wal-Mart, conducts market basket analysis to find out which product sells the best in conjunction with another, during certain periods of time. Often stated, but cited as an urban legend[7], was the story that the combination of beer and diapers sold as a set on Friday nights.

---

[6] to the extent that it is not giving away its own trade secrets
[7] Beer and Nappies -- A Data Mining Urban Legend
(Source: http://web.onetel.net.uk/~hibou/Beer%20and%20Nappies.html)

Suppliers, through sales at each retail store, constantly gather data in real time to see which products are hot and which ones are not. The actual data mining is performed with specialized software like Cognos or MicroStrategy in the business world, and i2 in the intelligence and investigative world. Databases like SAS and Oracle also create their own data mining interfaces.

Mining is never random, whether in diamond mining, coal mining, or information mining. In information collection, data mining is known as the data warehouse[8].

Information Anxiety

Information Anxiety is what most Internet newcomers experience when they click through Web page after Web page, often gaining very little insight into their query. As a business investigator, you are the cure to the information anxiety that the executive experiences. Your task is to gather the **data** from the ether called the Web, verify this data until you know that it is factual **information**, and can be analyzed and translated into **knowledge** as you write the report for your client.

This takes information anxiety and turns it into **knowledge ecology.**

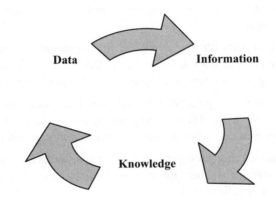

Data   **Information**

Knowledge

Primary Research

Primary research is first-hand experience, interviewing, collecting data onsite, and pulling records from courthouses. This is the traditional method of most investigators and interviewers.

---

[8] "A *data warehouse* is a repository storing integrated information for efficient querying and analysis. Information is extracted from heterogeneous sources as it is generated or updated. The information is then translated into a common data model and integrated with existing data at the warehouse. When a user query is submitted to the warehouse, the needed information is already there, with inconsistencies and differences already resolved. This makes it much easier and more efficient to run queries over data that originally came from different sources."
(Source: http://infolab.stanford.edu/warehousing/warehouse.html)

Secondary Research

Secondary research is utilizing databases, online services, Web sites, gathering information from books, magazines, and other second-hand sources. Remember, when using secondary sources for your reports, verify the information you are relaying or quote the source.

Hearsay

Hearsay is rumor, and unless you can substantiate a bit of the data gathered, either by primary or secondary research, you always should cite it in your report as hearsay and unverified information.

Selling Information

For secondary research, anyone with a library card, a car (to drive to clerks' offices and courthouses), and a good deal of time on his hands can do his own research. There are some high-end databases that are invaluable to the craft and their real value is time savings. If obtaining a personal, comprehensive report was that valuable to the data alone, it would be much more expensive. However, the public record vendors who produce these documents know that they are selling convenience, not private information. This is especially true with companies that are selling reports that have redacted Social Security and drivers' license numbers.

Investigators hone the ability to gather information from online databases and through the Internet, as well as offline in interviews, site visits, and observations.

After gathering everything that is available online and offline, it is time for report writing, which involves the analysis, conclusion, and recommendations.

Cynthia's Key Chapter Points

Here are my **Top Ten Characteristics** that are necessary to be a successful business investigator—

1. An understanding of the business world, the players, the language, and the challenges your client faces.

2. An understanding of the law, both foreign and domestic, as it applies to your work and your client's case.

3. Knowing the shortcomings of the information available online and onsite.

4. Interviewing skills.

5. Analytical abilities.

6. Determination for those complicated cases and patience when you are getting nowhere.

7. A professional network of investigators with whom to share information.

8. Always having access to the Internet and if necessary, subscription services.

9. A library of resources both in text and online.

10. Business decorum, know-how, and personal ethics.

Chapter 2

Learning to CRAWL

(What Makes a Good Investigator)

Success is a journey, not a destination.

—Ben Sweetland

In a fast-paced, answers-now business environment it is important to recognize the roles patience and precision play. Before you race into databases, charge into courthouses and relay facts to clients, you must first learn to CRAWL.

- **C**ommunicate
- **R**esearch
- **A**nalyze
- **W**rite
- **L**isten

With CRAWL, you will learn a rudimentary process for receiving new projects, reporting your findings and transcending your competitors in customer-service response.

You most likely will be very good at one or several of these steps. Good investigators say that **research** is the most important step. Successful investigators say that **analysis** and good report **writing** can be very profitable. Great investigators know it is all in **communicating** with their clients, with an emphasis on **listening**. A solid investigator who is profitable, well-respected and seeking steady work needs all five components.

Veteran investigators know that there are specialists in certain fields of research. Some fields of specialization are arson, surveillance, business backgrounds, organized crime, matrimonial, defense, and legal. As varied as these fields are, these experts all need to know the fundamentals of CRAWLing.

CRAWLing demands skills beyond the investigator's specialization. CRAWLing is the business model for investigators, just as the scientific method is a constant for scientists.

Without a fundamental application of the principles of CRAWL, an investigator may have a short career because he will not see return business, will become frustrated over inconsistent reports, and will not understand why the phone is not ringing.

Communicate

A good deal can be learned from your own clients, as they tend to be lawyers, business professionals and executives. When pressed for time, often there is little to spare on chit-chat when they are engaging your services. There will be a litany of questions about your services, fees, deliverable products and timeline. Also, a well-versed client should ask you about any ethics-related issues that might be associated with your investigation.

Confidence is key when engaging your clients. But this only addresses one half of the equation when it comes to communications. This half talks about style, finesse and politicking your clients and colleagues. The other half is expressing sincerity. It's about connecting with your client. Law enforcement is often noted for its jaded demeanor at crime scenes. That is a self-protection method that is necessary for them to perform their jobs effectively. However, you will find as I did, that it does not work in private practice. As a "for-hire investigator" or researcher, you do not want to appear cocky or jaded. This is serious stuff with no room for showboating. Even if the client's judgment seems stretched thinly, or if it is your fifth matrimonial case in a week, you *need* to connect with this client. He must feel that you are competent like impressive attorneys with their "lawyer speak," yet you must be personable like a good neighbor.

The first application to communication is honesty. You must create a connective line of communication with your client. He may come to you with an important need, a sensitive situation, or a business requirement. So, **that first conversation is very important**; it will set the standard for all future conversations. The best thing you can do is listen, absorb and collect, and to try to engage him in conversation that forces out the information about his project, as well as himself. This approach is to engage him as a person and win his trust. He is about to spend a considerable sum of money with your firm. You want him to be as closely connected to you as he is to his family doctor or his brother the priest. In the end, you will hold as many secrets regarding his case as the doctor holds about his medical history.

Communicating can happen in many terrains no matter how short the encounter. If your first meeting with a client is face-to-face, show your sincerity about his concerns. Body language, appearance, and demeanor may contribute to a good connection, or the face-to-face could serve as a warning of boundaries or expectations. If you cannot have that initial face-time, make sure to create a follow-up visit during or after your case. In the meanwhile, every time you talk to the client, he needs to know that he has your undivided attention, especially when you are in talks on the phone.

Phone conversations with a client are NOT time to multi-task. As in the story on page 28 – *Learn From a Rookie Mistake* – do not let other tasks distract you from hearing something crucial.

Logistics to Communicating

Establish Criteria and Expectations

What is the Big Picture? Find out what the client wants. Examine what outcome he is seeking.

Talking to clients in a professional yet sincere manner allows the investigator to understand the final goal. A key question to always ask during the initial interview with the client is "What outcome are you expecting from my investigation?"

Do not promise him a particular outcome; it may not be obtainable or legal. I always explain to my clients that "I will do my best to support their position but there are no guarantees." In either event, I will report my findings.

Timetable

Establish goals for the following:

- report style
- budget
- time constraints

"How fast and how much" are generally the first questions you get from a client. But your final product development should be based on "inexpensive, complete and time sensitive." Some clients have ongoing cases that can take months or even years, and turnaround time is not the major factor. These longer engagements allow for expert work within decent budgets. Still, **these long-term projects should be set up with short-term goals**.

When working with the client, do establish expectations for immediate, mid- and long-term goals. For example, your short-term reporting may consist of interviews and some database research. The client is informed that he will get a call and subsequent update by email within a few weeks. The mid-term goals may be for on-site records collection and deeper research needs. The client should understand this may take from several days to several months, depending on the records needed and the scope of the investigation. Finally, the final, in-depth report delivery could be promised a month or longer from your original sit-down engagement.

Here is an example of timing: Conduct a pre-employment background check on a retired military professional. Immediately, you can inform the client on your validations of certain information such as a check of the Social Security Number and current address. Perhaps in a week or so you can report on any criminal records as well as courthouse filings (litigation, judgments, etc.) you have uncovered. Finally your client needs to understand that military records themselves can take several months to obtain from the government agency, and not to expect an exception.

Informing the client of your time constraints in advance and putting this in your letter of engagement from the outset will always help to keep you on schedule and will make the client happy knowing the dates and expectations. Knowing the time constraints will also keep you motivated. And, any time there is a problem in retrieving information that affects your time budget, inform the client immediately.

Budget

Similar to time, it is important to inform the client about your budget. For example—

- Itemize the financial cost details within the letter of engagement.
- If you are working on an hourly rate, does it include database fees and vendors? If not, make sure the client knows he is paying your hourly rate plus these additional research fees.
- Inform the client if you are working with several rates. For example, researchers may work at $200 per hour, while an attorney will be reviewing the folio at a rate of $450 per hour.

It takes some experience to understand how many hours it will take an investigator to conduct a particular investigation. Even with a best guesstimate, some cases that seem easy and direct at the onset often turn into long-winded investigations no one could have predicted. As with the time budget, if you see your case is going to exceed the budget, inform your client prior to continuing. Even the best results will be met with criticism when the final invoice arrives at twice the price.

It is also possible to set a **per-project price approach**, instead of working on an hourly rate. This can be very successful for repetitive work. A per-project price allows your client to budget for their case needs. A good example is pre-employment checks. Most costs are known ahead of time, so most pre-employment searches come in at the same price every time. Domestic due diligence on small companies is also somewhat predictable and can be quoted in one lump sum.

Deliverables

Does the client want a formal report that can be submitted to management, or is court-ready deposition required? These reports tend to be reviewed by a peer investigator or an attorney before being submitted. An informal report will give the client the details of request, without the hours and budget spent on formalities or a review by counsel. Final report style is very informal; as requested, you convey the information gathered to the client via email, fax, face-to-face, or in a phone conversation. It is important to record the details of this conversation for your records, just in case this information is called into question at a later time. In the case of a phone call or an informal report, always follow-up with a fax or email restating your findings, then file it in your case file.

Research

Introduction to Research

Research is one of those words that can mean one thing to one person, and something else to another. "Research" covers a lot of areas. The topic is too broad to accurately describe what you do and what you produce. When I tell people I'm a "researcher," they tend to look for a white coat hanging on a peg in my office or lab animals in cages. The title "investigative researcher" makes you think of journalists and investigative reporters. And "librarian researcher" puts an academic spin on the title.

Research is strictly the process that you undertake to achieve an answer. It could be as complex as nuclear physics, or as straightforward as asking a question of the town assessor.

To be clear, investigative research is the task undertaken by "an investigator, analyst or researcher" to locate information that creates, supports or makes his case. How he or she goes about this will depend a lot on the type of case. With investigations being as varied as the areas they cover, let us narrow the basic research functions to the following four types of investigations—

- **Investigative Due Diligence**
- **Competitive Intelligence**
- **Background Research**
- **Internet Investigations**

During the interview with your client, you will understand the nature of your project as being one of these.

Investigative Due Diligence is conducted for projects such as mergers and acquisitions, pre-acquisition, vendor or supply alliances or any type of corporate background that requires you to know everything about a certain company, including its principals and the factors that affect its products.

Competitive Intelligence, sometimes called business or competitor intelligence, is crystal-ball research. In part, it is investigative due diligence with an emphasis on the future. The goal of competitive intelligence is usually either to gather data so a company can learn about it competition or to help a company bring a new product to the market place. Much of the investigation is a strategic examination of strengths, weaknesses, product offerings, pricing, markets served, prospects, suppliers, distributors, and competitors. You also could conduct traditional research and make some analytical predictions based on your knowledge of the companies, the market, and the facts as you understand them.

Background Research encompasses many fields such as pre-employment verification and market research. It is broader in scope and usually is a combination of several companies or persons being examined.

Internet Investigation is the newest of investigative types and one that is really taking off in the business marketplace. With Internet investigations, you are scanning the World Wide Web, newsrooms, chat boards, RSS feeds, even personal Web sites, and other Internet protocols for content relative to your case.

Watch For Imponderables

The specific type of investigation will give you a sense of the kinds of deliverables the client is expecting, the services you will need to enlist to perform your research, and the approximate amount of time it will take. However, be prepared for a bump in the road on time management. For example, if you are working on foreign corporate research, check a calendar from that country to insure that there are no unforeseen holidays and days off. When you do not know government buildings are closed is likely to make you look unprepared for a rush assignment.

Analyze

Analysis begins once the research has been conducted and the sources that were examined for pertinent material have been exhausted, begin processing the information. The methods you use in an analysis to process the information will vary depending on the type of case.

But the key factor is that analysis is not about summarizing data. Analysis is a combination of scientific and non-scientific interpretation of data or information to produce insightful, intelligent findings.

Probably the most popular of analysis models is **SWOT**. SWOT is an acronym for **strengths**, **weaknesses**, **opportunities**, and **threats**—the SWOT method breaks down any subject, whether it be a person or a company, into these four components.

For example, an orange grove in Florida may seem attractive for acquisition by an orange juice producer. Using the SWOT method, the investigator will analyze the issues related to that grove, but only after gathering all the research, data and facts that make the analysis possible.

- Strengths would include location, size of grove, and a present and established workforce.

- Weaknesses could include old on-site machinery, which might need repairing or replacing, or the trees themselves may be older and declining in productivity.

- Opportunity comes in the future potential to purchase adjacent property and expand the grove into a larger producing farm.

- Threats are present when the Food and Drug Administration tests produce for bacteria-related illnesses due to bad well-water.

All of these points come into play in the decision to purchase because of the information the investigator has gathered and verified.

I will cover SWOT and a few useful popular analysis methods in the next chapter.

> **Author Tip** ➡ Many informative books are available to explain the whys and whats of analysis. Recommended reading on analytical methods is the book *Strategic and Competitive Analysis: Methods and Techniques for Analyzing Business Competition* by Craig S. Fleisher and Babette Bensoussan. Fleisher and Bensoussan pull together more than twenty different types of analysis used in competitive intelligence, and place a strong emphasis on the practical application of each method. Their book is a virtual how-to manual for new investigators learning analysis. Some methods covered in their book are gap analysis, country-risk analysis, trend analysis, strategic intent, value chain, and war games.

Write

Creating a written report for your client should be done according to the expectations that were established when the project was assigned. Basic ingredients of your report are a restating of the objective, using the provided information and the results of your investigation with any recommendations. Also consider adding your search technique, disclaimers, and the always important contact information.

> **Author Tip ➜** While there are many styles used to write reports, using a format that is simple, clean, and professional is a definite must. An excellent reference for report writing is what I have called my "go to guide" since college – *The Publication Manual of the American Psychological Association* aka APA Style Manual. Although using this reference may seem like overkill for some reports, keep in mind the report *could* be read by attorneys and judges. By using a format commonly used in graduate schools, your client will understand the style and appreciate the attention to detail.

Examples of how to prepare investigative reports are presented in **Chapter 12**.

Clients may also request a visual presentation be prepared to be shared with an audience. This is primarily done using Microsoft PowerPoint. I have done a few of these, and admit to enjoying this style. Using PowerPoint allows you to hit just the key points of your investigation and avoid much of the laborious detail that sometimes fills pages. Even if you use a presentation tool, I always recommend to follow-up with a written report, and make available the support material you are bullet pointing for a presentation.

Remember When Writing:

- Be clear, concise and use proper grammar.
- Be wary of using nebulous words like comprehensive, complete, and conclusive.
- Stick to standardized, minimal set of fonts. Getting too fancy is distracting. If a report is reformatted on the client's computer and fonts are substituted, the report could look quite different from what you intended.
- Indicate what task is pending and make recommendations if warranted.

Listen

Good listening is a necessary skill for an investigator that applies not only to conducting interviews, but also when communicating with a client.

Learn From a Rookie Mistake

In my rookie days working a very tight deadline, I was typing a client report when a call came in from a new client. Although it would have been best to explain that I would call back immediately since I needed only five minutes to finish the other work, in my haste I began listening to the new client's needs. The entire time I was discussing what the client wanted and replying with the probable cost and turnaround time, I was also busy and noisily typing my other report. I got caught in the act. The phone client asked me to stop what I was doing and to give me his undivided attention. Since I was embarrassed, I tried covering up by saying I was taking notes for his case. But it was obvious that was an excuse when I need to ask him to repeat points I missed because I was not paying attention.

Since then I do not answer the phone if I am on a deadline, and when I do answer the phone, I turn my back from the computer and put a smile on. If you think the smile is silly, how many times have you spoken to someone on the phone who is obviously frowning, or stressed or upset? It can be heard, if not seen.

Good listening skills include—

- Giving full attention to the speaker, maintain eye contact if in person.
- Stay active mentally by determining what the key points are. Since you will think faster than the speaker can talk, stay on tract.
- Let the speaker finish before you begin to talk.
- Ask questions and give feedback.

The opportunity to use good listening can actually take place during four different phases with your client – when hired, during the investigation, the presentation of the report, and your follow-up after completion. Each phase is important and should never be overlooked.

Of course, at the outset it is important to understand the client's intentions. Make sure to listen thoroughly and attentively to the request. Keep in mind the client will most likely tell you what he thinks you can do, and not what he wants. So be sure to ask many questions, even if they seem out of place. You want to be very thorough and get all the initial information needed.

Depending on the size of the case, the importance of the timeline and if the client requests updates, I will stay in contact with the client throughout the investigation. It is a bad sign for any business if a client has to call you for an update. You should always initiate the communications, even if you have limited information to share. This practice is a constant reminder that you are working on their matter and that they are important to you.

Tips When Handing off the Completed Report and Follow-Up

When a case is completed, try to hand off your final report in person. This practice gives you an opportunity to vocalize your findings. This is especially helpful for sensitive cases where you may want to tell the client something like "Hey, keep an eye on this character." More importantly, in person reporting gives your client a chance to ask questions. The client will sometimes remember these answers more so than the material in the report. And once again, face time with the client is priceless.

Finally, never put a report in the client's hand and wait a week before contact. By then the report will have been read by many and facts may be distorted.

Do contact the client again within a week of sending your report. Customer service is rare in the investigative industry and the competition is great so take advantage of being visible and available.

Follow up with the client to learn if the information is useful, and ask if there are any other indicator items that need researched. Inquire if he wants you to follow through on your recommendations. Ask if he is satisfied with your findings.

If he is satisfied with your work, ask if there are any other opportunities within the organization. If so, ask for references to other contacts. For example, "I am glad to hear you are satisfied with my work, and I appreciate your business. Is there someone else in your company who else could use my services?"

Later, follow up with a letter or card thanking him for assigning you the engagement and for the co-worker reference.

On the down note, if you realize during the follow-up that the client is not as pleased as you anticipated, be certain to have your initial instructions and assignment on hand for review. A review will help you understand where expectations were not met, or where expectations may have exceeded your agreement.

Below is an excellent article written by a good friend of mine – Mr. Bill Majeski. Bill is an author and noted lecturer and I sincerely thank him for allowing us to reprint his article.

I Can Hear You but I Don't Know What You're Saying

By Bill Majeski

Is listening easy? We do it all the time, so it should be. However, listening is so natural that we don't always hear what is being said. We just kind of hear the words. Picture yourself sitting at home and your significant other starts telling you about their day. How much will you remember the next morning? Now picture yourself in a crowded restaurant and the person at the next table begins to talk about a new hot stock which is about to quadruple. I bet you will find yourself leaning ever so slightly towards that table, your heartrate will increase, your blood will flow a little faster, your eyes will open wider, and your body temperature will rise slightly. You're using energy to listen intently because you want to get the name of that stock.

There are physiological and physical manifestations which occur when we hear something we deem to be important. Our mental attitude adjusts to absorb what is being said. There are good listeners, casual listeners and bad listeners. Most people are casual listeners who have developed the habit of tuning out much of the information being disseminated. They have relinquished their ability to listen intently. If you do not concentrate, you will not hear, if you do not hear, you will not know, and without knowledge, you can't understand. You can train yourself to be a good listener by using what I call the "Funnel Effect". Picture an imaginary funnel – normally we listen through the wide end. But to listen intently, you must listen through the narrow end. Your goal is not only to absorb what you hear, but also to comprehend it more fully. The technique can be perfected if you make a conscious effort concentrate on what you are hearing. When you learn to intently listen to the spoken word, you're halfway to becoming a good listener.

Words are the conscious part of a person's message. Words are often chosen for their effect and they are relatively easy to control. Be mindful that there are also a wide range of unconscious "Sound Signals" that are an integral part of the communication process. A sampling of these Sound Signals would be: change in rate or rhythm, change in tone, change in pitch, cracking voice, sudden stammer or stutter, slurring, grunt, groan, moan, gasp, gulp, snort, sniff, hum, whistle, teeth grinding, hesitation, pause and silence. Other signals are word choice, word sequence, over-persuasion and Freudian slips. Sound Signals are as important as words because sounds are nearly always unconscious and therefore uncontrolled. Remember, an instinctive unrehearsed sound is more telling than the prepared, well formulated phrase. Just as you learn to absorb words using the "Funnel Effect", you can learn to absorb "Sound Signals". When you listen through the narrow end of the funnel, the inconsistency of a Sound Signal becomes more pronounced.

Using the Funnel Effect takes some practice. I found that one of the best ways to practice identifying the interplay of words and Sound Signals is over the telephone. It is easy to limit distractions and you can intensify your concentration by simply closing your eyes. Many people view a telephone as a shielding device. They believe that facial expressions and body movement are not factors. But, if you are listening intently, your 'mind's eye' will 'see' the smile, frown, or scowl. You will 'see' the body action.

Be a good listener; intensify your conscious level of concentration. The results will be positive. You'll probably be a little tired for the effort because good listening is hard work.

Bill Majeski, of Majeski and Associates, Inc., is the author of *The Lie Detection Book* (a book on body language), published by Ballantine Publications. Additionally he is a co-compiler of a textbook titled *Corporate Investigations*, published by Lawyers & Judges Publishing Company. You can reach Bill at www.majeski.net and bill@majeski.net

Cynthia's Key Chapter Points

- As you read this book – or as you train your own staff the basics of research and investigations – keep the fundamentals of CRAWL in mind. As former California Governor Jerry Brown once said, "What we need is a flexible plan for an ever changing world."

- Your client is your sole focus when starting a new investigation, so give them your undivided attention. A sincere relationship necessary helps them trust and work with you.

- Using the fundamentals of CRAWL guarantees consistent, productive reports – return clients.

- When communicating, establish criteria and expectations for timeline, budget and deliverables.

- Due diligence, competitive intelligence, background research and Internet investigations are four types of investigative projects. Researching doesn't change much, but how you report will vary on the type of investigation.

- Analysis will also vary on the type of investigation you conduct. Of the dozens of analytical methods, S.W.O.T. is the most general/popular and works in most cases.

- Write reports as professionally as possible, unless the client asks for something otherwise.

- Professional reports should be clear and concise, with correct spelling and grammar. Fancy is nice for invitations; in your reports, simple and direct is the best approach.

- If the client is not happy with the results – perhaps you did not meet expectations – then be prepared to throw yourself on the sword by offering to rip up the invoice or do the next case for free. In the end it's all about customer service – service the customer expects you to provide.

- Follow up a week, a month, or a year after the project is complete. See that they were happy with the results. Ask them for a referral.

Chapter 3

Research & Analysis Fundamentals

*Some people drink from the fountain of knowledge,
others just gargle.*

—Robert Newton Anthony

Research and analysis are necessary steps in any type of investigation. Research requires knowledge of available sources and services to accurately answer the questions asked. Analysis is the ability to discern the gathered information and decide which possible conclusions to offer.

Whether you are a researcher, a special agent or private investigator, it is necessary to implement a consistent methodology that allows you to approach your research in a systematic way, record your findings and report your analysis.

Research Basics

Strategically-directed research is a key to a successful investigation. Conducting investigative research today requires identifying the best resources associated with specific topics. Some resources are geared toward the legal market, others with fraud or motor-vehicle reconstruction or Internet investigations, and the list goes on.

When teaching a research class, one of my first instructions involves teaching investigators:

- where to obtain information;
- how to know its limitations and biases; and
- how to compile all the information that is available.

Resource tools and in-depth training aids also are helpful to investigators in taking an organized approach to research. These tools and aids include—

1. **Case Management Software**

2. **Books on Managing Investigations**

3. **Training Offered by Associations**

4. **Downloadable Checklists**

PI Magazine presents a great list of investigative organizations and resources which can be found at www.pimagazine.com/links.htm. The various state and national associations will advise, endorse or recommend on any of the four points above.

Online and Offline Sources

The Internet has made many of us lazy. Log onto ChoicePoint or Experian and we can easily get a report on a subject. Gone are the days when we had to write letters requesting alpha searches to be conducted county by county, and then waiting months to receive the results. I do not wish to return to that inefficient way for the bulk of my information gathering, but it still represents a methodology that should be taught to all new investigators.

Most database services I utilize for my investigations do not create information—they aggregate it from public sources. ChoicePoint, LexisNexis, Westlaw and others do not produce a single document that has not been pulled from public records. A team of investigators at LexisNexis do not provide me with dossiers on subjects I am evaluating. More likely, supercomputers gather information from thousands of sources to create a single document or report.

The most sizable report I can purchase from a database vendor, such as ChoicePoint or IRBsearch, is called a *comprehensive report*. Comprehensive reports are used to enlighten the investigator about the subject (person or company) they are investigating. A typical report contains addresses, relatives' names, business associates, phone numbers, etc., and is really a catalog of information aggregated from multiple state, Federal, county and vendor databases. For example, a comprehensive report on myself include the data from the New Jersey Division of Motor Vehicles, credit report companies (i.e. Experian and Trans Union), the local county Office of Deeds, the U.S. Postal Service, my phone provider, coupon-card distributors, and data from other agencies that sell personal information to commercial entities.

> **Author Tip ➡** One of my biggest criticisms of some investigators is their level of reliance on specific databases, without the foreknowledge of the material they are investigating. Dismissing any source or service without fully understanding the information received, and the purpose it serves, can hinder an investigation.
>
> A perfect example of this is a Dun & Bradstreet (D&B) report. D&B Reports are often dismissed as self-reported false information. Although some D&B information can be self-reported, it also checks state and federal legal findings, vendors and suppliers, trade boards (if a publicly traded company) and public records.

The Internet is Only One Source

The World Wide Web is not taking over the role of the library, archives or a county docket index, so do not consider this useful but often frustrating tool the only one to use.

There is a bevy of sources available that never make it to the Web. Many county courts are offline, with public records still in file cabinets. Market research and annual reports are deliberately kept in printed form to curtail copyright infringement.

If your investigation leads you to research at the local level, a town library is a good place to usually find localized data cataloged, indexed, and archived. Some towns maintain history rooms or designate a few shelves in their town halls for books written by local authors, and small-town newspapers often report stories from the local residents' perspective. If General Motors decided to close plants in Springfield, Illinois, the *New York Times* might report on GM's financial burden to maintain such large facilities as the purpose for the closings. However, a newspaper in suburban Springfield is more likely to report on the families who were losing incomes because of the closings.

> **Author Tip ➡** Locate a town's public library using an Internet phone book source or call the information operator. Then call or email the reference librarian to inquire about the local collection. It might take a visit to view the actual documents, because your answers may be in an old file cabinet that is rarely used or noticed.

Collecting and Tracking Information

When starting your investigation, create an initial word list of terms and expressions. This technique will help you develop additional, helpful words to add that you might not have thought of before.

For example, I had a case involving maintenance men who had been in escalator accidents. The client did not want information about accidents involving patrons, of which there are hundreds, but, specifically, he wanted to know about the workers who repair and maintain movable floors and stairs.

Using a Taxonomy

Taxonomy is a classification system. Using the above example, search Google or another search engines for the key terms "escalator, accident, maintenance." Once you start typing these words, you will realize there are other terms that can work for this search, too. You are now developing *word taxonomy* – meaning a list of all possible terms and expressions that can get you closer to the answers you need.

Organized into three columns, your taxonomy list for the above example would look like this—

Escalator	Accident	Maintenance
movable floor	injure	worker
	hurt	laborer
	harm	employee
	dead	mechanic
	killed	repairman
		union

Keep this list on your computer or in a notepad. In this same document, keep descriptive notes for yourself. You may be searching in one direction, find a brand new lead, and want to pursue that lead. However, you will be better served if you finish the original inquiry, and then return to the new lead. This disciplined "to-the- end" approach keeps you from scatterbrained and wandering searches on the Internet.

> **Author Tip ➡** It is easy when searching the Internet or using an electronic database to wander off on a lead and forget where you were originally. Using a notebook or notepad program, record where you were visiting, copy and paste the results, and leave yourself a note. You also can capture a Web page as an Adobe Acrobat document and save it for printing later. Whichever way works for you, be consistent so that you will always know where you left off.

Tracking your words and leads in one document always pays off when you have to follow up later in the investigation and need to refer to your notes. You can search one document versus digging through a pile of notes, post-it stickers and saved documents. Plus, if you electronically manage a word and subject directory, you can easily incorporate into your final report the items you searched for and where you looked.

Recording Your Findings

An important component of research is to establish a methodology that keeps you attuned with your research results. I recommend the combination approach of finding and recording information in the initial stages of the gathering mode—

- Record the findings in a consistent way so that you can return to the search and repeat the steps. Recording your findings in a consistent manner will help you create a more professional looking report that will benefit the client.

- You can choose an actual style manual, such as in Chicago Style or APA method, or create a style that is clear and continual.

If you are uncertain if your reports are of high quality, show your report style to a trusted friend or colleague and ask for feedback on flow, content, and readability. I mention style and not an actual report because the information you are reporting should be subject to non-disclosure. However having redacted reports on hand, with vital information removed or edited, is also a handy way to a report writing style to a potential client.

Know the Market or Industry

"I may not have a lot of knowledge, but I know where to find mountains of information."

Good investigators locate information by knowing where to focus their research efforts. Looking for data about an insurance company or an auto manufacturer will still require a Dun & Bradstreet report. Knowing that A.M. Best Company and International Insurance Industry are sources for rating insurance companies will enhance the report from standard off-the-shelf generalist information.

A great resource tool for industry and corporate research for general-business information is www.hoovers.com. Hoovers has both free and fee services that offer quick and concise information. Hoovers provides key points such as geography, industry, people, company description and competitor identification; however, it will not tell you how a company's property and casualty insurance compares to its competitors.

Using media sources, you may find there may be a hundred articles written about Ford Motor Company. However, you will not see any detail of union concerns or gain insight as to why its plants are closing, until you search further and read the trade magazines that focus on auto manufacturers.

As cases come and go, you will be exposed to many new, unique markets that you did not know a thing about before you started; but as you finish your final report, you will feel like an expert.

In one case, I was tasked with locating peanut processing plants in South America. My client wanted to sell his peanut factory and requested that I find the top three likely purchasers. I started searching by peanut processors, but was too limited in my approach. So using the taxonomy principle, I built a word list that included the term "nut." However, searching for nut processors broadened the search too much resulting in a list that included all legitimate and inappropriate contenders. Once I realized that I was searching too broadly, I stepped back and decided to educate myself on the peanut industry. I went to Hoovers and searched by industry keyword "nuts." The results come back as follows—

- Crop Production (found within Agriculture)
- Fresh Fruit & Vegetable Production (found within Agriculture - Crop Production)
- Hardware & Fastener Manufacturing (found within Industrial Manufacturing)
- Industrial Manufacturing
- Snack Foods (found within Food)
- Steel Production (found within Metals & Mining)

Choosing Crop Production offered an insight into this industry, defining it as companies that grow, harvest, process and package agricultural crops both for food and non-food products. Further research also lead to the following—

- Most-Viewed Crop Producers
- Other Industries Related to Crop Production

By using a combination of taxonomy, tracking, and common sense research, I was able to get a sense of the market, who the players are, and what other industries are associated with peanuts.

Using Industry Journals

Specialized trade journals, reference sources and industry-specific publications offer in-depth analysis of the minutiae within their targeted industry. Industry journal writers are generally experts in their fields. Since the writers may be business developers, company presidents and chief executive officers, they tend to write at a higher level of specificity. Generalization is exchanged for details. Interviews with key people turn into personal exchanges between interviewer and interviewee. Mutual trust and respect between journalist and interviewee increases because each speaks the same language, resulting in a knowledge–based exchange that can be very insightful. Often, movers and shakers in the industry are profiled in each issue, noting who is moving to which company, who is been bought or sold and what new products are being released. These specialized journals are published by trade associations, industry-targeted publishers or companies themselves. Keep in mind that advertisers need to be appeased, so there will be some bias.

See **Appendix 2** for a resource list of industry specific journals.

Using Government Agency Resources

Researching government agencies is an important component of standard sources that are used in business investigations. Most investigators think of public records, such as court cases, business registrations or Securities and Exchange Commission (SEC) filings, when they hear "government documents." Often these types of government documents, or at least an index of the documents, are available on various government agency various Web sites for free or for a nominal cost. A one-stop free shopping site for an enormous and updated collection U.S. sources is found www.brbpub.com.[9]

Other publicly available government publications that also can come in handy are industry reports, government studies and surveys, military reports, historical documents and white papers. Every single industry, country, scientific or medical endeavor has some government documents written about it. Getting to these documents can be cumbersome. But much of the information is now available at various Web sites, and the perfect place to start searching for them is through the U.S. Government search engine.

If you are diligent, you will want to visit the government depository library Web site www.gpoaccess.gov/libraries.html. Government depositories are excruciatingly complex information arsenals. Since the government produces more paper, media and source material than standard publishers, it has created its own classification system called the Superintendent of Documents (SuDoc.) SuDoc numbers change with every new administration. Before the creation of the Department of Homeland Security, most agencies fell under the Department of Treasury, Department of Justice or other law- enforcement organizations. Classification for Dept. of Justice documents all began with the letter "J" until the Dept. of Homeland Security was formed. Now, that same type of document is classified as "HS."

Visiting a government depository can be a vital part of your research assignments. But avail yourself to the specialized government-documents librarian who can help you navigate through the vast amount of source material and help find what you need. To find a library depository

---

[9] BRB maintains subscription product for professionals looking beyond a links list. The Public Record Research System (PRRS) product gives extensive details, describing the record access policies and procedures for over 20,000 government agencies. Also available in book form; there are no other references like this available.

location near you visit www.gpoaccess.gov/libraries.html. The first visit should be in person in order to establish a relationship with this valuable research asset.

Vendors and Government Documents

On the opposite side of the coin, companies like LexisNexis, Westlaw and Dialog are enterprises based on cataloging, indexing and making available government information that would not be accessible if it was not for their aggregation services. For the professional researcher, time is a very important budget item, so subscribing to these services can get information quickly. You can visit your local depository for a report on a Congressional hearing, but it is faster to search Dialog's Web site and download the same available document for a fee. However, aggregators can be expensive.

The good news is that between the government, Internet, media and other available sources, there are more than enough places to find research information.

Definitive information about finding and using certain government information sources is found throughout this book, per the chapter by topic.

The Basics on Analysis

"Cheap Fish aren't good. Good Fish aren't cheap."[10]

Business investigations that focus on mergers and acquisitions, competitive intelligence, vendor and supplier evaluations, or data mining research all require analysis. Simply collecting information and making claims is *not* an investigation. That is just finding "stuff" and reporting it.

The Returning Client

A longtime client called me after he had taken a few months' hiatus. When I asked him if work was just slow, or if he had chosen another company, he unabashedly admitted that he had tried a cheaper investigative firm. My reply to him was, "Did the new firm disappoint you? Did you get what you paid for?"

He sheepishly agreed that he had been disappointed. Evidently, the way that the other firm reported to him was through a series of haphazard emails and phone calls that related the facts as they occurred. This made it impossible for him to track and manage the case. He was glad to return to my firm.

Unfortunately, this story is all too common. Some investigators can find details, but they lack the ability to analyze and report their findings properly. In a case with time limitations, when the investigation uncovers key information contacting the client is welcomed. The client is part of

---

[10] Anonymous, but timely.

the process and can make decisions based on the findings. However, following up with a report that includes all the findings and your analysis is the professional way to close the investigation.

Hence, much of the analysis occurs during the report writing. When spelling out the details to the client, page-by-page, you not only should be rehashing the days' events, but also focusing on the purpose of the content. That said, always keep in mind that you need to answer the questions your client had when he came to you in the first place.

Having high-level analysis will make investigations easier to write, and will help with your firm's marketing strategies. As you start relationships with new clients, you can decide which analysis method would work best with the specific request, and then pitch that method to them.

Three analysis methods are reviewed here; however, there are many books dedicated to analysis methods. A good source for finding these works is to visit the Society of Competitive Intelligence Professionals' online store at www.scip.org.

SWOT Analysis

SWOT is an analyst methodology that is used for business, and its analysis is the most common and easiest style to work with. SWOT is an acronym for—

- **Strengths**
- **Weaknesses**
- **Opportunities**
- **Threats**

It is flexible, easy to learn and greatly utilized in business reports.

SWOT is the simplest of analyst methods and offers more benefits than merely the analysis itself. A common mistake some investigators make is to get caught up in the details of where a person lives and the person's affiliations. The SWOT method breaks down any subject, whether it is a person or a company, into these four components. This is a great way for an investigator to analyze details in a manner that can lead to other investigative tracks. For example, if a company is showing $750,000 in annual revenue, but similarly sized companies in the same market and type are bringing in $1.5 to $2.0 million, this is an indicator of a weakness to research. Perhaps the sales force is ineffective, the company is young to the market, or a bad reputation is involved.

Using SWOT, the client is properly prepared for your work and will anticipate a formula in the report you prepare

Writing Benefits

Writing the report, by filling in the blanks for SWOT, is an easy way for an investigator to create the report. But perhaps more important, it is putting the details on paper, in a specific formula, that brings to light the issues that otherwise might not have been noticed. For example, while considering the opportunities that were presented in the orange grove case, it came to light that the adjacent properties were for sale. This information was uncovered, because I did not see any other real opportunities that were obvious and worth reporting. However, the SWOT method made me find something to put in the "opportunities" section, which, in turn, forced that information to come to light. Conversely, if I had written a standard, detailed report about the orange grove case, the neighborhood properties for sale would not have been mentioned and the clients would not have benefited in the end.

Presentation Benefits

Using the SWOT method will result in a final report that will read very smoothly, be easy to navigate, and will probably look attractive. The client will appreciate the ability to find key information. He can go directly to the "weaknesses" or "threats" section of the report, if he wishes to read about a competitor, or turn to the "opportunities" section and read about a potential acquisition.

Marketing Benefits of SWOT

When you speak to your clients in business language, using the SWOT methodology, they will have an easier time understanding what you are proposing, and will hire you more readily. As in the orange grove case, as discussed in Chapter 2 under CRAWL, when the client mentioned the predicament he was confronted with, I suggested a SWOT analysis and he was onboard immediately with the project.

The client was prepared for a report that highlighted the four key points: strengths, weaknesses, opportunities, and threats. So, selling him my services was simple, because I anticipated his needs, and spoke his language.

Value Chain and Supply Chain Analysis

Value Chains

Value Chain Analysis (VCA) differs from SWOT because it performs specific functions within certain tasks. For example, VCA is used for examining the core competencies of internal to external resource allocation – i.e. how does a client manage, build, maintain, ship, sell, and protect products.

Created in a text, titled *Competitive Advantage11* by Michael Porter in 1985, VCA has become a stable methodology that is used in many industries, because of its value in identifying and increasing profit margins.

Investigators only need a portion of this analysis to help identify key players in a business or potentially fraudulent vendors and suppliers. I prefer to call this simplified version supply chain analysis, because it demonstrates who are the suppliers and who are the vendors involved in the business process.

---

[11] Porter, M. E. (1985). *Competitive Advantage*. New York: The Free Press.

Supply Chains

Supply chain analysis looks at logistics, both inbound and outbound, operations, support teams, human resources, infrastructure, and technology. By locating the information for each of these areas, and defining the respective roles within the company, this analysis method will create opportunities and/or demonstrate where a company is strongest and most powerful or where its weaknesses are in the chain.

Adapting this method to a business investigation will help assess who is providing assets to the company, whether financially or as a vendor. It also can be instrumental in security assessments and business-continuity planning.

Key components of **supply chain analysis** are—

1. Logistics - Inbound – Warehousing and Internal Handing Of Products

   What are the warehouse conditions? Be ready to define how the product is handled and stored. If refrigeration is necessary, is that addressed? Which vendors are being used to service and repair the air conditioners? If the company produces a controlled substance, food, or a potentially hazardous product, then consider which oversight agency (EPA, FDA, local labor commission, union heads, etc.) would be on-site and writing reports about the internal logistics.

2. Logistics – Outbound – Distribution

   How are the products shipped? Are the products packaged and shipped by the company or does the company use an outside contractor as part of the fulfillment procedure, such as transporting the products to distribution centers, stores, or some other final location.

3. Operations – Product Development and Manufacturing

   Who is making the product? Is there special machinery involved in the creation of the manufactured good? Keep in mind that many products, such as cola and beer, are not actually manufactured by the parent company, but are shipped from a participating vendor or supply partner. For example, a company like Georgia-based Coca-Cola contracts with companies all around the world to manufacturer its product, in accordance with its recipe and standards, and to bottle and distribute locally.

4. Support Teams – Research and Development, Manufacturing-Related Groups, and Unions

   Recognize that the workforce for the product could be made up of research and development in one country, and union workers in another. Software companies also may be spread out in this fashion. Perhaps the research and development labs are located in New York or Tel Aviv, the customer support in India, and the products actually packaged and shipped from China. Discovering where all the employees are will help locate and determine if any regional laws or rules apply.

5. Human Resources – Support for Support Teams and Management

   This is management analysis. The sole purpose of management is to make sure that the staff is provided with the proper environment to work in, the tools and resources needed to conduct the work, and adequate leadership to guide the company. Analysis of the management will help discern if they are up to the task to create a productive environment and, thereby are producing a consistent product.

6. Infrastructure – Location, Security, and Risk Management

Consider what would happen if a catastrophe were to strike the building where the products were manufactured or stored. What contingency plans are in place to get the business back to manufacturing? Are compliance and security policies in place and are the employees aware of the standard operating procedures for emergencies?

Most manufacturing companies abide the technical standards that were established by the International Organization of Standardization (ISO). This means that they meet and are qualified for an international standard that is accepted as a benchmark for companies in their respective industries. Qualification is an expensive and painstaking process. For investigators, finding a company ISO-qualified indicates that the plans of operation are on file with the standards board.

Also, any large plant operating in a community will, no doubt, have emergency plans on file with local law enforcement, the zoning commission, or another oversight agency.

7. Technology – Tracking Products, Customer Intelligence, and Market Basket Analysis.

Customer relationship management (CRM) tools are standard for companies selling products. The CRM allows a purchaser access to his account to purchase more supplies, manage the shipments and analyze the usage.

Wal-Mart is famous for its Retail Link®, (www.retailright.ca/), which allows suppliers to globally access sales data and manage their product inventory.

Tying all these pieces together on a company investigation can demonstrate weaknesses that otherwise would not be apparent in the traditional "who, what, and where" investigative report.

Woes

The ABC Needle Company is responsible for manufacturing pediatric hypodermic needles. It has created a special process to make custom, tiny injectors and is the sole supplier of this product to Farley Pharmaceutical Co. These needles are so precise that Farley uses them exclusively for its infant insulin-injector guns. Also, part of Farley's process involves the plungers, stoppers, and other mechanics that go into making insulin guns for babies.

One day in Little Town, Kansas, where ABC is located, a tornado strikes and tears the roof off its building, destroying a nearby school, and devastating families in a 20-mile radius.

The damages at the ABC facility not only include the immediate products, but also the manufacturing equipment and machines. ABC cannot produce any new needles until the equipment is fixed. But, even if the equipment worked, the employees are too overwhelmed by their own grief and troubles to go to work, as they are cleaning up their own homes.

The company president realizes the only viable products he has left are the tractor-trailers that were away from the factory at the time of the storm. Because he cannot immediately get his machines repaired and operating, he will be unable to continue producing the hypodermics in the short term. Therefore, he has to contact a competitor, if there is one, or expect to lose the contract with Farley, and potentially file for bankruptcy.

As a protection, Farley now must look for another needle manufacturer. Without a supplier that can provide needles to its specifications, Farley will be unable to produce the infant insulin-injector guns.

Finally, without infant insulin-injector guns available, doctors are forced to find alternatives for families who rely on this technology to treat their children.

If that story sounds a tad preposterous, then consider that once every three years the U.S. runs out of the influenza vaccine. There is such a limited supply, because only a few companies manufacture the vaccine. If one of those companies is devastated and its extended resources are damaged, a flu epidemic could easily turn into a pandemic.

The goal of supply chain analysis is to find the weakest link. Establish that all links are either substantial, offer redundancy or have solid contingency plans. But then look for the weakest link and try to imagine a worst-case scenario based on its failure. Of course, when reporting to your client, be specific that you are creating only a supposition of events that may never occur. Your client needs to be aware of the possibilities.

CARA Analysis

The third analysis model is known as CARA, an acronym for characteristics, associations, reputation, and affiliations. CARA is used for analyzing individuals.

Characteristics

Characteristics give a sense of the subject's personality. Look at his rank or position, and the type of car he drives. Is he litigious? Has he been convicted of any crimes or rewarded for any heroic acts?

Associations

Associations with other people, either professional or personal, help in understanding the socio-economic position of the subject, whether he is wealthy, an average worker or a criminal.

Reputation

Reputation searches present the best opportunities to hear what people say about the person and his affiliates.

Affiliations

Affiliations with certain companies, organizations, associations, and educational facilities are very telling.

All four CARA indicators mirror each other. The point of separating them is to focus on analysis and report writing.

CARA is a bit of an anomaly, introduced to me years ago by a former Federal Agent. I wish I could say I created a new analysis method, but I can claim to have adopted it for all my investigations. Reputation and associations are important no matter if you are investigating a person or a company. Even as adults we are judged by association. Establishing with whom your target individual associates, consorts, does business or maintains relations will be very important factors to your client.

Presenting CARA Analysis

Be careful when presenting your analysis. Unless you want to gamble on making bold statements based solely on research findings, you cannot say for certain that "Mr. So-and-so" is a mob lawyer. Instead, you should convey the information as you interpret it based on CARA. For example, you can state that "Mr. So-and-so" is an attorney with a high net worth, and he is considered to be a savvy businessman. He is attended, according to the media, six recent engagements, all organized by reputed mob bosses and their families.

With all of the information you have gathered, examine any unusual relationships between the associates, addresses, or businesses. Remember that fraudulent people will go to great lengths to hide common threads linking them with other parties.

For leads that seem to go nowhere, be prepared to explain your search strategy and your pursuit of a false lead that ultimately resulted in a dead end or an unexpected outcome.

Cynthia's Key Chapter Points

Using one or all of these analysis methods are extremely important to a business background investigation. Keep these methods in mind as you read the chapters to follow. Good and effective use of these analytical methods will help you produce a consistent report, which will be appreciated by your clients.

♦ An investigator may not have the necessary information at hand, but does know where to find it.

♦ More importantly, that investigator knows, or will expect to learn, the limitations of available information and that there are biases in certain sources.

♦ If you have never done analysis before, look into classes, conferences or books teaching the various analytical methods.

♦ With so many online resources available, it is easy to neglect the traditional offline repositories. Don't!

♦ Local libraries are like an Intranet specific to your investigation. See what they offer in the way of local press indexes, town historian registrars, etc.

♦ Taxonomy, or word lists, should always be developed at the beginning of your research so that you know to try all the variants of an expression. This helps you not miss vital information.

♦ Use an official style manual to help record your findings and for report writing.

♦ Learn about the subject as a whole (i.e. market or industry) before delving into specifics, more so when a significant market change could be the reason for the investigation.

♦ Free government documents are really what public record vendors are reselling at a premium. If you have the time, cut costs by finding the source information through the original sources like the Government Printing Office (gpo.gov).

♦ Depending on your type of investigation, S.W.O.T., Value and Supply Chain Analysis and C.A.R.A Analysis are three best ways to view the research. Each of these would cover most investigative report needs.

Section 2

Performing the Investigation

The foundation is set and the fundamentals should be clear. With an actual case in hand, it is time to start investigating.

Section Two examines the intricacies of business information. Here is the path to locating leads, understanding given information for actual use and finally how to interpret the results.

We will dissect people and companies by regulatory and legal issues, discover their assets and liens, and disclose their affiliations and industries.

Chapter 4

Discovering and Dissecting Company Information

The business of America is business.
                                        —Calvin Coolidge
The business of government is to keep the government out of business – that is, unless business needs government aid.
                                        —Will Rogers

Companies come in multiple sizes, jurisdictions, ownership structures and sectors. The quest for information about companies will vary depending on how long they have been in business, how large they are, how many customers they serve, where they are located, and the principals behind them. Narrowing the structure and logistics of the company you are investigating will set the stage for the budget and timeline. **Having in-depth knowledge on all of these issues is a must for an investigator.**

This chapter is lengthy, but important since it will examine, in detail, the following topics—

- Types and structures of business entities
- Publicly owned companies and private ownership
- Large companies vs. small companies
- Location issues
- Locating company headquarters
- Subsidiaries, divisions, satellite offices, affiliates, plants
- Non-profits and foundations
- Recommended online investigative resources

Identify the Type of Business Entity

Determining the entity's structure will give you an invaluable sense and understanding of what is available from an information perspective and how to launch your investigation. A few norms can be supposed.

- Generally, a publicly traded company has more information readily available, and the data is easy to obtain and is apparent. However, these types of companies also tend to be large, multi-layered organizations that can be cumbersome to examine as you peel away the layers of management, subsidiaries, and partnerships. A publicly traded company will have a large volume of data and information to cull through, but it is still readily available.

- Investigating private companies is challenging since there are fewer regulations that demand these firms to file or report publicly available data, especially financial-related records. Private company financials are always questionable when gathering information from off- the-shelf business services, because of their self-reported value.

- A company based in the U.S. will be easier to investigate than a foreign entity.

- Small and/or young companies are difficult to research because of the lack of information available. You will have to search deeper into the history of the principal's prior companies.

To lay a proper foundation, let us examine the types of U.S. business entities that you will encounter.

Corporation

A corporation is a legal entity or structure created under the authority of state law. A corporation is owned by shareholders or stockholders. A corporation can enter into contracts, sue or be sued, and is liable for its own debts and obligations, including income taxes. When ownership changes in a corporation, the corporation does not dissolve.

There are two common forms of a corporation – a "C" and a subchapter "S" corporation. A "C" corporation is, as described above, a legal separate entity, but with limited personal liability for business debts. An "S" corporation is not a taxable entity; the corporate earnings and profits are passed directly to the personal tax return of the shareholder on a prorated basis equal to the share of ownership.

Foreign Corporation

Also called an out-of-state corporation, a foreign corporation is an existing corporation that registered to do business in another state. A foreign corporation is able to operate in multiple states or jurisdictions as one organization. (Note: there are actually two definitions. Do not confuse this with a corporation formed and operating in a foreign country – these are two entirely different types of entities.) The alternative – to register a separate corporation in each jurisdiction where operations are taking place– would be extremely cumbersome.

Non Profit

A non-profit corporation is formed to carry out a specific purpose that is charitable, educational, religious, literary or scientific in nature. A non-profit corporation does not pay federal or state income taxes on its profits because the IRS perceives that the public derives benefits from this organization. Non-profits are often referred to as a "501C3" which comes from Section 501(c)(3) of the Internal Revenue Code.

Partnerships

A partnership is a business with more than one owner who has not filed papers with the state to become a corporation or a limited liability company (see below). There are two basic types of partnerships – general partnerships and limited partnerships. The general partnership is the simplest and least expensive co-owned business structure to create and maintain. Many states allow the creation of special limited liability partnerships (LLPs).

A limited liability limited partnership (LLLP) is a relatively new modification of the limited partnership, a form of business entity recognized under U.S. commercial law. Like a limited partnership, an LLLP is a limited partnership and, as such, consists of one or more general partners and one or more limited partners. Many LLLPs deal with real estate ownership and management.

Limited Liability Company

A limited liability company (LLC) combines the advantages of a corporation with the tax advantages and management flexibility of a partnership. Similar to a corporation, an LLC is created by a state filing, protects personal assets from business liabilities, and has few ownership restrictions. Perhaps the biggest difference between LLCs and corporations is that LLCs do not issue stock. Like partnerships, LLCs are simply owned by the members and/or the managers of the company.

Because of the simplicity and flexibility, an LLC is very popular for both start-up businesses and more mature businesses. In many states, the number of new LLCs being formed is outpacing new corporation filings.

Watch for Trade Names, Fictitious Names, and Assumed Names

"Trade names" is relative term. Trade names may be referred to as "fictitious names," "assumed names," or "DBAs." States (or counties) allow business owners to operate a company using a name other than its real name. Registering the name insures two entities will not use the same or close to the same name.

Typically, the state agency that oversees corporation records usually maintains the files for trade names. Most states will allow verbal or Web status checks of names. Some states will administer "fictitious names" at the state level while county agencies administer "trade names," or vice versa.

Researching Publicly Owned Companies

A publicly owned company is a corporation whose securities, i.e. stocks, are available for sale to the open market. These shares are exchanged on stock markets, such as the American Stock Exchange (AMEX), New York Stock Exchange (NYSE) and the National Association of Securities Dealers Automated Quotations (NASDAQ). Companies that do not qualify to have shares sold in one of these three exchanges are often found listed in one of the lesser exchanges, often known as the over-the-counter (OTC) market or on the "Pink Sheets." These stocks, often referred to as *penny stocks,* represent companies that still offer opportunity and value, but are not traded on the major markets.

Companies also may be traded on foreign stock exchanges. Examples are the Toyko Exchange (www.tse.or.jp), the Toronto Exchange (www.tsx.com), and the Jamaican Stock Exchange (www.jamstockex.com). Each exchange and country will have its own oversight group. Below are two resources to find a list of foreign exchanges—

- www.tdd.lt/slnews/Stock_Exchanges/Stock.Exchanges.htm
- http://en.wikipedia.org/wiki/List_of_stock_exchanges

Publicly traded companies operating in the U.S. are required by Federal law to register with the Securities and Exchange Commission (SEC) and submit filings quarterly and annually to the SEC. However, publicly owned companies that only operate within a particular state may file with their state's bureau of securities instead of the SEC. Both the SEC and these state agencies also monitor these companies for any irregularities or potential fraudulent behavior.

Fortunately, it is very easy to find out if your subject company is traded or not. First, the company itself will give you its stock symbol, a short coded identifier such as Ebay's "EBA" or General Electric's "GE." All major brokerage firms with a Web presence offer research on stock symbols and detailed overviews of the company's profits and operations. If you do not have a stock account, I recommend visiting either www.finance.yahoo.com or www.finance.google.com. Similar in offerings, both give symbol look-ups, news on the company in question, and a plethora of corporate-structure details for free.

Some companies that have experienced tough times or troubles with regulator will be delisted from a major exchange and listed on the OTC. Most companies are delisted because they are acquired by another company, they merge with another company, the stock price does not meet the exchange's minimum, they fail to file proper papers or they have solvency problems. In fact, companies also can be demerged, decentralized, demutualized or re-privatized.

As you examine the particular filings of the company you are investigating, a good idea is to keep a financial dictionary within arm's reach. Or, you may want to place a Web site like www.business.com, on your favorites list, as a resource to define financial expressions.

Regulatory Sources—SEC, FINRA & NFA

There are three primary regulatory agencies that over see regulatory and compliance issues with publicly traded securities or with security dealers.

- **Securities & Exchange Commission (SEC)**
- **Financial Industry Regulatory Authority (FINRA)**[12]
- **National Futures Association (NFA)**

The SEC is a Federal government agency. FINRA and NFA are self-regulatory bodies.

Each agency is excellent resource for investigating compliance issues and enforcement actions. Chapter 6 examines in detail how to access the databases from these agencies when investigating compliance issues and sanctions. For the purposes of this chapter, we will examine EDGAR – the SEC's repository of filings from publicly owned companies.

EDGAR

EDGAR – the **E**lectronic **D**ata **G**athering **A**nalysis and **R**etrieval system – was established by the SEC to allow companies to make required filings to the SEC by direct transmission. As of May 6, 1996, all public domestic companies are required to make their filings on EDGAR, except for filings made to the SEC's regional offices and those filings made on paper due to a hardship exemption.

EDGAR has an extensive repository of U.S. corporation information, most of which is available online. Companies must file the following reports with the SEC—

- 10-K– an annual financial report that includes audited year-end financial statements.
- 10-Q – a quarterly, un-audited report.
- 8K – report detailing significant or unscheduled corporate changes or events.
- Securities offerings, trading registrations, and the final prospectus.

The list above is not conclusive. There are other miscellaneous reports filed, including those dealing with security holdings by institutions and insiders. Access to these documents provides a wealth of information.

How to Access EDGAR Online

Search EDGAR at www.sec.gov/edgar/searchedgar/webusers.htm. Also, a number of private vendors offer access to EDGAR records. LexisNexis acts as the data wholesaler or distributor on behalf of the government. LexisNexis sells data to information retailers, including its own Nexis service.

---

[12] Formerly the National Association of Securities Dealers – NASD

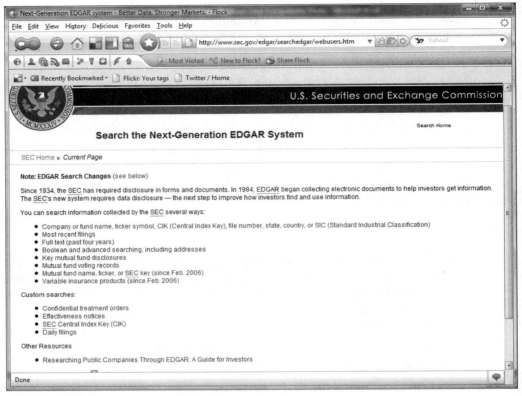

(Source: www.sec.gov/edgar/searchedgar/webusers.htm)

EDGAR's search features have been expanded considerably in the recent past. Companies can be searched by name, and by filing specifics, such as just the DEF14 reports (good for getting executive compensation information). Also searchable are Mutual Funds, historical findings and Variable Insurance Products back to February of 2006. EDGAR also offers full-text searching, a feature newly added that lets the investigator search by a keyword. Keyword searches allow you to search by personal name or company name. Results are "keyword-like." This means if the person or company you are searching for is mentioned in a filing, the keyword will appear, even if it is ancillary, and what will not appear is the focus of the report. Sample searches in EDGAR for "Barack Obama" turned up 10 matches, "Robert Nardelli" had 37 matches, and "Mickey Mouse" turned up 66 matches.

For more information on how to use the SEC and EDGAR for investigations see Chapter 6.

Researching Foreign Country Company Designations

In the U.S., most companies are designated as Inc. or LLC. If you see a U.S.-based company name with Ltd. at the end, then you know to look for a foreign parent. Foreign designations can be confusing if you have not seen them in the course of your work. After a while, however, you get accustomed to seeing designations like GmbH, Ltd. and S.A.

Below are some examples of foreign company designations. An expanded list of 193 countries' foreign designations, graciously provided by Winthrop Corporation for publication in this book, (www.CorporateInformation.com) is found in Appendix 1.

- Gesellschaft mit beschränkter Haftung, or GmbH, is German and literally translates to *company with limited liability*. GmbH indicates the company is incorporated, but not publicly traded. And Aktiengesellschaft, or AG, is a loosely translated German term for publicly traded companies. A GmbH must have at least two partners and a nominal amount of capital. Subsidiaries of AGs can be GmbHs.

- Limited, denoted as Ltd., is commonly used in the United Kingdom and in the Commonwealth, in Japan, and in the United States. Ltd. indicates that the company is incorporated and that the owners have limited liability.

- S.A. is a very popular corporate type that is used in many Latin countries. In general terms, the abbreviation stands for "anonymous society/corporation." In addition, Greece, Luxembourg, France, and Belgium mark companies with an S.A. It is difficult to generalize a definition of S.A for all these countries; however, S.A. is a private entity, with a minimum capital ownership required of at least two parties.

- B.V., a common Dutch symbol for Besloten Vennootschap, can be found with companies in the Dutch Antilles, the Netherlands and Belgium.

Using the information in the Appendix, you can quickly surmise where to begin when investigating a company that has an unusual incorporation mark. Each country will offer different amounts of information on each company.

> **Author Tip ➡** Most foreign countries that have an embassy in the U.S., will also maintain an embassy Web page in English. These pages represent an excellent resource for investigation more about that particular country's government agencies. A links list to these Web addresses is found at www.brbpub.com/freeresources/pubrecsites.aspx. Click on *Foreign Sites – Other*.

Understanding Private Ownership and Investors

Private ownership of a company essentially means that a single shareholder owns the company, like the local plumber up the street, or Mars, Inc., famous for its candy bars. Private companies have less reporting requirements to the government than public companies. The SEC does not require quarterly or yearly statements to insure the legitimacy and honesty of a company for its shareholders.

Sizable private companies may be involved with private investors known as venture capitalists, private equity investors, or even public companies. Note that a public company can have a private venture, and vice versa. In this instance, use EDGAR to find ownership or involvement.

It can be difficult, if not impossible, to find the terms of a private deal between two private entities, especially if they do not want the details disclosed. Perhaps you may find a press release that says a little more than, "ABC Company was purchased for an undisclosed amount by the DEX Firm."

Perhaps the best option to finding financial information on private companies is to valuate their known assets and liabilities (see Chapter 7`), as well as reviewing business and credit reports from vendors, such as Dun & Bradstreet (D&B) and Experian.

Who owns the company is sometimes the most complicated question to answer. One or many persons or entities may be involved, and sometimes ownership is a matter of one percent difference in shareholder value. Breaking down company ownership by small and large corporations helps to get started into this research endeavor.

Identifying Small Companies

According to the U.S. Small Business Administration, "Small firms represent 99.7 percent of all employer firms."[13]

Given the vast number of companies considered "small," there is a strong probability most investigations will involve a small companies. Even though small companies can still be million dollar firms, their corporate structure is generally easier to assess than huge conglomerates. These companies tend to be private entities, and can be as small as the local pizzeria, and as large as a multi-million dollar, multi-state organization. Keeping subsidiaries out of this, tracing the origin of ownership of a company *should* be as easy as obtaining its annual report from the Secretary of State's office. Unfortunately, not all states require ownership information to be on file, and only request the contact information for Service for Process, where legal papers should be sent in case the company is sued.

The first place to look for a small company is through the Secretary of State Business Registration. Remember to follow up with a request for an actual photocopy of a report, or a TIFF[14] file, as you can obtain online in Florida, and not just accept what is delivered via the Web. If a filing is written and submitted to the state, and you find that the filer has crossed out some information, like an address, you will not see the error online.

The Proof is on the Paper

A large company contracted me to assist on an employee fraud issue. The subject employee was a real estate manager for the company's Midwest division in Michigan. He was having an affair with a young Chinese woman, who was of interest to the U.S. authorities. Beyond the original reason for launching the investigation, the company also was told that the

---

[13] Source: www.sba.gov/advo/stats/sbfaq.pdf
[14] TIFF - Tagged Image File Format is a file format for storing images, including photographs and line art

couple was working together in real estate. If true, this would have been an employee violation of the non-compete clause the manager had signed. My task was to find out what he was doing outside of company business.

Both parties had created businesses, filed in the state of Michigan. His filing listed him as a corporate officer, and her filing listed her as a corporate officer. Unfortunately, they did not list each other in the same documents. Looking at the Web page that provided this information, I thought it would be interesting to see the actual documents. So, I ordered copies of the corporate registrations and waited patiently, as it took Michigan' Corporation Division a few weeks to send.

When the copies arrived, I noticed a few, very distinct and obvious clues. First, both applications were typed, using the same typewriter. Who has a typewriter anymore?! The typing was similar on each form, using the same indenting and spacing style. I was feeling like Sherlock Holmes making these odd, but important, discoveries, until I realized the most obvious clue of all. Both forms had her home address typed on them for the Service of Process. But on his form, the typed information had an "X" through it, and she carefully had written his address next to it. I knew it was her handwriting because she had used the same cursive style in her own signature on her own form. That never would have been seen without obtaining hard copies of the actual filing documents.

Business registrations, changes and annual reports can be found at each state's Secretary of State Web site. The site list can be obtained at www.brbpub.com's public records directory. Another source for locating small business information is through a town's Chamber of Commerce. For example, www.worldchambers.com is a good start.

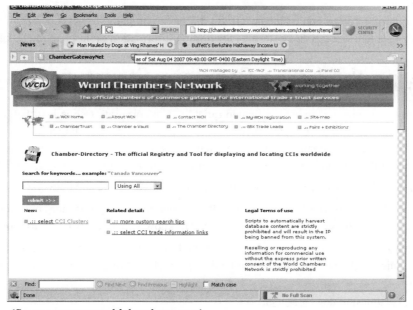

(Source: www.worldchambers.com)

Small Company — Big Web Presence

Do not underestimate news stories, press releases, and a company's Web site. The "About Us" section may accurately offer company history and ownership information. However, it is best to verify any company-produced literature.

Given that investigators always verify their leads, take a look to see what is on the Web site that offers clues. Visiting the Web site will give you a sense of what the company has to say.

Remember Peter Steiner's "On the Internet nobody knows you're a dog" cartoon published in *The New Yorker* (pg 61 of July 5, 1993)?[15] Some very impressive looking Web sites are just fronts for small garage operations. At-home moms, people working side jobs, and any number of individuals are "doing business on the Internet" by selling travel services, financial advice, or providing consulting on a variety. These entities may or may not be illegitimate.

When you view a Web site and you are skeptical as to the validity of the product or company, a good starting point to weed out the truth is the About Us section. This section is reflects how the people who put up these sites are presenting themselves and their company.

The key to writing the "About Us" section is to share with the readers how talented and capable the leaders of a company are in their respective roles. These biographies always discuss their history, talents and education. The rule to reading through this is to remember there is a bias. Also, "you get what you pay for," so verify all the information being provided on the "About Us" Web pages.

If that information is freely given, then fee-based services can only enhance the return for the investigator. For small and large companies, fee-based information services are rich resources for gathering data quickly on a company. See the discussion on databases at the end of the chapter.

Let us look at other end of the spectrum, the large company, to get a perspective on the unique challenges and free-service offerings for finding information on large to mega-large companies.

Identifying the Large Company Structure

Large companies become complicated quickly. The corporate tree is just that, a top-down view of companies and who owns them. Also, it provides a clear understanding about who the ultimate parent company is. Publicly traded companies will have their corporate structures written in their annual reports. Even so, that information is not easy to discern.

You would think Coca-Cola is the ultimate parent of Coke, the soda beverage.

But is it? Is Coca-Cola Enterprises the ultimate parent? Tricky question, but important if you are working on a product-liability case, and need to know who to track down for your client.

Chances are a canning company, contracted to can soda for Coca-Cola as well as other companies, is liable. Yet, to find culpable parties, litigators will search for the deepest pockets.

---

[15] www.epatric.com/funstuff/dog/index.html

The canning company may be simply a contract firm, signed to can a beverage by contract only. It also can be partially or completely owned by Coca-Cola Enterprises. There is never one single answer to this issue, and each matter must be researched thoroughly to understand the unique circumstances.

Fast-food service companies often go through this. You may never have heard of Yum! Brands, but its subsidiaries KFC and Taco Bell are familiar to most Americans. Visit a Web site like www.yumfranchises.com and see how many opportunities there are for partnership.

Interestingly, on most of the large company investigations I have worked, the target company is actually a subsidiary that was five "branches" removed from the ultimate parent.

Using Web sites for research are as effective for large companies as they are for the smaller ones. Be sure to search the actual company Web site's "About Us" section, as well as any "Investor" or "Financial" Web pages.

Finding the Parent

When the question comes down to "who owns whom?" I can recommend two valuable resources for finding the ultimate parent of a company—

- The Directory of Corporate Affiliations - www.corporateaffiliations.com, owned by LexisNexis.

  Per their web page..."Looking for authoritative business intelligence on corporate families?...Our database provides current, accurate corporate linkage information and company profiles on nearly 200,000 of the most prominent global public and private parent companies and their affiliates, subsidiaries and divisions—down to the seventh level of corporate linkage."

  Not only does Corporate Affiliations publish corporate family trees, the database also contains over 700,000 corporate contacts, 110,000 board members, 150,000 brand names and 140,000 competitors."

- Who Owns Whom" - https://solutions.dnb.com/wow - www.dialog.com (File 522), owned by Dun & Bradstreet

  This international database covers the following industries since January 2006— "...manufacturing, retail trade , wholesale trade , agriculture, mining, construction, financial services, educational institutions, business services, professional services, public, private and government-run companies."

Recognize Location Issues

Location, location, location! This is the mantra of many real estate investors. The same is true for many businesses. An investigator must keep in mind that businesses will locate their headquarters, offices, plants, and warehouses in the precise location(s) that works best for their situation.

Perhaps a major, international law firm, wanting to impress and capture the attention of wealthy potential clients, will be located center stage in New York City, London, Hong Kong, Singapore, or other prestigious and expensive real estate locations. Some companies must locate near specific transportation resources, such as railroad yards, freeways, waterways, or airports, for ease of operation. Corporations, especially larger ones, may operate in more than one country. Some mega-companies, such as Coca-Cola and Microsoft, can claim more than 100 different locations. A customer-support team for a software company does not necessarily need downtown views of a seaport, nor does it necessarily need to be in the same country as the company's headquarters. Today, many firms outsource their tech support to locations in Third World countries, such as in Asia or in South America. This trend allows companies to man their customer-service lines 24/7 with inexpensive labor.

Of course, retail companies, looking for local clients, will be found in the middle of residential and business neighborhoods, where their neon signs and other forms of advertising will lure new customers.

Knowing where to investigate companies with more than one location, whether the company has two offices in two cities, or is a multinational firm with subsidiaries, branches, satellites, plants, and help desks located in multiple nations, is an important factor. A research starting point is to obtain business reports from vendors such as Kompass, Hoovers, SkyMinder or Dun & Bradstreet, as covered at the end of this chapter). Each vendor should offer a view of the corporate structure, or, at the very least, the highest level of the company with its immediate subsidiaries.

A good starting point is to find the company's true headquarters.

How to Locate the Company Headquarters

Multinational is the wave of business these days. As discussed above, with the improvement of technology and advantages of cheaper labor, tax shelters, and weak environmental and labor laws in some countries, it is no wonder that many American businesses move overseas to set up companies in foreign countries. Researching these company headquarters can sometimes be a little like playing the game "Pin the Tail on the Donkey." Where is the true location of a company's headquarters, and where does the CEO actually report to work?

Use Annual Reports

One of the first steps is to locate annual reports. With a simple Google search, you can find many Web services that provide annual reports, such as www.annualreports.com.

Many times, these informative reports may be found on the company's Web site or in SEC filings, if available. First, look to see if "headquarter-friendly" locations are shown. For example, many American businesses use the tax advantages of registering their corporations in Delaware. Yet, you will not see any population booms in Dover tied to the numbers of new registrations. The same is true in the Bahamas, British Virgin Islands and other offshore locations. These locations are commonly not the true headquarters. For example, a search in the Dun & Bradstreet database for a specific location, known as "Road Town" in the British Virgin Islands, returns thousands of companies, all registered in care of trust companies. An example is "Lexus Investment Group c/o Mission Trust Company." If all these companies actually had physical headquarters on the island, there would be very little space to move around. Technically, there is nothing wrong with this practice. This is a way for companies to take advantage of foreign offshore offerings, such as easier taxation, anonymity and asset protection. However, if an investigator sees a British Virgin Islands address as a company's headquarters or comes across addresses in the Bahamas or another tropical resort country, known more for tourism than industry, then the investigator should immediately consider that the company is registered there, but operating elsewhere.

Watch for Emerging Markets

Another trend to watch is when a company decides to place its headquarters in an area where emerging markets are connected to its product line. Dubai is now considered a prestigious location for wealthy enterprising companies. Many corporations in the petroleum, infrastructure, and manufacturing industries will set up headquarters, or a substantial presence, in Dubai to service the needs of their clients in the Middle East.

Firms serving the technology market may take a similar approach. In order to demonstrate commitment to their current clients and be near potentially new clients, technology firms often set up their headquarters in marketing facilities that are geographically close to their clients. These firms may merely maintain a paper headquarters somewhere else, perhaps in the British Virgin Islands, but physically maintain their headquarters in one of their main sales and marketing facilities in the United States. This pattern also is similar for many technology companies that are created in the U.S., but send the majority of their work overseas to contractors, or subsidiaries in India, Pakistan and other Asian countries.

Also, trying to discern which office location is the actual headquarters can be vexing, because of the nuances these corporations place themselves into. For example, some Israeli technology companies have research and development divisions in one country, their founders and lead scientists in another country, and their headquarters in a U.S. location, like the Silicon Valley in California. In this case, placing the headquarters in the U.S. provides a cost savings for the company, because the tax burden on companies in Israel is steep.

Use Media Sources

Using the media as a source is also a good investigative route to take. One Dun & Bradstreet business report might indicate the ultimate parent company, ABC, being in India, whereas a news article on the same company might have an executive claiming, "our parent company here in the U.S. . . . " This certainly can cause confusion. Keep in mind that both statements may be true. You might be looking at the American division of a company, whose headquarters is in the U.S., and yet the parent company is actually the subsidiary of a larger group that operates overseas. An excellent example is the Tata family of businesses.

Tata Tea Example

Tata Tea is a rich and complicated company, larger than Coca-Cola. However, in the U.S., you would know it by one of its brand names, such as Tetley, and not by Tata Tea. Tetley is a subsidiary of Tata Tea Limited and Tetley Group U.K., and is known as Tata Tetley. In the U.S., two other subsidiaries are Tata Tea Inc. and Tata Coffee.

If that is not confusing enough, there are 28 publicly listed Tata enterprises and they have a combined market capitalisation of some $60 billion, and a shareholder base of 3.5 million. The major Tata companies are Tata Steel, Tata Motors, Tata Consultancy Services (TCS), Tata Power, Tata Chemicals, Tata Tea, Indian Hotels and Tata Communications.

(Source: www.tatatea.com/tata_tetley.htm)

> **Author Tip ➡** Since there are many industries that Tata is involved with, it is a company that is a perfect example for new investigators to use in practicing investigative research and analysis. Tata provides a great deal of information on its Web site, and a myriad of additional information can be found in vendor business and finance reports, legal sources, and through the media and other open sources.

Investigating the HQ Address

Once the headquarters is located, there are some additional steps to take. If the subject company is a large operation, then the headquarters could be in a prestigious location, such as a metropolitan city or center of commerce. Check your property-records resource to see if the company owns the building. If it does not, then you need to determine if the company only occupies a few floors of a skyscraper or shares the address with other businesses.

> **Author Tip** ➡ Be sure to check out who else is at the same address, since there may be some cooperative entities, partners or business associates also located at the same address. This is a vital requirement if your investigation is on a smaller company, such as entity with only one address. The possibility exists that not only are there collusive parties in the same building, but also they are located in the same suite.

Examples of Searches

For example, if you did a search using Dun & Bradstreet on the address 409 Washington Street, Hoboken, New Jersey, you might find 45 companies are located in this single building, telling me it is a multiple tenant facility, like an apartment building or office building.

There are a number of excellent vendors that supply business reports. D&B, perhaps the largest database provider of company information worldwide, offers researchers and investigators the ability to search by address. Whether performing a large or small company research, a subscription to D&B is an immediate help.

By location

Street number starting with [ ]   ending with [ ]

Check for ○ Odd street numbers   ○ Even street numbers   ◉ Both

*Street name: [ ]

*City/Town: [ ]   *State: [————US States———— ▼]   Zip code: [ ]

[Search]

(Source: www.dnb.com)

Even search engines like Google can be helpful. Run the following address search on Google: "409 Washington Hoboken" but add "Street, Road, Avenue, or Court" to in your query, but do not search using "NJ" or "N.J." Even though you might receive more results than necessary, in this case, it is better to be overwhelmed with hits than miss a vital link. Another technique is to view the initial results and then re-search using some filters, such as "street or road". This will help you whittle the results to a more useful list.

Another research key is to search by a telephone number. Again, searching D&B or similar vendors is a good route to go. When searching a phone number in Google or other search engines, leave out the usual dashes, parenthesis, backslashes and other phone number separators. The search should look like this: "xxx xxx xxxx" or "212 555 1212." In most search engines, particularly Google, those marks are considered stop symbols that are automatically ignored by the engine. However, the space is respected. So, anything can occur between the 2 and the 5 and Google will return results.

A search on the phone number "212 555 1212" returned more than 75,000 hits in Google. The actual number goes to Verizon 411 service. In a real phone, fax or cell number search, investigators may find leads and links between companies. A common red flag to spot is if multiple companies are using the same phone number. While this can be a legitimate sign of a spin-offs or subsidiaries, it can also mean some fraudulent companies are piggy-backing off of the same address and phone number.

Also, do not discount the importance of searching a fax number. Sometimes a company's main telephone numbers is merely overlays and searching by the fax number may lead to the physical address

Let us use the ABC Company for another example, using the 409 Washington Street, Hoboken, N.J., with a phone number 201-555-1234 and a fax number 201-555-1233.

The phone number and address indeed may be authentic. However, when searching the address "409 Washington Hoboken," you might find six or more companies that are listed. Now, perform the search using the fax number and you might find three different company names that appear. Following the links back, you might have located three companies, all with the same address and fax number, but each with a different phone number. Hence, you have uncovered the fact that there is some sort of cooperation of shared office space, which means potential collusion. Another avenue to explore is to see if these companies are using rented office space, which might be rented by the hour, month or week.

So, your analysis should note, "ABC Company resides at 409 Washington Street in Hoboken, N.J. Also, the DEX Company and the XYZ Investment Group are located at this address and share the same fax number."

Parent Companies, Subsidiaries, Divisions and Affiliates

A **parent** company is a company that operates and controls separately chartered businesses. The businesses beneath it are known as subsidiaries.

A **subsidiary** operates as a separate entity, but is controlled by the parent company that also wholly or partially (50% or more) owns it.

A **division** is a functional area of the company that specializes in services or product offerings.

An **affiliate** is a chartered business whose shares are owned by one or more companies, with each company owning less than 50%.

Subsidiaries—Who and Where Are They?

As mentioned above, a company that is owned in majority by another company is called a subsidiary. Subsidiary research requires that you investigate who the parent company is. You should determine how much of a shareholder the parent company is and who the shareholders are. Also, an investigator must be aware of the possibility that a subsidiary could be an acquired company. Maybe the company has continued with its own brand name and logo and has not taken the parent's name. It is not readily apparent that it is a subsidiary. And finally, be cognizant that the management of subsidiary companies usually has multiple roles in the larger company, and perhaps in other subsidiaries as well.

Here are two examples.

1. The following is a mock-up example. Coca-Cola is the parent company and it manages the many Coke companies under the Coca-Cola banner. One of the subsidiaries is Coke Enterprises. Coke Enterprises manages the bottling and shipping of Coca-Cola products. Coke Productions is a division of Coca-Cola. It is a small production company that creates Coca-Cola commercials and ad design work. Coca-Cola HBC Polska, a bottling plant in Poland, is partly owned by Coca-Cola and it is considered an affiliate.

2. When evaluating a company, especially an international one, it is not uncommon to see a long line of subsidiaries. For example—

Groupo de Brazil (Brazil) Ultimate Parent

GDB Services Company (Brazil) Headquarters

GDB Services Telecom (Brazil) Subsidiary

GDB Telecom (Brazil) Subsidiary of Subsidiary

Brazil Telecom (NY, U.S.) Subsidiary of Subsidiary, U.S. Headquarters

Brazil Telco Corp (CO, U.S.) Final Subsidiary, actual operating company

A good deal of information about subsidiary relationships can be located in the company's annual report, on its Web site, in the media, in press releases, and in corporate reports. The fee side of D&B and Hoovers does a great job of family hierarchies, as well.

Sometimes, subsidiaries can be discovered quite easily. Using Tata Tea Limited as an example, you find that the company is based in India and is the 100 percent shareholder/owner of Tata Tea Inc. (U.S.), located in Plant City, Florida. According to the financials link on the company's Web site, the majority shareholder, with 20 percent of the shares, is Tata Sons Limited. Look at the list on the next page for the "Top Ten" shareholders in this corporation.

Top Ten Shareholders on March 31, 2009

NAME OF THE SHAREHOLDER	NO. OF SHARES	PERCENTAGE OF SHAREHOLDING
Tata Sons Limited	1,40,87,207	22.78
Life Insurance Corporation of India	73,54,569	11.89

Tata Chemicals Limited	43,17,514	6.98
Tata Investment Corporation Limited	28,00,000	4.53
Bajaj Allianz Life Insurance Company Ltd	22,31,099	3.61
Arisaig Partners(Asia)PTE Ltd A/C Arisaig India Fund Ltd	16,73,320	2.71
National Insurance Company Ltd	9,28,078	1.50
UTI- Unit Linked Insurance Plan	9,00,000	1.45
Norges Bank A/c Government Petroleum Fund	7,58,996	1.23
The Royal Bank of Scotland Ltd as Depository of First State Asia Pacific Fund – A sub fund of First State Investments ICVC	6,97,260	1.13

(Source: www.tatatea.com/invest_relation.htm#16)

One percent, or less, ownership of a company may seem insignificant. However, consider that to obtain the product "VitaminWater" in 2007, Coca-Cola acquired Glaceau for more than $4 billion. Further research shows that Tata Tea and Tata Group were 30 percent shareholders of Glaceau. This change of hands may be significant to a background investigation. An asset search of an individual (see Chapter 7) that uncovers ownership of a company in transition could mean that the individual is sitting on thousands or hundreds of thousands of dollars in stock.

Since subsidiaries do not necessarily have the same brand name or logo as the parent company, investigating subsidiaries will turn up an array of investigative leads to track.

Take, for example, the famous red "Innovation Ring" of Lucent, used before being acquired by Alcatel in 2007. Alcatel's own logo changed with the acquisition as well. However, both company names are still being used, since each is recognizable.

Another pattern to watch for in a subsidiary investigation is when a subsidiary has its own senior management, but the parent company's board of advisors oversees the actions. Often the chief executive officer of a subsidiary is a vice president of the parent company. For example, Percy T. Siganporia is the managing director of Tata Tea. He also sits on the board of Eight O'Clock Coffee, another Tata-owned company.[16]

Satellite Offices and Plants

Sometimes a business background investigation will necessitate research on a company's secondary sites. These satellite offices could house entire divisions of the company, or merely two employees in a rented office to give a local business presence for a company. The satellite office may be in a major metropolitan area, in the suburbs, or in another country, where the office houses a research and development team or a group in charge of a certain product line.

To find these secondary sites, a good place to start is the company's Web site, under "Contact Us" or a similar page. Another search resource is an online phone directory, such as www.yellowpages.com or www.superpages.com. If you search Google for additional sites, use the company name and the city name in the same search sequence.

Sometimes, an investigation of a subsidiary location will turn up interesting results.

Who is Answering the Phone?

A branch of a well-known insurance firm was located 40 miles from the nearest major city. That branch, actually a small office, had been at the location for more than six years. In a cost reduction effort, the parent company decided to close the branch and relocate the employees. Not long after the office had closed, a group of individuals moved into that same space. This group of rogue individuals placed advertisements in small, foreign-language newspapers and advertised itself as the same company as the former tenant. The group successfully "sold" a number of insurance policies. However, after a few months without receiving their insurance documents, the policy owners became frustrated with "the branch" office and began calling the corporate headquarters for assistance. Unfortunately by that time, the rogue individuals were long gone with the policy owners' money.

This corporate identity theft was brilliant, because these individuals took the identity of an established company. Therefore, if a suspicious customer had called the Better Business Bureau or Chamber of Commerce, he would have received glowing reports for that company. And even if you pulled a D&B report, there would be an indicator that the branch had been located there for six years.

Even the parent company had to check the location and records to make sure it had closed the branch.

---

[16] Source: www.tata.com/company/Media/inside.aspx?artid=iN+Yn858a2g

Plants located outside of the corporate headquarters are easy to locate by using the same resource when looking for satellite offices. In addition, there are several excellent manufacturer directories to turn to. The most popular is the Thomas Register of Manufacturers (see www.thomasnet.com).

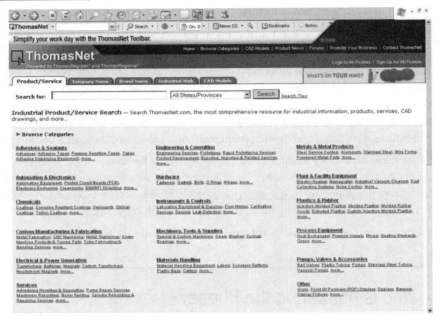

(Source: www.thomasnet.com)

One can Search at ThomasNet by product/brand name, company name, and product type. The level of detail provided for each company listing is very useful.

For example, a search of "bicycle locks" turned up 16 matches, including Courage Industries. In the example below, you can see the details in the registry and find the company's home page.

(Source: www.thomasnet.com)

This resource is helpful, not only for looking up a specific plant or facility, but also it is incredibly useful when trying to locate potential suppliers that a company might enlist for a project. For example, if your investigation involves a brewery opening a new plant in Arkansas, anticipate the brewery will be looking for aluminum-can manufacturers for its product. In Arkansas, one manufacturer appeared—Ball Company in Springdale.

For additional searching tips within targeted industries, turn to Chapter 9 on Industry Focused Research.

Franchises

A franchise is an enterprise that sells or provides products or services, and is owned and supplied by a manufacturer, supplier, or parent. Typical franchise operations are fast-food restaurants, fitness clubs, financial-service entities, tanning salons, construction groups, hotels, and medical groups. A franchise contract, or agreement between the parties, is finalized with specific terms and conditions. Franchise ownership can be in almost any form of a business entity, including a subsidiary. There is no limit to what type of corporation can be doled out as a franchise opportunity. The pervasive theme to franchise is to maintain the brand and quality of service that the supplier or parent requires.

> **Author Tip ➡**   For example, a Dunkin Donuts in the Italian section of New York City could not offer zeppolles (Italian donut with no hole), since this would violate the brand Dunkin Donuts was trying to establish.

However, parent-company kitchens do try new recipes in specific cities. Burger King tried its vegetarian burger first in the U.K., before it slowly made its way into U.S. stores.

The most common type of ownership in a franchise is a small investment group that owns 10 stores in a particular region of the country, versus a single owner/operator store.

When a patron of a restaurant is served substandard food and decides to sue the company, the lawsuit must first establish the chain of ownership. A Taco Bell located in Harrisburg, Pennsylvania, might be owned by "Harrisburg Investment Group," which owns six Taco Bells, two Long John Silver's, and one KFC. The plaintiff may insist on going to the top of Taco Bell's corporate ladder, but the litigating attorney will have to create an issue for the case to go that high. While not that complicated, considering the brand is owned and guaranteed by the corporate entity, suing a franchise can add a layer of individuals named in a lawsuit.

Finding who owns a particular franchise is sometimes as easy as visiting the store, or hotel, or shop. There is usually a sign somewhere in the facility that states, "This Taco Bell is owned by. . . ." And hotels usually post a sign by the lobby front door.

Obtaining a business report from one of the fee-based services mentioned at the end of this chapter is a good search resource. You may see the company name as a "doing business as" (DBA), with the true franchise owner's name as the company name. Also, search the particular state's business registration database, usually held by the Secretary of State, for filings.

Searching a franchise by address should produce two company names: one for the franchise and one for the franchise owner.

Once you obtain a franchise owner's name, begin looking for other franchises under that name. Lawsuits that may have occurred in the past also can lead to future investigations involving media attention.

Franchisers also have been known to form their own trade associations, which can be a great investigative resource. For example, The American Franchisee Association offers an interesting list of who's who in franchiser-specific associations at its Web site www.franchisee.org/supporters.htm.

Again, do not underestimate the type of company that can be franchised, such as major hotel chains, retailers, pharmacies, and gourmet restaurants. They are not all fast-food chains.

Non-profit and Charitable Entities

Private foundations, charities, non-profits, churches, hospitals, schools, or publicly supported organizations all are subject to special considerations when it comes to federal taxes. These entities file different forms with the IRS, and all must contribute detailed financial and member information, which can be a great asset for the online intelligence investigator.

Whether you are looking to reveal experts in the field, local interests to a region, or the financial participation of a particular foundation, these organizations can open a bevy of investigative leads. Finding out what organizations or affiliations a person belongs to can give you insight into the person's character. Categories can include religious, athletic, health, child focused, or specific-interest related. For example, there are two non-profit associations dedicated just to avocados.

Using Non-profits as Corporate Shells

Although many professionals will join organizations for networking purposes, some professionals realize having an opportunity to lend their name, time and finances to a group carries more weight than networking potential.

Often, while doing a name search in an investigation, you will locate a foundation named after the subject. This may be a technique to divert assets into a non-profit status, thereby creating a tax shelter.

Given the choice to pay more taxes to the government or to give money to a charity of your choice, the obvious answer is to support your cause. What better way for a corporation to do this than to create a charity or foundation and support it directly? Not every company that creates a foundation does so to avoid paying taxes, but a few do create these foundations to shelter money that would otherwise leave their coffers. As a foundation, they can appoint board members, directors, and management. Spending can be influenced by the parent organization, unless the bylaws of the foundation specifically state otherwise.

Finding Information About Non-profits

Below are some recommended resources to find information on non-profits, foundations, and the wealthy—

- **GuideStar** www.guidestar.org
- **The Foundation Center** foundationcenter.org
- **The Taft Group** www.taftgroup.com/taft.htm
- **Noza990pf** www.noza990pf.com

The information regarding officers and the financials in a non-profit organization is completely transparent in the Form 990, an annual reporting return that certain federally tax-exempt organizations must file with the IRS. Form 990 provides information on the filing organization's mission, programs, and finances.

Below you can see Part 8 of a random Form 990 taken from GuideStar. The names are blocked out to protect the identities, but I can mention that they all have the same last name as the foundation itself. They appear to be siblings and children of the corporate owner. In other words, what better way to take care of your children than to appoint them as trustees of your own foundation!

Form 990-PF (2005)   Page **6**

Part VIII Information About Officers, Directors, Trustees, Foundation Managers, Highly Paid Employees, and Contractors

1 List all officers, directors, trustees, foundation managers and their compensation (see page 21 of the instructions).

(a) Name and address	(b) Title, and average hours per week devoted to position	(c) Compensation (If not paid, enter -0-)	(d) Contributions to employee benefit plans and deferred compensation	(e) Expense account, other allowances
	Trustee 40	400,000		
	Trustee 40	400,000		
4965	Trustee 40	400,000		

Identifying and Researching Key Location Concerns

Each business location, whether the corporate headquarters, franchise, satellite office, or manufacturing plant is in the U.S. or abroad, will have unique regional concerns. These issues may be environmental or cultural in nature, or may have legal or sanction requirements.

Licenses and Permits

Company regional issues represent an investigation avenue for business research. Specific knowledge of state, county or town laws, governances, and local codes often come into play.

A simple example of how a very large, multinational company has to abide by small-town laws is when a communications company, like Verizon, decides to locate a retail store in a prominently historical neighborhood. It has to abide by the local codes for building design and signage, yet skillfully maintain its logo integrity without compromising the design requirements of the neighborhood.

There are many small-town laws, such as blue laws (no shopping on Sunday), liquor- licensing laws (bars closing for two hours), dry counties (no alcohol served), or environmental codes. Knowing these laws, codes, and issues that a company faces, within the town and county of operation, can be important to an investigation.

Not in My Bailiwick

Once, an investigator called me for assistance on a case that involved a traffic accident outside of San Diego. I thought it odd that a West Coast investigator would contact a New Jersey investigator for a California traffic accident. Of course, nothing is normal or to be expected in this business, so I took the call and received the assignment.

Apparently, the defendant was in a fender bender with a man who claimed that he was mentally traumatized by the accident that occurred between the two of them. There was no question of the accident itself, and the automobile-insurance claim was satisfied for the incident. However, the mental-trauma claim created a lawsuit for the client.

The claim was filed, because the man had been reminded of the deaths of his wife and two daughters in New Jersey in the 1970s. His story was that on the Sunday following Thanksgiving, his wife took their children shopping to the Bergen Mall in Paramus, New Jersey. While exiting the mall parking lot, her car was struck by a semi-trailer truck, crushing his wife and children, and killing them instantly.

Since his accident occurred in California almost thirty years later, he was unable to do anything else, but think of the loss of his entire family back in New Jersey.

Truly a sad story, but if not for my research, he might have gotten away with the blatant lie he told.

As the investigator was telling me the story, I stopped him when he mentioned the location and time. I said, "Wait a minute. Did you say the Bergen Mall on the Sunday after Thanksgiving?" He replied, "Yes." I responded that it wasn't possible for this accident to have occurred as the man asserted. The Bergen Mall is located in Bergen County, New Jersey, which has had a blue law for decades. The Bergen County Blue Law forbids the sale of non-necessary items, such as clothing, shoes, and other retail items commonly found at the mall.

Of course, to verify this statement, I visited the Paramus public library and scrolled through the newspapers, following the said date, to make sure that I was not mistaken, and that the county had not changed the law for one year, or even for one weekend. I looked for two major items: First, to read any mention of the accident. An accident that horrific would certainly have gained the attention of the local press. Second, I researched the week prior to Thanksgiving to insure that there were no advertisements mentioning open hours on

Sunday. In fact, the advertisements specifically stated the Sunday hours for stores in nearby Passaic and Hudson Counties, but indicated that the Bergen County stores were closed on that Sunday.

After giving that vital detail to the investigator, I asked him to look into the man's history a little further. It turned out that, during the supposed time of his family's accident, he was in a state prison. Furthermore, he was never married.

This story demonstrates three key investigative facts.

1. First, be aware of the local laws and customs of the region you are working in. If you are not familiar with them, then call a local investigator in that area and ask him of any issues that you should be aware. If you are not sure you want to discuss your case with another investigator, then call the local library or city clerk's office. The California investigator followed up my research by calling the Paramus Police Department and talking with a captain, who had joined the force in the late '70s.

2. The second issue is the use of the local library for regional research. Local newspapers are so important for more reasons than I cover in the chapter on media. In this instance, I utilized the local press to get information that is not available in a database. Anything prior to 1980 is sketchy, at best. And you will never see advertisements in media database searches outside of ProQuest databases, which highlight only very popular historical newspapers, like the *New York Times*. This kind of newspaper captures full-screen shots.

3. The third piece is to check the obvious. Check facts if you have a history of an individual who has mental lapses regarding time. In the previous story, it did not cost the West Coast investigator a lot of money to hire me to run to the library; however, he could have saved that budget and his own time, if he had interviewed the subject a little further and had seen the incongruent details of his story.

Be cognizant of other types of laws and different inspectors that could also be involved with your investigation. For example, if a company operates an air hanger, the Federal Aviation Administration (www.faa.gov) will have documentation and inspection records on that particular hanger or company. If your case involves media broadcasting, the Federal Communications Commission (www.fcc.gov) oversees licensing for radio, television, satellite, and all other communications within the U.S.

> **Author Tip ➡** There really is no limit on how involved federal, state, and local governments will get with a business. This is a good place for a little imagination. Ask yourself when presented with a new company to investigate, "Who in the government would care?" Chances are, there is a license, permit, or inspection involved with the particular company. Visit the state's Web site, search the occupation in the generic search box for the state and see what types of links come up. If there are too many, then simply search the occupation + license (or) + permit.

Environmental Issues

Producers and manufacturers will have some sort of oversight organization involved in insuring they are in compliance with environmental laws. County, state and federal boards all will have special interest in the pollution concerns of the community.

The federal government has the Environmental Protection Agency (EPA) with regional offices throughout the U.S.

State environmental agencies also protect property through enforcement. The EPA Web site has a convenient link to these state pages at www.epa.gov/epahome/state.htm.

Counties and towns also have health departments, with appointed health officers, who are the regional guardians, and are usually a part of the first response when a toxic spill occurs or a pandemic/epidemic begins. Locate the official county and town Web sites and you will find a link to them, or their actual contact information.

These agencies will be important when trying to find out if the plant or factory you are investigating has followed regulations and passed inspections. These documents are available for review, and, sometimes, offer a good deal of information about the plants and their managers.

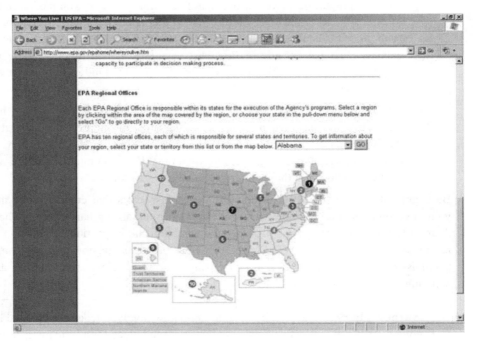

(Source: www.epa.gov/epahome/whereyoulive.htm)

Civic and Cultural Laws

Regionally located companies are not only hosted by the cities where they are located, but also they become a *part of the community*. You will find that large companies, with key offices, manufacturing plants, and operational facilities located outside of company headquarters, are usually involved with outreach efforts in the community. This involvement is good for business and demonstrates civic responsibility and respect for the communities. Communities will sometimes develop around a large plant facility. Unfortunately, when a company decides to move its operations abroad or to another region, the town often collectively fails.

Key investigative leads may be found through the local economy supporting these companies. The plants and satellite offices are not only filled with people, but also with people who need goods and services. They hire local cleaning companies, eat in local restaurants, buy gas, and organize events, like holiday parties at local hotels. Local retail and hospitality venues are good places for interviewing employees and establishing dialog, when a company is trying to understand how the locals feel about it.

There may be two sides to this story, however. Often you will find the locals need the company in town to help their shops thrive, but they may hold some resentment for the employees, the company, or both. "Outsiders" often are not welcomed right away.

Investigative Resources

One excellent way to learn more about how a community feels toward its local company is to read the local newspapers and interview the residents. Contact the local public library or visit it online to see what regional newspapers cover the neighborhoods. Factiva is one of the better sites for getting very small newspapers on its database. However, the real service provider is www.townnews.com. The caveat here is that it can not be searched direct from its Web site, but has to be accessed through a third party, like a town newspaper. Keep in mind you may find that visiting medium to small communities' in-person is needed, because there are few Internet alternatives.

On the business front, to locate how active a company is within the community, research www.noza990pf.com for a company's foundation or charity work in a specific community. You can search by company name and geography within the advanced-search feature. Also contact support organizations like the chamber of commerce, VFW, rotary, etc. You can usually find people who like to talk about their community.

Dealing with Cultural Issues

Cultural issues can come as a surprise to many new investigators who are located overseas or working with foreign guests. With corporations becoming global so quickly, it is difficult to keep up with the cultural norms of guests or host countries. Does a woman wear a headdress? Do you bow or shake the hand of your Asian client? Who eats first and do you eat everything on your plate, or leave just a little to show you are satisfied?

Pick a Card, Any Card

When playing host to Japanese software developers many years ago, I was given a half-day instruction on Japanese business etiquette. Many of the rules escape me now, but I clearly recall that I was supposed to stare at the visitor's business card, with reverence, for at least 15 seconds. That is a long time when you have six cards in front of you. However, I decided to maintain this practice, and find that I clearly remember a person by his business card now.

Although there are books with plenty of good information about dealing with other cultures, I have found that working with a consultant is the most efficient means to educate yourself. For example, visit www.globalimmersions.com. If the owner can not help you, she will find someone who can.

Local Unions

Put three people on the payroll, and one will call himself a manager and the other two will be organizers. The labor movement, or as several bumper stickers profess, "The people who brought you the weekend," has left its mark on many companies. Whether for good, bad, or indifferent, unions and organized parties are a necessary and apparent part of the workforce in the U.S. and abroad.

(Source: www.indymedia.ie/attachments/feb2006/unite.jpg)

Investigators who specialize in strike forces tend to work from the security standpoint, a necessary and helpful function when a company is preparing to lay off entire divisions, because of financial cutbacks. When combining intelligence with security, it is beneficial to gain perspective on how the union operates, how the employees will be affected, and if the employees are planning any legal, physical, or verbal retaliation.

An Associated Press story in 2004 told of a protest, organized by the Communication Workers of America, at the home of their company's CEO. The story originally contained the CEO's true home address, and was wired to more than 1,000 Associated Press affiliates globally until AP discovered the oops and redacted the address.

Unions have their own Web sites that offer news, updates, and rally information. Keep in mind that these are working-class individuals, not gang members. They normally use bargaining strategies and legal means to achieve their goals, and only strike as a last resort. However, some of these organized parties are well known for their bullying of contractors, who have brought non-union help, or "scabs," onto a job site. They also may try to coerce non-union shops into organizing. Anytime an investigator finds himself at a corporate location with management and unions involved, he should assume that there will be two sides: an "us" and a "them."

A source location for investigating union activity is blogs. Not your typical www.myspace.com profile, but actual blogs that are linked to the union's Web site, like http://blog.aflcio.org/. The quickest way to finding organizational blogs is to locate the parent organization's Web site. Then visit http://technorati.com/, using its advanced- search feature. Search by the URL, such as www.aflcio.org, and see how many blogs - personal or otherwise - are linked to the AFL-CIO's Web site.

(Source: www.technorati.com/search?advanced)

Recommended Online Database Services

The key to learning more a company is to find out who the administration is, what type of financials can be obtained, how many locations it has, and what type of industry it is involved in.

There are numerous online services to research both large and small corporations. The given for large companies, is that the bigger they are, the easier it is to gather information on them. The tasking issues are discerning the volumes of data and deciding on what is valuable and current and what is not. Researching the target company by using online database vendors is a must.

The rest of this chapter is devoted to services to turn to first when researching companies.

Dun & Bradstreet

Dun & Bradstreet is the largest provider of business reports internationally, with more than 100 million companies in its database. Very small, one-man companies and very large, mega corporations are in its international collection. For investigators who conduct a lot of due diligence or find themselves looking into companies often, D&B is worth the starting subscription price of several thousand dollars.

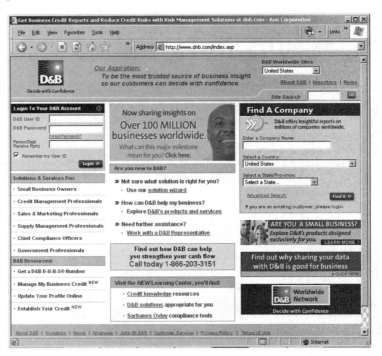

The shortcoming of this service is its price. However, you can search for your company for free. Looking at the above screen shot, you will see the "Find a Company" search box. This "Find a Company" search box extends to international searches. Therefore, look to see if your company is even listed.

Special Tip for Searching D&B

Search by the person's last name or full name, instead of the company name. This is especially handy for small companies. D&B will find the owner's name and cite it as "Also Trades As:." For example, I searched on "Cynthia Hetherington" in New Jersey and came up with:

> HETHERINGTON INFORMATION SERVICES LLC
>
> Also Trades As: CYNTHIA HETERINGTON [sic]

Key things to know about searching D&B reports include—

- For information that contributes to your report, use D&B reports as a lead, not the answer.

- The best part of the reports is not the financial information.

- The best parts of a report for investigators are:

  o Name of company and owner

  o Phone and fax

  o History of company and principals

  o Public filings

  o And the really best part of D&B is being able to search inside its database.

Here are some practical reasons that illustrate the need to use D&B—

- Fraudulent companies often share fax numbers, even though they generate new phone numbers for business. ALWAYS SEARCH the FAX!

- Searching by the principal's name will often show former company interests or current company interests.

- Dun & Bradstreet automatically does Soundex searching. The name *Bill* will generate *William* hits.

- Address searches will show other companies listed at the same address, including mail drops and suspicious addresses.

If you can not afford D&B directly, you can access their reports through one of B&B's resellers, such as Dialog, SkyMinder, LexisNexis and Bureau van Dijk. If you are a licensed investigator with ChoicePoint or Accurint, both resell D&B reports. However, keep in mind that direct service subscribers get much better pricing.

Kompass.com

Kompass originated in Switzerland and is now present in 70 countries. It offers a very reasonably priced collection of information on more than two million companies globally. With a subscription, you can locate the executives of companies, obtain addresses, corporate structures, names of key figures, company turnover information, company descriptions, product names and services, trade and brand names, and location of branches. Kompass offers free searches for the following topics—

- Region – Geographically locate all companies
- Products/Services – Type of product (i.e. clocks, telephones, hamburgers)
- Companies – Name of company
- Trade names – Name of product
- Executives – Search by person at the top
- Codes – NAICS, SIC and other government-related codes

I searched the company and family name Bugshan in Saudi Arabia and discovered multiple choices to explore.

Without incurring any cost, I then selected the Bugshan Sweets & Tahina Factory and received the following—

Bugshan Sweets & Tahina Factory

Industrial City, Phase No.4
Jeddah 21411
Saudi Arabia
Phone : +966 2 6883636
Fax : +966 2 6883300

Number of employees (total in the company) From 11 to 20

This is a considerable amount of information when you are starting from nothing. The address and phone numbers are leads that can be explored at Google or at other databases, such as D&B. Having a ballpark number of employees also is helpful.

The minimum amount of credit units you can buy is 50, which costs $150.00 (USD). Opting to purchase the complete Bughsan Sweets & Tahina Factory record will cost one unit or $3.00.

The information gathered also includes their office hours and time zone, (Saturday to Thursday 7 A.M to 3 P.M) a post office box address (PO Box 181) and the general manager's name (Saleh Omar S Bugshan). In addition, the products and services section catalogs the Bugshan Sweets & Tahina Factory as a manufacturer of "Spreads and pastes, fruit or vegetable."

Author Tip ➡ For a list of state Web pages that offer free access to U.S. corporation and business entity records, go to pages 256-257 in **Appendix 2.**

SkyMinder.com

SkyMinder, located in Tampa, Florida, is an affiliate of CRIBIS S.p.A., based in Bologna, Italy. SkyMinder is an incredible aggregator of other corporate business and credit reports. Consider the following—

- Used by more than 330 Italian banking and financial institutions and more than 14,000 Italian, European and U.S. companies.

- Supplies online credit and business information on more than 50 million companies in 230 countries.

- Only works with Internet Explorer version 5.0 and newer.

- One of the best places to buy inexpensive D&B header reports.

- Available data (per their Web page) includes: marketing data, line of business, incorporation details, shareholders/owners, executives, employees, office and facilities, business structure (headquarters, parent, branches, subsidiaries), rating, credit limit, payment information, financials, banking relationships and accountants, litigations, etc.

A complete source list for Skyminder can be located on its Web site at www.skyminder.com/basic/info_sources.asp. The source list includes a note on how often the data is updated for each of the 46 sources.

A search for "Bugshan" in the company section automatically seeks credit reports. The return offers 32 matches under "Credit Info" and 10 matches under "Company Info."

Bugshan Sweets & Tahina is not named in either corporate or credit results lists. However, the Abdullah Said Bugshan & Bros. listing at the top of the "Company Info" results page states that it is the headquarters. This could be the parent of Bugshan Sweets.

The following is a description for this company, available for free.

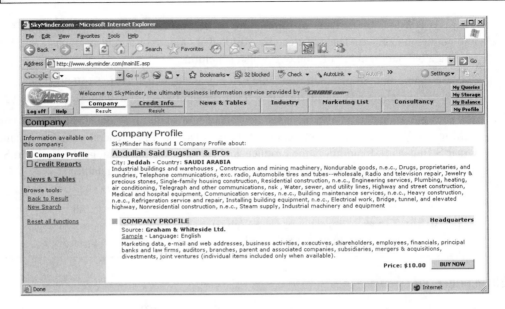

This listing may be the parent of the Sweets branch, considering it is naming just about every type of manufactured product from construction materials to sundries.

The key here is to see what sort of reports www.skyminder.com is selling. In this case, Graham & Whiteside Ltd. has a document for sale that includes contact information, employee size, principals, banking and finance and associated companies. For $10, that's a bargain.

The Graham & Whiteside report shown on the next page was purchased from www.skyminder.com. The information contained here is phenomenal. The investigator can see industry specifics, banking information, the majority ownership (Saudi Wiemer & Trachte Ltd.), and a great amount of detail, which would cost hundreds of dollars from Dun & Bradstreet.

SkyMinder also resells credit reports, which are similar to business reports, but with more financial offerings, such as payment history, credit ratings and profit, loss and reported financials. These reports tend to be ordered on-the-fly, and a certain amount of time is taken to generate the documents. In other words, once the report is ordered, a local researcher actually conducts the investigation in that country and delivers the results within a week or more.

As an example of prices, credit reports for Abdullah Said Bugshan & Bros. are available from Dun & Bradstreet at a price slightly over $200, at Asian CIS the fee is about $140. At RIME Information Bureau, CreditInfo Middle East Ltd., and ICP the fee ranges from $130 to more than $200, depending on how quickly you want the information.

Bureau van Dijk (BvDEP)

Because there is so much that Bureau van Dijk (www.bvdep.com) offers, it is difficult to catalog the many databases it offers. With a unique name for each service, international databases, such as ORBIS and Osiris, are teamed up with country-specific services like Ruslana (Russia), Sabi (Spain) and Jade (Japan).

ORBIS (www.bvdinfo.com/ProductContainer/Orbis.aspx) is a global database with information on more than 65 million companies. ORBIS covers—

- 60,000+ "publicly listed" companies worldwide
- 28,000+ banks and 7,700+ insurance companies
- 26 million+ European companies
- 19 million+ North America companies
- 6 million+ South and Central American companies
- 4 million+ Japanese companies
- 400,000+ Chinese companies
- 2.5 million+ Companies in rest of the world

The information is sourced from more than 40 different information providers, all experts in their regions or disciplines. With descriptive information and company financials, ORBIS contains extensive detail on items such as news, market research, ratings and country reports, scanned reports, ownership and mergers and acquisitions data.

ORBIS has several different reports for each company. You can view a summary report, a report that automatically compares a company to its peers or view more detailed reports that are taken from BvDEP's specialist products. For listed companies, banks and insurance companies, plus major, private companies, more detailed information is available.

Searching ORBIS can be done in basic or advanced modes. The advanced mode, as seen in this screen shot on the next page, offers searches by company names, locations, board member and executive names, specific financials, mergers and acquisitions deals, etc.

Once a name is searched, a page with the number of results is offered. You can pay to look at all the results or choose a free preview to see if you are close to the results you wanted.

A search for Bugshan in this service returned only one match in Germany. But reviewing the offerings, there are 65,000 companies listed in East and Central Asia. The Bugshan corporate name is well known, so the result of one match is surprising. With this service, as with any service, once you have questionable or no results, call customer service and ask the representative to check your findings. Customer-service representatives should be experts in their own database products and it is to the investigator's advantage to tap into that intellect. Because Bureau van Dijk has thousands of subscribers, you being one of them, its representatives will assist in the research. In this case, the researcher verifies that there are no Bugshan reports of value in ORBIS, and he either recommends searching in another Bureau database, or offers to create a report that can take several days to generate and deliver.

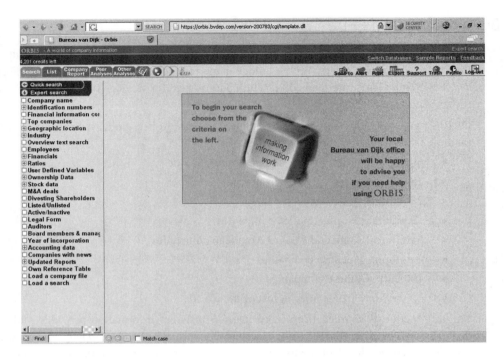

(Source: www.bvdep.com/en/ORBIS.html)

The other Bureau databases can be examined by viewing their brochures online at www.bvd.co.uk/companyinformationbrochure/cib.pdf.

Other unique database services of Bureau van Dijk include—

- **ZEPHYR** - A worldwide database of detailed information on rumored, announced or completed financial deals; it includes approximately 80,000 new deals a year.

- **FAME** - Company accounts, ratios, activities, ownership and management of the largest 2.8 million British and Irish companies, and summary information for an additional one million smaller businesses.

- **ODIN** - Standardized annual accounts, financial ratios, activities and ownership information for one million companies in Scandinavia.

- **QIN** - Company accounts and financial ratios for 300,000 companies in mainland China in both standardized and local detailed formats.

Other Sources of Note

Not everything is in a database. Corporate research, especially of foreign companies, will require expertise in that country. Hire licensed, if required, private investigators who know the laws, limitations and public records for their country. Be very clear about what you are looking for, and what you do not want. Sad, but true in many cases, investigators will break laws to gain information. This not only reflects poorly on them, but also on the company that hired them. If it is a large company that hired the rogue investigator, that company can be held responsible for the offense. And, it can be cited for breaking several federal and state laws, such as the Economic Espionage Act (www.usdoj.gov/criminal/cybercrime/eea.html), Fair Credit Reporting Act (www.ftc.gov/os/statutes/031224fcra.pdf) or other laws or statutes.

Other unusual places to find assistance are in libraries, associations, personal Web sites and embassies.

Domestic and Foreign Libraries

For local information on a company, the local librarian probably will be able to offer as little as some directory information to as much as a personal clipping file on the firm itself. To find these librarians, simply search www.google.com and type the words "public library" +<town name state> (i.e. "public library" Springfield Illinois).

For foreign companies, not only will the librarian overseas offer all the regional information that she can find, but also she will search for it in her own language, and in her own databases. I recommend that you contact an American university within that country for the most cooperative librarian you can find.

Associations

Check association Web sites that are akin to the company being researched. The association may have some historical pages, or share insight into its members. The Encyclopedia of Associations (Thomson Gale) is offered through www.dialog.com (File 114) and LexisNexis. It is also a very common resource found in the reference collection of most public libraries.

Personal Histories

Look for personal histories, biographies, tear sheets and resumes of the lead professionals at the particular company being investigated. A personal history may reveal an interesting perspective as to why a particular company started. An example is the following statement from Anita Roddick, founder of the Body Shop.

> "It wasn't only economic necessity [a woman's struggle to earn a living for herself and two young daughters] that inspired the birth of The Body Shop. My early travels had given me a wealth of experience. I had spent time in farming and fishing communities with pre-industrial peoples, and been exposed to body rituals of women from all over the world. Also the frugality that my mother exercised during the war years made me question retail conventions. Why waste a container when you can refill it? And why buy more of something than you can use? We behaved as she did in the Second World War, we reused everything, we refilled everything and we recycled all we could. The foundation of The Body Shop's environmental activism was born out of ideas like these."[17]

---

[17] Source: http://www.anitaroddick.com/aboutanita.php

Before reading and understanding Ms. Roddick's personal history, one might think of this multi-national company as just another product manufacturer, and not for its unique approach to green business and female empowerment that this corporation embraces.

Foreign Press and Foreign Embassies

When researching a foreign company, do not neglect contacting a business-affairs correspondent in the country of the company being investigated. Prepare to have a lot of patience and time when waiting for the information to be delivered. A list of U.S. embassy locations abroad is found at www.usembassy.gov/.

Just as discussing in using foreign libraries, do not hesitate to contact a librarian overseas and request that he or she conduct a brief search through a local regional news index for your company. Again, patience and a great deal of appreciation should be given to these individuals who agree to assist. In the meantime check two very large, general news databases that cover an extensive amount of foreign press check at www.factiva.com and www.lexis.com. In addition, www.dialog.com is another resource that offers specialized media databases.

Cynthia's Key Chapter Points

- ◆ Determine if the firm is private or public, small or large, domestic or foreign.

- ◆ Find the location of the company's headquarters and look for subsidiaries or franchises to uncover additional assets and liabilities.

- ◆ Non-profits and charities is a resource to uncover incredible assets - look up their Form 990's with the IRS to check for officers and directors, and their salaries.

- ◆ Get local in your search. Not only do you need to understand the customs and legal issues of another country that can affect a business. You also need to learn any local nuances that affect local business locations.

- ◆ Multiple jurisdictional agencies such as environmental and/or regulatory agencies might have key information on your company or its plants.

- ◆ The use of standard database providers always apply, but also stay on top of new or unique services that might hold key information on your subject.

- ◆ Foreign source information is limited compared to the U.S.-based sources. Be aware that for a long time services like Kompass, Skyminder and Bureau van Dijk have been aggregating foreign corporation information at a reasonable price.

- ◆ When researching in a foreign country, contact the U.S. embassy attaché for assistance. Check for any U.S. universities in that country. Contact their libraries for assistance.

- ◆ To get a sense of history and ownership, read the company Web site, especially the About Us section.

Chapter 5

Corporate Officers & Employees

I think any man in business would be foolish to fool around with his secretary. If it's somebody else's secretary, fine!

—Senator Barry Goldwater

Corporate Officers

The crux of any investigation is the people who are being researched. Although a corporate investigation includes business filings, lawsuits, and subsidiaries and so on, the real issue is people. Buildings do not commit fraud or make business decisions, people do. So with any investigation into a corporation, the investigator researches the individuals behind the scenes.

Investigators learn in their careers that there are four types of individuals who they research in business. Those four are—

- **Unremarkable**
- **Lime-Lighters**
- **Fraudulent**
- **Incompetent**

Unremarkable

This individual has very little published about him. He is rarely a corporate giant, but if he is, he is new to his role. This individual is not significant enough for reporters to contact, interview and write about, or for him to appear in the news in any way. He does not sign too many official documents, and his legal background is minimal, if at all. He steers clear of too much activity that can be recorded.

This is the ideal position for an individual trying to avoid a paper trail, because as an open-source researcher, you will come up flat when you are documenting your report. With all the services you use to locate data about this individual, you still are unable to find anything on him.

The exception is the corporate leader who has been well groomed to insure his statement is consistent. For example, usually the only comments this officer makes are when he is discussing company business. No personal comments are addressed to reporters. His wife and kids are not a topic for conversation. He is meticulous about the events he attends, and cooperative with his own corporate security and legal counsel on all travel, personal safety and public-profile issues.

A great example of this type of individual is an American foreign diplomat. There are mountains of information written about this individual; however, you will gather very little from the public statements and personas you obtain through the embassy's Web site.

Lime-Lighters

Many morning news programs show the crowds that gather outside the network studios. NBC's *Today Show*, for example, makes use of this crowd and often shoots part of its program among the masses. As the cameraman pans the crowd, everyone gets a bit giddy and starts screaming and waving because they can see themselves on TV. Being on national television and holding up a "Love You Mom" banner is not an everyday occurrence for most people; so it is no surprise that everyone jockeys for position to get in front of that camera.

But then there are those, like celebrities, who cannot avoid the camera. They realize their images are tied to the public's perception of them. They strive for as much camera time, press releases and "look at me" action as they can receive.

Researching a celebrity can be tricky because he knows how to work the media and will massage his imagine into just the right view, so that he is projected as tall, smart, powerful, wealthy, talented or whatever image he is seeking. Some of you may remember William Hung as he auditioned on *American Idol* with his rendition of singer Ricky Martin's song *She Bangs*? His portrayal of the song was so painful to watch, yet you could not turn away. And if you search for *She Bangs* on google.com, you will find the top ten links go to Hung and not Martin.

The key lime-lighters in the business world are Chief Executive Officers (CEOs) of companies. You might recognize Donald Trump, Martha Stewart and Emeril Lagasse right off the cuff. However, can you name the CEOs of McDonald's, Coca-Cola or Starbucks? It is all a matter of how they use the media to showcase their companies, products or even themselves.

> **Author Tip ➡** When investigating the CEO or any upper-management executive lime-lighter, a few focus points are necessary to keep in mind. First, if the stories you are reading are press releases distributed by PR Newswire or similar wire services, then consider the stories have been paid for by the company and are probably biased. Second, discount any talking points coming direct from the executives. Remember, they are masters of ceremony and will always take an opportunity to self-puff about the business, its brands, or themselves.

The best way to truly find out about a lime-lighter is to check what is being written about him. For every celebrity, there is a critic. In business, the critics come from multiple places such as competing companies, industries or trade sources, like magazines, conference proceedings and product reviews. In addition, you will want to look for older articles that talk about the individual. These early articles may offer quite a bit of insight into what the person was like before he was at the C-level (CEO,CIO, CFO, etc). And, those stories will give you a sense of the character of the professional you are investigating.

Fraudulent

Who Are You?

An executive client called me recently, fresh from an investment seminar in his community. He was so taken in by the presenter's intelligence and charisma that he spoke with the presenter after the seminar and was offered a follow-up meeting to discuss some investment opportunities.

But a quick search showed that this Wall Street-wise presenter was also known by a federal prison number. The year prior, the presenter was convicted of various corporate crimes.

Does it get more obvious than this? Sure it seems straightforward, however you have to take into account that you could be misreading your subject as a lime-lighter, and it turns out he is fraudulent. In fact, most fraudulent characters are lime-lighters. One of the greatest talents of a fraud is his charisma. So, as you are being taken in on what a great person he is, his great company or superior product he has to offer, it is really the charisma of the fraudulent person you are buying into.

Incompetent

There are a few reasons to be considered incompetent. The executive is too busy to manage all his tasks and mistakenly thinks someone else is taking care of the details. The executive is entering a realm that is unfamiliar, and he does not realize the laws or does not think to see if the laws apply to his new project (i.e. SOX[18], HIPAA[19]). Finally, he could be a "go-getter" who hopes the ends justify the means, and thereby ignores the compliance, legal, and ethical concerns of his company in order to achieve his goal.

With these types of individuals being the target of the investigation, it is imperative to look at the different roles they may take, the information that surrounds them, and the circumstances that have affected their business and personal decisions.

The more investigations you do the more you might shake your head and wonder how some executives have made their way into the positions they are in. Many times an investigation starts with the premise that something nefarious or fraudulent has occurred. But what you find is that

---

[18] The Sarbanes-Oxley Act of 2002 (often shortened to *SOX*), was enacted because of high-profile financial scandals (Enron). SOX protects shareholders and the general public from accounting errors and fraudulent practices. The SEC administers this act.

[19] HIPAA is the United States Health Insurance Portability and Accountability Act of 1996. It established mandatory regulations regarding the way that health providers conduct business. See www.hhs.gov/ocr/hipaa

the person driving the project is more likely unprepared to handle the task. As the saying goes, "Ignorance of the law is not a defense." But, it certainly explains why some executives do stupid things.

The following will be discussed in detail

- Corporate Board Positions
- Political Affiliations
- Criminal and Civil Records
- Economic Information

- Organization Lists
- Assets
- Sanctions
- Media

Corporate Board Positions

Who are Board Members?

According to www.investorwords.com, Board Members are—

> *Individuals elected by a corporation's shareholders to oversee the management of the corporation. The members of a Board of Directors are paid in cash and/or stock, meet several times each year, and assume legal responsibility for corporate activities.*

There is no schooling or training involved in becoming a board member. The general sense is that board members get their seats based on influence. They are there to use their influence to help run the organization, establish merit for the company, or sometimes to merely fill in a seat and "keep out of the way."

Board members who help run the company establish and maintain the mission of the organization. Their focus is to remain true to the goals set forth by the shareholders. Many board members are often major investors in the company. For example, a start-up technology company most likely will have one or two of its biggest investors sitting on its board, because, quite frankly, the investors want to see their investment profit.

Those who help establish merit also could be board members. These individuals are well-respected captains of industry, such as scientists, writers, sports figures or celebrities. Having their name on your board will bring instant name recognition and credibility to the company.

And, the "keeping-out-the-way" seat holders are those family members who do not need a job because they are wealthy, but it looks good if you have them occupied in a useful function. These board members tend to sit on philanthropic boards. Political figures often have their spouses involved with non-profit organizations, such as a board member of an "ABC" fund-raiser.

When investigating a company, it is important to find out who the board members are, and what their roles are on the board. Investigators especially will want to look for collusion among board members or corporate officers. Your investigation should focus on such questions as—

- Do they sit individually or together on other boards?

- Have they been investigated in the past or accused of any type of corruption?
- Are any of them also a vendor for the company?
- Have they or their companies/families or organizations received any special treatment or pricing?
- Who appointed each board member and when?

Finding out who sits on what board, as well as getting the lists of corporate officers, depends on the sources you have at hand. The next portion of this chapter takes a look at the resources available to find this information.

Organizational lists

The following are some key organizational lists or resources that should be used when finding and investigating corporate officers.

Annual Reports

Publicly traded companies issue annual reports. Past and present reports will be of value. This report will list board members, their backgrounds, and if they sit on other boards. This report also will disclose ongoing investigations.

The Company's Web Site

This should always be your first source to check. There is really no reason to hide the board from the general public, especially since having a board gives a sense of credibility to the company. You will find board members under one of three common links: About Us, Investor Relations, or Management.

Securities and Exchange Commission (SEC) Filings for Public Companies

Next up for researching company boards is finding the annual reports filed with the SEC or its foreign equivalent. Visit www.sec.gov, search by company name and then obtain the company's proxy statement, also known as the **DEF-14 filing**.[20] The proxy will show the compensation for each board member and corporate officer. More information about using the SEC for investigations is found in Chapter 6.

Phone Lists of Private Companies

Services such as www.infousa.com and www.zapdata.com (a Dun & Bradstreet company) offer mailing-list services. Through various public records, news accounts and telephone interviews, D&B has amassed a large amount of very specific contact information that can be purchased by the batch or in small doses. The lists are targeted for marketing purposes, but investigators can use purchased lists to locate a target or subject by occupation, geography, or hobby.

---

[20] See www.sec.gov/info/edgar/forms/edgform.pdf

Former Employees and Officers

If it is an option, do not hesitate to try interviewing former employees to find out who may be still working at the company. Do not discount the importance of researching at least several good names of individuals who are either on the employee roster, are former board members or are now, or in the past affiliated with the company.

Finding these former employees may turn up real leads to former workers who are disgruntled, or to others who love to talk about the past and all the problems their companies suffered, or all the great people they worked with. Until you actually speak to them, it will not be clear what information they can provide.

Political Affiliations

According to Oscar Ameringer...*Politics is the gentle art of getting votes from the poor and campaign funds from the rich, by promising to protect each from the other.*

The higher in power your executive subject rises, the more politically involved he or she will become. This can be by choice or as a result of a position in the senior-management group. Companies spend billions of dollars every year on lobbyists to help their company succeed. Certainly petroleum companies would like to open up the Alaskan wilderness to tap into the rich supply of oil underneath the earth's crust, even though these wild preserves are on protected land. Conversely, animal-rights groups, like People for the Ethical Treatment of Animals (PETA), are supported by name-brand products that you see on the store shelves everyday. While the discussion about corporations and their active role in politics is beyond the scope of my work, the corporate employee's sponsorship of certain political parties and non-profit organizations are of concern to the investigation.

A fast way to locate information about the political donations and activities of an executive is to go to the Federal Election Commission's Web site at www.fec.gov. Under the Campaign Finance Reports and Data tab, you will see the Disclosure Database. This database can be searched by party, by contributor or committee. If you want to find all the contributors for a particular company, use the advanced search feature and search by company. Investigators also can download an entire list of people and view it in comma-delimited format through File Transfer Protocol (FTP), a common way to move large files via the Internet. The list can be sorted and viewed easily in applications such as Microsoft Excel.

The Federal Election Commission administers and enforces federal campaign-finance laws, insuring that companies, parties and persons do not abuse the campaign-finance laws that are in place. If a company offers an automatic withdrawal from an employee's paycheck and donates that money to a campaign, then it must report this transaction to the FEC in its annual reporting.

The chart on the following page is an example of an actual report filed by a company with the names redacted.

SCHEDULE A	ITEMIZED RECEIPTS	Use separate schedules for each category of the Detailed Summary Page	PAGE 29 OF 64 FOR LINE NUMBER 11(a)(i)

Any information copied from such Reports and Statements may not be sold or used by any person for the purpose of soliciting contributions or for commercial purposes, other than using the name and address of any political committee to solicit contributions from such committee.

NAME OF COMMITTEE (In Full) NJ REPUBLICAN STATE COMMITTEE

Full Name, Mailing Address and Zip Code	Name of Employer / Occupation	Date (month, day, year)	Amount of Each Receipt this Period
A. ▮▮▮▮▮▮▮▮	Name of Employer: Allied Beverage Group, L.L.C.	07/24/2000	2,500.00
	Occupation: Partner		
Receipt For: ☐ Primary ☐ General ☐ Other (specify)	Aggregate Year-to-Date -> 2,500.00		MEMO
B. ▮▮▮▮▮▮▮▮	Name of Employer: self-employed	07/24/2000	900.00
	Occupation: Financial Advisor		
Receipt For: ☐ Primary ☐ General ☐ Other (specify)	Aggregate Year-to-Date -> 900.00		
C. ▮▮▮▮▮▮▮▮	Name of Employer: Self employed	09/19/2000	5,000.00
	Occupation: Artist		
Receipt For: ☐ Primary ☐ General ☐ Other (specify)	Aggregate Year-to-Date -> 5,000.00		
D. ▮▮▮▮▮▮▮▮	Name of Employer: Self employed	07/19/2000	400.00
	Occupation: Realtor		
Receipt For: ☐ Primary ☐ General ☐ Other (specify)	Aggregate Year-to-Date -> 500.00		
E. ▮▮▮▮▮▮▮▮	Name of Employer: PSE&G	07/20/2000	400.00
	Occupation: Supervisor		
Receipt For: ☐ Primary ☐ General ☐ Other (specify)	Aggregate Year-to-Date -> 400.00		
F. ▮▮▮▮▮▮▮▮	Name of Employer: Chubb & Son Inc.	09/13/2000	1,000.00
	Occupation: President & CEO		
Receipt For: ☐ Primary ☐ General ☐ Other (specify)	Aggregate Year-to-Date -> 1,000.00		
G. ▮▮▮▮▮▮▮▮	Name of Employer: Net 2 Phone	07/06/2000	5,000.00
	Occupation: President		
Receipt For: ☐ Primary ☐ General ☐ Other (specify)	Aggregate Year-to-Date -> 5,000.00		

SUBTOTAL of Receipts This Page (optional)	12,600.00
TOTAL This Period (last page this line number only)	

(Source: Federal Election Commission at www.fec.gov)

Two excellent private Web sites to find political donations are www.followthemoney.org and www.opensecrets.org. More Web sites are out there, but these two are very comprehensive and good places to start on tracking contributions at the state level.

After searching the federal, state and local contributions, where possible, start a media search. See if the executive is talking openly about a political issue or attending fund-raisers sponsored by the Democrats or Republicans. These executives are not shy about who they support. In fact, knowing their attendance at rallies and fund-raisers most likely will be reported in the media, they use their positions to lend support to their party. How to perform a media search is covered in Chapter 10.

One issue to be aware of is that it is not unusual to see a company, or its executives, supporting multiple parties. The reason is that contributors know they have a greater chance of winning influence if they play both sides of the coin. As Will Rogers once said…*A fool and his money are soon elected!*

Charitable Works

Using the lesson on non-profits and charity research in the previous chapter, look for any charitable works your executive may be involved. Of course these charitable interests may be sincere, but they could also be just a front for laundering money.

A Profitable Non-Profit

An East Coast building developer was the recipient of every major, new building project within the city limits. Just about every school, hospital or government building was built by this developer or by his father, since the developer was a second-generation owner of the company. His major competitor believed something underhanded or unfair was occurring that was leading every new project to this man's company and hired me to investigate.

After days of researching his business reports and filings, I learned that his buildings were structurally sound, he did not have too many negative stories written about him in the press and his legal troubles were minimal. For a second-generation business developer, his history was a bit too free of trouble. So, I looked to see if he was involved in any non-profit organizations. I discovered he had a non-profit organization named after him and the organization had received more than $1 million a year in donations. The leading donator was his own company. He recently had won building contracts with the schools and hospitals that were the recipients of these donations. The Form 990 revealed a highly suggestive kick-back scheme connected to the projects he won contracts to build.

Assets

There are two types of assets: **physical** and **financial**.

Physical assets include automobiles, vessels, airplanes, real estate, property, personal possessions, and collectibles. The "stuff" that people associate with status and wealth, whether driving a nice car, living in a beautiful home or owning an incredible baseball-card collection, are considered to be assets and can be insured or repossessed.

Each one of these physical possessions is usually associated with some type of public record, thus creating a paper trail. For example, a car, boat and plane all have to be registered within an operating jurisdiction, such as state motor-vehicle agency for cars and pleasure boats, the U.S. Coast Guard for commercial boats, and Federal Aviation Administration for planes. Real estate property records are kept at the county, parish, or city level, depending on the state.

Other personal property includes collections or business equipment. These assets will not show on a public record unless the owner has borrowed against them and the lender has recorded a lien known as a Uniform Commercial Code (UCC) filing.

Personal financials assets are trust accounts, UCCs, stocks and securities, retirement plans, insurance clauses, funds and other financial entities that you invest in or own. The assets are evidence by the paperwork mélange that most people accumulate in their lives, and if anything, try to increase as they near retirement.

Only so much about financial assets is available in open source for the investigator. Bank accounts and financial statements are protected by the Fair Credit Reporting Act (www.ftc.gov/os/statutes/fcradoc.pdf). However, other financial documents are accessible from the government agency where the liens are recorded. For example, a good place to perform a name search of a lien index is at the local recorder's office or at a state agency such as the Secretary of State. Other legal filings to investigate that will lead to assets include bankruptcies at federal courts, divorce proceedings and other civil lawsuits at the local level. Additionally, you will see financial information in the Federal SEC filings, if the person is a corporate officer.

Check for open source leads as well through Google, in newspaper stories and press releases. Search for stories about donations to charities, hosting big events, such as fundraisers, purchasing a new home, some property, or even a yacht. Sometimes individuals reveal more then should be mentioned in the press, or take pictures in front of their fancy new boat or car. The open source searches can generate a lot of leads towards finding actual assets.

Another type of asset is intellectual property. As an investigator, I like to distinguish my services from others and I always mention that, along with the standard physical and financial assets, I will be looking for intellectual property, as well. In some cases, intellectual property is more valuable than homes, planes and stocks. Imagine investigating an individual whose physical assets amount to a home in the suburbs, a three-year-old car and a 401K plan. Then, you research further into intellectual property holdings and find that the subject also holds the patent to the latest "widget" or Ronco kitchen appliance.

How to investigate assets is covered in-depth in Chapter 7.

A Few Words about Criminal Records, Civil Records, and Sanctions

Connecting Criminal and Civil Records to Your Subject

Although the topic of how to search for court records is covered in detail in the next chapter, it certainly bears mention in a discussion of corporate officers and key personnel. Legal research of criminal and civil records is very fruitful and necessary for any investigation, and especially to corporate investigations. It is important to know where companies have fallen down, lost sight of their ethics or got caught with their hands in the cookie jar. Not to give too much weight to the defense side, the company you are researching also could be litigious, suing other companies or persons for debts unpaid, trademark infringement, contract disputes or any number of pertinent issues.

Both criminal and civil research should be done carefully, as the availability to information changes from jurisdiction to jurisdiction. The rule of thumb is to start online, but always finish the research in person.

When researching overseas companies, try to locate an investigator in that particular country who can assist you in understanding the legal system there, and help you conduct the research on-site.

To discuss the differences between criminal and civil research, I have borrowed text from *The Criminal Records Manual* by Derek Hinton and Larry Henry. Their work, from which I've learned a great amount, includes the chart below which he has graciously allowed us to reprint, and will help you begin to understand the differences between the two cases.

Subject	Criminal Case	Civil Case
Who brings the case	A government prosecutor	A private party, normally through an attorney
Name of case	People vs. Smith (if state court) or the United States of America vs. Smith (if federal court)	Adams vs. Smith (names of the parties)
Outcome if Plaintiff successful	Criminal sanctions, including imprisonment, fine and probationary terms.	Monetary damages. In some lawsuits, the plaintiff may be seeking injunctive relief.

Jurors who must agree with the plaintiff	All twelve jurors - unanimous verdict	Nine jurors out of twelve
Standard of proof	Government must overcome the presumption of innocence by proving guilt beyond a reasonable doubt.	Plaintiff only needs to show that his side is more convincing, and that it's more probable he's right.

Again, see the next chapter for additional details on how to conduct criminal and civil record investigations.

Sanctions

Sanctions are administrative actions, usually involving punishment or restrictions, taken against and individual or entity by a government agency or trade-related association.

Sanctions come from many places and are imposed for many reasons. Law enforcement, compliance, professional disciplinary actions, as well as regulatory enforcements, are all forms of sanctions. Depending on the type of professional you are researching, the sources you check will vary.

The next chapter covers in depth the investigation of various sanctions, but it is worth mentioning here some examples of what is available to research online.

- **The Excluded Parties List System (EPLS)** published by the General Services Administration (GSA) and available at www.epls.gov is a great U.S. government site. According to the privacy notice on the Web site, "The EPLS includes information regarding entities debarred, suspended, proposed for debarment, excluded or disqualified under the non-procurement common rule, or otherwise declared ineligible from receiving Federal contracts, certain subcontracts, and certain Federal assistance and benefits." The EPLS is made up of 60 U.S. government agencies, including NASA and the Departments of Army and Justice. Even if you check the EPLS, I recommend also going directly to the agency site as well, and checking with its system. For example, the Department of Health and Human Services is in the EPLS, but also it has its own direct search (see below). I recommend you check both.

- Many Professional License Sanctions can be found online via state agency Web sites. In fact, over 5,000 of the nearly 8,800 state boards offer some degree of online verification of individuals' licensing. Some boards report on disciplinary actions including lawsuits filed for malpractice. Most professions are regulated by state licensing boards, but there are certain, specific occupations that involve the federal regulation, such as the air-traffic controllers regulated by the FAA. Go to www.verifyprolicense.com for links to these 5,000+ searchable sites.

- When investigating a physician, start by checking with the state regulatory board to insure that the physician has not been barred from practicing or has not had disciplinary actions taken against him in the past, or been sued for malpractice.

- For many years the Congress of the United States has worked diligently to protect the health and welfare of the nation's elderly and poor by implementing legislation to prevent certain individuals and businesses from participating in Federally-funded health care programs. The OIG, under this Congressional mandate, established a program to exclude individuals and entities affected by these various legal authorities, contained in sections 1128 and 1156 of the Social Security Act, and maintains a list of all currently excluded parties called the List of Excluded Individuals/Entities. See http://oig.hhs.gov/fraud/exclusions.asp

- The key oversight committees for securities and financial markets are the SEC and the National Association of Securities Dealers (NASD). Oversight groups, such as NASD, monitor brokerage houses and brokers. The SEC Web site has a litigation section to peruse, but it redirects you to the NASD Web site. Each state also monitors securities dealers in its jurisdiction; so, that is the next step to researching your subject. Visit www.sec.gov/litigation.shtml.

Some Recommended Database Sources

Professional, albeit expensive, services like www.capitaliq.com from Standard & Poor's and www.boardex.com by Management Diagnostics Limited are phenomenal in their coverage of people and companies. Their analysts actually offer summarized data in their reports, much like investigators do, and biographies online.

Another service is *Corporate Board Member* magazine (www.boardmember.com). They maintain an extensive, proprietary database that can be used to not only search the information on the directors and officers, but also to illustrate relationships among directors and boards.

Random-services Web sites such as www.theyrule.net make a great attempt at pulling together information and reporting it, but there can be limitations. For example, the currency of the data in www.theyrule.net is from 2004.

Accurint's Web site for private investigators, found at www.irbsearch.com[21], offers many of the same public records searches that all the major information companies servicing the investigative profession offer. However, one unique service that puts this vendor above the rest is its People-at-Work search. The database is aggregated from secretary of state filings, Web site registrations, credit headers and other public records.

Another great source for free searching is www.zoominfo.com. Information is collated from Web sites that the Zoominfo software bots, also known as intelligent agents, have captured and matched to a particular person or company. You can search by company, person or industry and truly, it is the most useful specialist search engine on the Internet. You can locate an abundance

---

[21] Private investigators must use www.IRBSearch.com, all other professions use www.accurint.com

of who's who straight from www.zoominfo.com. Keep in mind, though, that this information is being generated from other Web sites and needs to be verified before passed to clients in a final report.

Once you have tried the resources stated above, remember that media searches in trade magazines affiliated with that particular profession may also offer some usable leads in your investigations. See Chapter 9 for more information on industry resources and Chapter 10 for more information on media database resources.

Cynthia's Key Chapter Points

- ◆ No matter what corporation, organization, or business entity is the subject of your search, eventually it will always be people you are investigating.

- ◆ People can be classified as unremarkable, lime-lighters, fraudulent, and incompetent.

- ◆ Try to locate the Board Members; they are the real stakeholders of most corporations.

- ◆ After the board holders, find organizational maps and lists of current and past employees. Past employees are excellent sources for interviews.

- ◆ Political affiliations offer insight into the leadership's leanings.

- ◆ Charitable projects, donations and affiliations are more than good marketing for a company; they are often tied to the management's personal agenda.

- ◆ There are two types of assets – physical and financial.

- ◆ Criminal and civil court filings are managed and retained differently depending on the courts they are filed in, the county, the state, and the country. Take time to learn the retention policy for the jurisdiction of your subject.

- ◆ Regulatory and sanctioning agencies exist for just about every type of profession or licensed occupation. Check on the federal, state, and local agencies first. Then look for a professional association oversight, like Bar Associations for attorneys.

- ◆ Use traditional online sources where possible to develop leads into business members - workers and leadership. Contact libraries to determine if they have the equivalent of expensive for-pay databases free in book format. Use Linkedin.com.

Chapter 6

Investigating Regulatory Enforcement Records

We have a criminal jury system which is superior to any in the world; and its efficiency is only marred by the difficulty of finding twelve men every day who don't know anything and can't read!
—Mark Twain

The Good, the Bad, and the Ugly

"Dirt" is a popular topic amongst investigators. No, they are not avid gardeners, but are often requested by clients to "Dig up the Dirt!" It seems an unlikely thing to request or fulfill, however, rarely does a person or a company get through an entire lifetime without a few skeletons in the closet. Some skeletons are slight, with perhaps a few speeding tickets for the CEO of a company or maybe a bankruptcy claim on the CFO. However, some skeletons can be quite substantial, such as corruption, racketeering, fraud, breaking international treaties, or other similar reputation and legal problems.

This chapter examines the various investigative trails that develop because of involvement with, or violation of, government regulatory issues. These "dirt" trails are grouped into six segments—

- Local, State, and Federal Court Records
- Licensing Boards and Disciplinary Actions
- Trails of Financial Crimes
- Publicly Traded Companies and Security Dealers Compliance Actions
- Government Watch Lists
- Sanctions, Terrorists, and Other Law Enforcement Sources

Author Tip ➡ Keep in mind that just because companies or people are found on regulatory lists does not necessary mean they are suspected of crimes or should be avoided completely. The circumstances should be examined and understood, especially when very large companies are involved.

Searching Court Records and State Criminal Agency Records

As previously discussed, many business background investigations involve investigations on individuals. Key areas of focus are criminal cases, civil actions, and sources of various disciplinary actions.

Criminal Records

Unless a violation of federal law is involved, the information trail of a criminal record starts at the county, parish, city, or even tribal courthouse. The information that *could be* disclosed on a criminal record includes the arrest record, criminal charges, fines, sentencing and incarceration information.

Criminal Record Searching

The first step in criminal record searching is determining where to search. A county courthouse search is the most accurate and least complicated search, but not always the most practical. There are over 6,000 courts in the U.S. that hold felony or significant (non-traffic related) misdemeanor records. For those of you who think everything is online, know that less than half of the courts offer online access to a searchable record index; and far less offer online access to the case file documents.[22]

Each state has a central judicial office, usually known as the State Court Administrator, which oversees the state court system. The state judicial Web site is a good place to find decisions and opinions from the state' supreme court appeals court. In some states, the state court administration office oversees a statewide online access system to court records. Some of these systems are commercial fee-based. Other systems offer free access, but search results are usually very limited in comparison. For example, in Alabama, Maryland, Minnesota, New Mexico, Oregon, Washington, and Wisconsin where "statewide" online systems are available, you still need to understand (1) the court structure in that state, (2) which particular courts are included in their online system, (3) what types of cases are included or not included, and (4) what personal identifiers are presented.

Criminal court records are eventually submitted to a central repository controlled by a state agency such as the State Police or Department of Public Safety.

There is a huge difference on the record access procedures between the state repositories and the courts. Records maintained by the court are generally open to the public, *but not all state criminal record repositories open their criminal records to the public*. Of those states that *will* release records to the public, many require the submission of fingerprints and/or signed release forms. Check www.brbpub.com to locate any possible open free database availability. Counties in Florida and Texas and the city of Los Angeles have a lot online. If you are a subscriber to BRB's *Public Record Research System*, you will have access to court info on 7,900+ courts as

---

[22] From *The Sourcebook to Public Records Information* by BRB Publications, Inc.

well as each state's court structure. If not, look up the state's court administration Web page to start.

Once You Find the Case

Once a civil or criminal matter is located it is important that you understand and repeat clearly what the citation, docket sheet or case file states. The docket sheet (list of events that occurred) will give you dates, parties and some idea as to the conclusion or disposition. However, it may be necessary to send a public record retriever on site to the court that is housing the case file. The retriever can photocopy the file and send you the proceedings. These large files can take hours or longer to review, but are worth the time. The details within the case files, especially civil business matters, will indicate many interesting details, such as associates that you have been trying to match up, perhaps brought in to testify as a witness. The appended case files also can help you find assets you may have been looking for.

Below are some recommended vendor resources—

- LexisNexis and Westlaw specialize in providing criminal record data to the legal industry.

- KnowX.com, a ChoicePoint service, is a leading consumer site.

- To find an on-site record searcher to visit a local court, go to www.prrn.us

> Author Tip ➡ There are a number of vendors who have assembled a proprietary database of criminal record data. While these database searches are low cost and may prove to be quite useful, they should be only considered as **supplemental**. Despite the sometimes mis-leading advertising, there is no national database of criminal record data.

There are two other significant state resources of criminal records—the **state prison system** (incarceration records) and the agency that maintains the **sexual offender** records. Most of these state agencies offer online access to portions of their records. Always worth a check is the sexual predator lists. It is hard to imagine an executive being noted as a sexual predator, yet there is no one type of person who decides to victimize others. Always check these handy and important state lists for your subject.

State Sex-Offender Registers can be located at most of the state registry Web sites, at a U.S. Department of Justice site at www.nsopr.gov/, and with vendors such as IRBsearch, AutoTrackXP, TracersInfo and LexisNexis to name a few.

To find state Web sites, check State Prison Inmate Locator at www.corrections.com/links and the state searches at https://www.vinelink.com/vinelink/initMap.do. In addition, search by using "sex offender" and the state name at www.usa.gov.

Outside of the United States, you will have to check on the laws of that country to see if criminal histories are available, and if so, if they require a signed release.

Federal Court Records

At the federal level, all cases involve federal or U.S. constitutional law or interstate commerce. Records of criminal acts that violate federal law are found at the 290 U.S. District Courts. The task of locating the right court is seemingly simplified by the nature of the federal system—

- All court locations are based upon the plaintiff's county of domicile.
- All civil and criminal cases go to the U.S. District Courts.
- All bankruptcy cases go to the U.S. Bankruptcy Courts.

Numerous programs have been developed for electronic access to federal court records. Over the years the Administrative Office of the United States Courts in Washington, DC has developed three innovative public access programs: VCIS, PACER, and most recently the Case Management/ Electronic Case Files (CM/ECF) project. The most useful program for online searching is now CM/ECF. VCIS access is via telephone is being phased out; PACER via Internet or remote dial-up is being replaced by CM/ECF.

Case Management/Electronic Case Files (CM/ECF)

CM/ECF is the case management system for the Federal Judiciary for all bankruptcy, district and appellate courts. CM/ECF allows courts to accept filings and provide access to filed documents over the Internet. CM/CDF replaced aging electronic docketing and case management systems in all federal courts in 2005. It is important to note that when you search ECF, you may be ONLY searching cases that have been filed electronically. A case may not have been filed electronically through CM/ECF, so you must still conduct a search using PACER if you want to know if a case exists.

To sign-up for CM/ECF access, visit http://pacer.psc.uscourts.gov/cmecf/index.html. Most courts offer tutorials on how to use CM/ECF.

PACER

PACER, the acronym for **P**ublic **A**ccess to **E**lectronic **C**ourt **R**ecords, provides docket information online for open cases at **all U.S. Bankruptcy courts** and **most U.S. District courts**. Currently most courts are available on the Internet. Cases for the U.S. Court of Federal Claims are also available.

Sign-up and technical support is handled at the PACER Service Center in San Antonio, Texas; phone 800-676-6856. You can sign up for all or multiple districts at once. In many judicial districts, when you sign up for PACER access, you will receive a PACER Primer that has been customized for each district. The primer contains a summary of how to access PACER, how to select cases, how to read case numbers and docket sheets, some searching tips, who to call for problem resolution, and district specific program variations.

A problem with PACER is that each court determines when records will be purged and how records will be indexed, leaving you to guess how a name is spelled or abbreviated and how much information about closed cases your search will uncover. A PACER search for anything but open cases **cannot** take the place of a full seven-year search of the federal court records available by written request from the court itself or through a local document retrieval company.

Many districts report that they have closed records back a number of years, but at the same time indicate they purge docket items every six months.

An excellent FAQ on PACER is found at http://pacer.psc.uscourts.gov/faq.html.

> **Author Tip ➡** There is a real problem when searching any federal court records – **the lack of identifiers**. Most federal courts do not show the full DOB on records available to the public. Thus, if a record searcher has a common name and gets one or more hits, each individual case file may need to be reviewed to determine if the case belongs to the subject in mind.

Other Federal Record Sources

Federal Bureau of Prisons – www.bop.gov

National Wants & Warrants – www.tracersinfo.com (a vendor)

Litigation and Civil Judgments

Civil litigation is a matter between two parties, not involving the government, as in a criminal suit. However some criminal cases turn into civil matters (as in the OJ Simpson Trial), and some civil matters turn into criminal trials (as in many financial fraud cases).

Civil cases can be tried, mediated or dismissed. Civil matters include bankruptcy, contract failures, real estate disputes, property, insurance and liability claims. Tort cases can be thought of as "do no harm" lawsuits. Product liability, neglect, and trespass are all examples of tort cases. These files are found in federal and state court systems, using the same sources federal and state research. However, when finding a product liability case, registered as a Tort, be sure to check for class action lawsuit.

Civil Record Searching

Searching a company for civil filings an investigator needs to be sure to look closely under the company name, their subsidiaries and the principals. Also be keenly aware that the company may have changed names. Even a large company will change its name to avoid being identified with its unscrupulous past.

Conduct a business search prior to legal search so you know all the names to look under, and not just the one you commonly know. The *ABC Company* may be the popular name, and is a good idea to search under, but the legal name, the one taken to court, could be *ABC Group.* If you do not look for ABC Group, the legal history may be missed.

Civil court records can be found in the same manner as described above in the Criminal Records section. There is one additional resource that is worthy of mention. Stanford University has a terrific open source, free, class action lawsuit database, as shown on the next page.

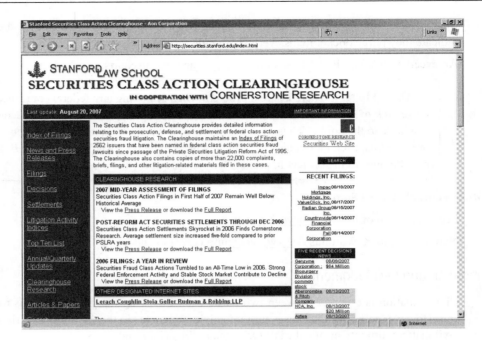

(Source: http://securities.stanford.edu)

Naming the chief principals of a company is also popular in lawsuits. Individual claims against the company will want to draw in all the parties responsible for their grievance.

A lawsuit against ABC Company may name 5 defendants, such as this example below—

Mark Johnson vs. ABC Group, et. al.

Defendants:

- ABC Group
- ABC Company, Subsidiary
- Robert Smith, Chief Employment Officer
- Michael Colfax, Chief Finance Officer
- John Roberts, General Counsel

Taxi to Tribal (Unfamiliar Court Systems)

Taxi Court

Taxi Court is a very unique court system, an almost underground version of traffic court, stationed in **New York City**. It is run by the NYC Tax and Limousine Commission. The home page for the Taxi Court online is www.nyc.gov/html/tlc/html/home/home.shtml. There will not be a business reason to search Taxi Court, it is here to serve as an example of how odd the legal system sometimes is. The point is, just because you know how court records are handled in your county or the next county over, never assume they are handled the same way in the next state or across the country.

Tribal Courts

Tribal Courts represent a unique legal system that works within the separate sovereignty of the Indian nations within the United States. The impact on using these courts in business investigations is considerable within the gaming industry. The key point here is that case information in tribal courts is NOT found in any level within the rest of the courts in the U.S.

Searching tribal courts is a must for any obvious Native American name. Also any particular cases which may be brought against any gambling facilities or casinos. These court systems encapsulate criminal, civil, summary judgments and similar cases. Below are several excellent sources to find tribal courts.

- National Tribal Justice Resource Center - www.tribalresourcecenter.org
- Tribal Court Clearinghouse - www.tribal-institute.org/index.htm
- A listing of Tribal Courts is also provided by www.versuslaw.com

International Courts

International legal issues involve treaties, tribunals and recognized global authorities.

The World Intellectual Property Organization, (WIPO), formed by the United Nations in 1967, is a recognized authority with jurisdiction on intellectual property. The WIPO mandate from Member States is:

> "…to promote the protection of IP throughout the world through cooperation among states and in collaboration with other international organizations."[23]

WIPO offers several database searches available at www.wipo.int for patent, trademark and copyright property. Web site domain names will often end up in WIPO courts for dispute mediation. As in the example of T.A. Hari (see story below), the case was based on an International recognized trademark, so eventually the case was tried in the internationally recognized WIPO court.

The United Nations also is involved with sanctions and embargos through the Security Council.

What's In a Name?

Several years ago I was called to investigate an individual with a unique name. His last name combined with first and middle initial spelled out matched a famous designer label. For example, T.A. Hari, when spelled together, would look like "Tahari" – is a noted women's clothier label. T.A. Hari registered the domain name tahari.com and used it for his own purposes, which were not related to the clothing industry. Tahari the clothier contacted him and sent him a 'cease and desist' letter for the use of their trademark. He offered to settle for a few thousand dollars, but the clothier felt it was their trademark and they had a right to take it back. The dispute went to ICANN for resolution, and T.A. Hari

---

[23] www.wipo.int/about-wipo/en/what_is_wipo.html

> was judged to be using his own name with permissible purpose. Since the name was his own, he had right to it. They informed him he could not use the name to resell clothes or for the clothier market because THEN it would be an intrusion on the Tahari trademark.

Another example of an international court is the **International Criminal Court (ICC)**. This independent, permanent court tries persons accused of serious crimes of international concern, such as use of genocide, crimes against humanity, and war crimes. The ICC was formed per a treaty, which now represents 104 countries. Visit www.icc-cpi.int.

There are other court systems as well, including military and tribunal. Think about jurisdiction when a case opens itself up. Remember to check for all the parties first, if there are name variations, or if the company is a subsidiary of a larger firm. Look for the principals behind the company, as well as any guarantors (investors) that also can be named as a party. Once you know the players involved consider first the location of the individual, in the United States or abroad. Second find out what sort of legal jurisdiction would be involved, if criminal or civil, or in a unique court perhaps on the International level or something more local like a tribal court.

Motor Vehicle Offenses

Motor vehicle checks are common used in background investigations and pre-employment searches. Much can be learned about an individual by obtaining their motor vehicle history. Traffic-related violations are tried in local courts and records of convictions are forwarded to a central state repository. The record retrieval industry often refers to driving records as "MVRs." Typical information on an MVR, besides the traffic infractions, might include full name, address, physical description and date of birth. Also, the license type, restrictions and/or endorsements can provide background data on an individual. If they received many tickets, lost their license, have DUI indictments, they could be just as reckless with the company car, or their personal habits. Other issues that surface, such as driving while suspended or under the influence, indicate poor judgment and bad decisions.

The Federal Driver's Privacy Protection Act (DPPA) regulates the policy of when identifiers found in motor vehicle information can be released to the public. Per DPPA, to determine who may receive a record containing personal information, states must differentiate between requesters with a permissible use (14 are designated in DPPA) vs. requests from casual requesters. For example, a state DMV may choose to sell a record to a "casual requester." However, the record can report personal information (address, etc.), ONLY if the subject has given written consent. Otherwise personal information in the report is cloaked.

Licensing Boards and Disciplinary Actions

Occupational Licensing Boards

There are literally thousands of government licensing authorities or "boards" that oversee and regulate the occupation of an individual or type of industry for a business. Certain licensing categories are more regulated than others. For example a food service company will have more licensing and permits than a bookstore. However that does not mean the bookstore is free from government bureaucracy requiring the store abide by town ordinances, county and state law. While some industries manage to self-regulate, and majority are over sighted by government agencies.

Searching for licenses and permits is a windfall opportunity for an investigator. Sometimes the only place you will find a true admission of business ownership, asset holders, or just get the right contact information is from a license registration.

The rule of hand when determining if a professional is licensed, is to **consider the consumer**. A perfect example is anything that deals with touching the body or hands on physical work, will be a licensed occupation. For example, manicurists, beauticians, massage therapists, doctors and dentists are all licensed in every state.

Florida's Department of Regulation and Business is a great example of the occupations that states will license. In Florida, everything appears to have a license authority, so if your subject has any affiliation with the State, be sure to check for a license there. You will find good information, even on a regional basis. For example, a recent check of *body wrappers* in Dade County located 68 licensed individuals. A licensing board may be willing to release part or all of the following—

- Field of Certification
- Status of License/Certificate
- Date License/Certificate Issued or Expires
- Current or Most Recent Employer
- Address of Subject
- Complaints, Violations or Disciplinary Actions

The New Hygienist

A female dental hygienist moved with her family to a suburb of Dallas. New to the neighborhood, she found a job at a local dentist's office. Se was the only hygienist on staff, as the dentist claimed to have recently lost a long-time employee.

Within a month the dentist sexually assaulted her. The case evolved to "her word against his" so we needed to find other past employees who could be interviewed and perhaps corroborate the story. Using the county Web site, we located a list of all the registered hygienists in the county, and then with a map, we plotted those closest to his office to call first.

Within four phone calls, we found a woman who also worked at his office, but only for a short period of time. She claimed that a colleague who worked with her there made statements that the dentist was fondling her. Both women left without calling the authorities. When I explained why I was calling, she was very helpful in providing her colleagues current contact information, which my client used to win the case.

Disciplinary Actions

Probably the most widely searched fields of licensing are the medical and legal fields. The licensing boards for these professions usually maintain disciplinary databases that are quite resourceful.

Below is an example of a search of disciplinary actions on three nurses from the state of New York. **Note:** The last name and license number have been changed, but the reported facts are taken straight from the Office of Professional Management at www.op.nysed.gov. Notice that two out of three received probation in lieu of having their license suspended, regardless of unethical and dangerous mishandling of their patients.

Kathleen T. Clive, Goldens Bridge, NY

Profession: Registered Professional Nurse; Lic. No. 126692; Cal. No. 13831

Regents Action Date: April 15, 1994

Action: Application to surrender license granted.

Summary: Licensee could not successfully defend against charges of documenting nine sessions with patients that she did not perform.

Charles O'Shea, Wyandanch, NY

Profession: Registered Professional Nurse; Lic. No. 291296; Cal. No. 10667

Regents Action Date: April 28, 1995

Action: 3 year suspension, execution of last 24 months of suspension stayed, probation for last 24 months.

Summary: Licensee was found guilty of charges of having placed a patient in a tub of running water, failing to insure that the temperature of the water was safe, and having placed the patient in such a manner that the patient's head was in close proximity to the metal spigot, the patient thereafter being diagnosed with first and second degree burns which caused his death.

Rosemary P. Ratchet, Valley Stream, NY

Profession: Registered Professional Nurse; Lic. No. 237207; Cal. No. 12614

Regents Action Date: April 28, 1995

Action: Suspension until successfully completes a course of treatment - upon termination of suspension, probation 2 years.

Summary: Licensee was found guilty of charges of practicing the profession while her ability to practice was impaired by alcohol and drugs, involving respondent practicing the profession under the influence of wine and Valium while on duty.

More Searching Tips for Licensing and Disciplinary Actions

As mentioned in the last chapter, there are approximately 8,800 state licensing boards in the U.S. and over 5,000 offer online access to at least some information about licensees.

To find these services or find the ones not online, there are several options.

- Visit www.usa.gov and look for the state and license type
- Visit www.verifyprolicense.com
- Visit the state home page (i.e. www.in.gov for Indiana) and do a search

If you are having a hard time researching a subject that you know works in a special profession, there could be several reasons. First, that state may not require licensing for a particular profession. In Colorado for example, private investigators are not required to be licensed by the state. Or, maybe your subject's profession is certified, but does not require licensing. Many groups self-certify, and some companies even do self-certification, such as a physical fitness club for trainers. But there may be a third reason which can be a red flag in an investigation – your subject may purposely be avoiding getting licensed by the state. This could signify the subject is avoiding paying taxes, is a felon and ineligible to be licensed, or practicing but does not meet the qualifications of the state to obtain the license.

Another vexing problem is to figure out which professional is the right one. Perhaps your subject works in a hospital, but per the list of Florida Health licenses found at www.doh.state.fl.us, there are a possible 142 health vocations, from "Anesthesiologist Assistants" to "Veterinary Prescription Drug Wholesaler."

If you can, start by calling the office in the off hours of the person you are investigating. The title may be in the voicemail box. i.e. "Hello you have reached Roger, Director of Radiology for Farmers Hospital." Fortunately some states, like Florida, let you conduct an "ALL" search at once, so you do not have to try and figure out if your subject is an EMS Service Provider ALS or an EMS Service Provider BLS (whatever that means).

Once you get a sense of what type of title this person holds, numerous state Web sites can be scanned. You may still need to contact the licensing authority. More information is found on file than online. Usually the licensing agent has the training, school, contact information, and other details on file.

Another way to verify, or establish a contact for a subject is to check with trade associations. An industry association can be regional or national in scope, similar to the profession of private investigators. These organizations are for networking, educational and legislative development and fraternity.

Remember that many industries require businesses to be licensed. Examples include manufacturing, contractors, automotive, hospitality, liquor, gaming, etc. Most of these industry workers are regulated by state. Check with the same state agency resources to find the proper authority regulating the industry in question. Follow the same searching procedures as searching individual professionals to determine if your subject is properly licensed or not, or has disciplinary actions.

Licensing Boards Are Always Good Lead Sources

Always remember that searching for a person or about a person, by license, is one of the few ways you can find an "average Joe" that does not show up in news stories, press releases, or on the company Web site. He is normally going back and forth to work with a big sense of obscurity. Using government oversight boards is a great information equalizer.

No matter the profession, if your subject has done something terrible enough to merit disciplinary action, chances are they were written about in the news, or prosecuted by a state or district attorney. There could also have been a fine, or public notice. Make sure you research the news and legal filings for this person and their company.

Legal research is not complete until you combine the legal records with the disciplinary actions and investigate all the possible excluded parties and regulatory sanctioned lists. These lists are formed by international groups, national agencies, and law enforcement bodies which have found persons or companies in violation of their state's laws.

Investigating Financial Crimes

Financial crime is no longer the practice of bank robbers and charlatans. Today's criminal can be found sitting behind a glossy boardroom table or on the Internet. The task of monitoring financial misdeeds falls to SEC, FINRA and state securities bureaus which will be outlined in detail later. These organizations protect the investor from modern day thieves who manage to steal millions through stocks and securities, and which we will cover them later in the section.

First, let us examine the some of the most common types of financial fraud that you may come across during investigations. Keep in mind many of these practices are legal by themselves, such as backdating and short selling. But the abuse of them through manipulative tactics can make them illegal. In fact, many company executives like Martha Stewart (Martha Stewart Omnimedia Publications) and Kenneth Lay (Enron) professed their innocence throughout their trials, claiming they were conducting legitimate stock maneuvers. When in fact, Stewart and Lay were taking advantage of loopholes in the trading market which generated fortunes for them. Since then the SEC has created an oversight commission and has backed compliance laws in order to keep shifty investors from committing crimes with securities.

Manipulation

The SEC defines Manipulation as the intentional conduct designed to deceive investors by controlling or artificially affecting the market for a security. Manipulation can involve a number of techniques to affect the supply of, or demand for, a stock. They include: spreading false or misleading information about a company; improperly limiting the number of publicly-available shares; or rigging quotes, prices or trades to create a false or deceptive picture of the demand for a security. Those found guilty of manipulation are subject to criminal and civil penalties[24]

Investment message boards, such as found on Yahoo.com, are well known to investigators for spreading rumors about a company giving the impression that the company is in trouble, which leads real investors to sell their shares, thereby deflating the security and driving the price of the security down.

Backdating Stocks

Backdating is dating any document earlier than the one on which the document was originally drawn up. Steve Jobs of Apple and Martha Stewart were both accused of backdating their stock options. They would, as would others, backdate the options to land on the date when the stock was at its lowest value, allowing them the highest return when it is sold. In small terms, if a company is trying to attract a talented executive to their employ, they may offer him stocks. To get the best deal for him, they may backdate them to a date when the value of the stock was at its lowest. The tactic to protect them, and keep this legal, would be to clear this first with the board of shareholders and to compensate any fees associated to offer. It becomes illegal when the backdating occurs and only the executive who is signing off on the document knows about it.

Extra Extra

SEC Charges Former General Counsel of RFI-Thames And ABC Company Inc. For Fraudulent Stock Option Backdating

ABC Company Settles Fraud Charges Brought by Commission

FOR IMMEDIATE RELEASE

2007-123

Washington, D.C., August 28, 20xx - The Securities and Exchange Commission today filed fraud charges against a Bay Area attorney for her role in illegally backdating stock option grants. The Commission charged Abby B. Cherry with routinely backdating option grants from 1997 to 2003, first as General Counsel of RFI-Thames Corporation and then as General Counsel of ABC Company, Inc. The Commission alleges that Cherry's misconduct caused the two companies to conceal hundreds of millions of dollars in stock option compensation expenses relating to undisclosed in-the-money options provided to company executives and employees.

Insider Trading

Insider trading is the act of buying and selling stocks with the foreknowledge that has not yet been release to the public. For example, imagine a pharmaceutical CEO's son finds out through

---

[24] http://www.sec.gov/answers/tmanipul.htm

conversations with his father that the company is on the verge of receiving approval from FDA on a new type of diet drug. The son then buys large quantities of stock at what will be a reduced stock price, prior to the press release. Once the press release about the FDA approval is published, the stock prices soar as everyone tries to get in early on the new purchase. His foreknowledge is insider information and therefore he utilized that information illegally in purchasing the stocks.

Short Selling

Most long-term investors are "Going Long" meaning they purchase stocks with the hope of gaining wealth as the price of the security increases. But a **Short Seller** borrows on a stock and sells hoping the price will decrease. Wikipedia.org offers a simple example of short selling.

> "For example, assume that shares in XYZ Company currently sell for $10 per share. A short seller would borrow 100 shares of XYZ Company, and then immediately sell those shares for a total of $1000. If the price of XYZ shares later falls to $8 per share, the short seller would then buy 100 shares back for $800, return the shares to their original owner, and make a $200 profit. This practice has the potential for an unlimited loss. For example, if the shares of XYZ that one borrowed and sold in fact went up to $25, the short seller would have to buy back all the shares at $2500, losing $1500."

(Source: www.wikipedia.org/wiki/Shorting)

And all of this is completely legal; shorting becomes illegal when it gets Naked. Naked Shorting is when you are selling stocks you do not even own.

An article found on Motley Fool (www.fool.com - a great resource for financial news on the Web) by Stephen D. Simpson, CFA titled "Manipulation and the Individual Investor"[25] states—

> "In regular shorting, the seller (or the seller's broker, rather) must locate the shares to be shorted, borrow them, and sell them. Can't find any shares to borrow and short? Well, you can't short the stock. Unless you want to try a naked short, that is.
>
> In a naked short, you just short the stock -- you don't make any attempt at actually locating the shares or borrowing them. Now, in theory there is a 13-day window in which those shares must be delivered. But brokerage houses have been known to hand off transactions to other houses and keep them moving around in such a way that they never settle.
>
> If the bird actually does come home to roost after 13 days and no shares have been delivered, the broker has to buy those shares back. But if the manipulators succeeded in their attempt to push the stock down, that buyback can still be at a price that gives the wrongdoer a profit. Neat little scam, huh?"

In this way, the Naked Shorter has moved the stock, profited and has never actually borrowed it or against it to begin.

---

[25] www.fool.com/investing/high-growth/2005/05/31/manipulation-and-the-individual-investor.aspx

Pump and Dump Schemes

Pump and dump schemes are illegal manipulation of stock prices based on fraudulent claims. Companies promise advances in science, bigger returns, cures for diseases, technology that exceeds all standards, and in return investors clamor to get behind the latest and greatest company. Then the company fails to deliver their products, the demand for new capital wanes and the company is stock is dumped.

Pump and dump schemes were very common during the tech bubble years, when companies would continually prophesize their emerging products, ability and knowledge trust. Reading their press releases would inspire investors to get in young and fast. Venture capitalists and everyday people were all jumping on the bandwagon, putting money into false promises. Once the promotion stopped, or the fraudulent truths were discovered, the demand is removed, causing a collapse in the price of the investment, leaving many investors out of pocket. Key indicators in a pump and dump scheme are monthly, or regular, press releases making outlandish claims but no support. The indicator is how the company is funded. Are they completely funded by venture capital, or do they produce some sort of other service or product that can support them? Finally, use common sense, "too good to be true" inventions probably are.

Not So Smart

My client was concerned that a competitor was outranking his Smartcards[26] in the market. This occurred in mid-1990's when Smartcards were still a hot item, with a lot of development yet to come. However this competitor claimed to build gigabyte cards that were indestructible. My client obviously was concerned that the current standard of megabyte cards were going to be surpassed, and being a top scientist and business professional in the industry, he was stumped as to how the competitor beat him to market.

This investigation immediately was suspect, because the competitor was only discussing the release of his Smartcards. The competitor actually did not have a product in place. When all the news articles were retrieved, I noticed that at the middle of every month this company placed its press release, discussing all sorts of improvements and relationships. Like clockwork each month one could read about how this company improved compression ratios, aligned themselves with a laminating company which had ballistics grade plastic to coat these cards in, and recent new investors to impress even the savviest of Wall Street tycoons. This ongoing "pump" of new information into the news generated a lot of buzz, and investors were hungry to buy shares and make investments in the company.

While researching the news, I focused on the management. They seem to come from Canada, recently settling into the Silicon Valley, California area. I then started looking for

---

[26] Smartcards, similar to credit cards, contain data which is used for a specific purpose. A room key pass, or identity badge is an example of a Smartcard.

past companies in Canada that these executives may have worked for. In short time I found a mention of the Toronto Stock Exchange delisting a company the CEO worked for. This company was producing portable medical testing units that could scan for viruses such as HIV, without the need for electricity – a sort of finger-prick analysis. While researching this company I discovered the same mantra of monthly articles professing major accomplishments every month, until one day they stopped. As it turned out, Canadian authorities suspected the claims as fraudulent. The CEO and others were investigated. The company remains open today, but the stock is close to worthless and many investors were left without reprise.

When then surmised that this same CEO was doing the same pump and dump in the U.S. with his Smartcard scam. For our client's sake, we knew the claimed technology did not exist and we exposed the fraudulent person to the SEC for further review.

Taking it Online

Pump and dumps, and misinformation campaigns can also be generated online. Online chat boards found on Yahoo.com and Ragingbull.com are famous for getting "insider news." The anonymity of the identities of the posters shields them from being exposed talking about fights in the boardrooms, product releases, marketing schemes, etc. Companies need to monitor their own message boards for any truths or half-truths. It is not uncommon for a former employee, or current disgruntled employee, to post proprietary information in these chat forums.

As in the case of Dendrite vs. John Doe, Dendrite, a Morristown, N.J. based provider of products and services for the pharmaceutical and consumer package goods industries. Dendrite went after several anonymous people who were posting defamatory information on the Yahoo Dendrite message board. Each poster was independent of the other, but all were suspected employees of the company. In at least two of the cases the court ruled that Yahoo did not have to expose the identity of the posters, claiming first amendment rights, and in the second case, no harm occurred. But according to court papers, Dendrite said "John Doe No. 3" made a series of posts on a Yahoo bulletin board specifically devoted to the company's financial matters. "The company alleged that negative comments by several posters about Dendrite and its management constituted breaches of contract, defamatory statements and misappropriated trade secrets." [27]

The misappropriation of trade secrets is what opens the individual up to criminal misconduct.

Individuals posting on the Internet, through blogs, message boards and in forums, do not realize they truly are not invisible. While they think they are sharing insider secrets, opinions, and bad feelings about their supervisor, they do not realize investigators and corporate security are also monitoring the boards for any intellectual property loss.

---

[27] Bartlett, Michael. (July 11, 2001). *New Jersey Court Upholds Anonymity On Net Bulletin Board - Dendrite International.* Newsbytes News Network

Undercover

The best tactic is to prepare a proactive approach by getting yourself involved before information starts flowing. As a contributor you are monitoring the news, participating in the exchange of information, bantering back and forth with the other investors, and gaining trust.

The captioned image below is from Martha Stewart's company Omnimedia Publishing. This company's message board attracts a good deal of attention, and is excellent for new investigators to use for training. Here's how. Everyday for a week visit this message board (or pick another company message board of interest). As you check everyday, you become familiar with who the frequent posters are, their biases, and the language they use to communicate with one another. When you are only observing it is known as **lurking**. Once you feel comfortable with the banter, start contributing small unimportant tidbits or opinions. This makes you active and seen by the other message board posters, and helps establish some credibility. It is like going undercover on the Internet. Hopefully you can continue to do this for your client before any issues arise on your identity. Thus when something of value to your case is posted, you are already "inside" on the message board and can ask some key questions without seeming to be suspicious.

There are many topical, random boards that you can access once you have created a profile in Yahoo. Again, this is to establish that you have some history in message boards and are not some Johnny Come Lately creating suspicion when you pipe up about a sensitive topic. If you do intercede on a new board, then at least when the other posters check out your profile they will see some history. The statement you open with is… "Hello I've been lurking on this board for a few months and…"

(Source: http://messages.finance.yahoo.com/mb/MSO)

With so many types of financial fraud, continuing education is necessary to understand and investigate in this arena.

Two resources for continuing education regarding financial investigations are first read the white paper titled, "Short Selling, Death Spiral Convertibles, And The Profitability Of Stock Manipulation" written by John D. Finnerty, Professor of Finance, Fordham University Graduate School of Business (March 2005)[28]. The second is to visit the Web site for the Association of Certified Fraud Examiners (www.acfe.org) and check out the Fraud Resource Center for articles on various financial frauds as well as class offerings and industry news.

Publicly Traded Companies and Securities Dealers

There are three primary agencies that oversee regulatory and compliance issues with publicly traded securities or with security dealers.

- **Securities and Exchange Commission (SEC)**
- **Financial Industry Regulatory Authority (FINRA)[29]**
- **National Futures Association (NFA)**

The SEC is a federal government agency. FINRA and NFA are self-regulatory bodies.

Another important entity, profiled later in this chapter, is the **North American Securities Administrators Association (NASAA)**.

Each agency is an excellent resource for investigating compliance issues and enforcement actions. In summary, each organization monitors public companies and brokers for impropriety; it also oversees securities dealers, brokerage firms, and compliance requirements. Each has the authority to investigate and enforce regulatory actions.

The types of investigations are pump and dump schemes, stock manipulation, backdating of stocks, short selling, and insider trading, as described earlier.

The Securities and Exchange Commission (SEC)

The SEC is the primary overseer and regulator of the U.S. securities markets. According to the SEC's Web site (www.sec.gov), "The mission of the U.S. Securities and Exchange Commission is to protect investors, maintain fair, orderly, and efficient markets, and facilitate capital formation… "

The SEC oversees the key participants in the securities world, including securities exchanges, securities brokers and dealers, investment advisors, and mutual funds. Here, the SEC is concerned primarily with promoting the disclosure of important market-related information, maintaining fair dealing, and protecting against fraud.

---

[28] www.sec.gov/rules/petitions/4-500/jdfinnerty050505.pdf
[29] Formerly the National Association of Securities Dealers – NASD

Part of the SEC function is the enforcement of civil actions against individuals and companies that violate securities laws. Typical infractions include insider trading, accounting fraud, and providing false or misleading information about securities and the companies that issue them. For more information, visit www.sec.gov/litigation.shtml.

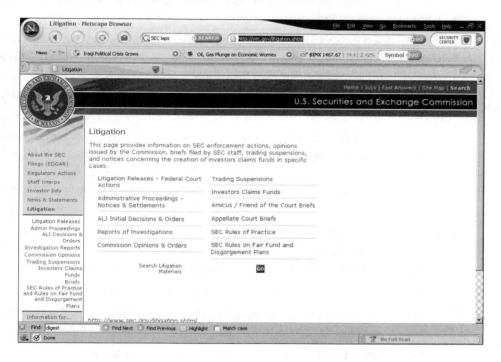

(Source: www.sec.gov/litigation.shtml)

These news releases concerning stock fraud and misappropriation of securities are issued daily. Below is a sample release—

U.S. SECURITIES AND EXCHANGE COMMISSION

SEC Charges Prominent Miami Beach Businessman in $900 Million Ponzi Scheme

FOR IMMEDIATE RELEASE

2010-63

Washington, D.C., April 21, 2010 — The Securities and Exchange Commission today charged a prominent Miami Beach-based businessman and philanthropist with fraud for orchestrating a $900 million offering fraud and Ponzi scheme.

The SEC alleges that Nevin K. Shapiro, the founder and president of Capitol Investments USA, Inc., sold investors securities that he claimed would fund Capitol's grocery diverting business. Shapiro told investors that the securities were risk-free with rates of return as high as 26 percent annually. Instead, Shapiro was actually conducting a Ponzi scheme and illegally using investor money to pay for other unrelated business ventures and fund his own lavish lifestyle. When investors questioned Capitol's business, Shapiro showed them fabricated invoices and purchase orders for nonexistent sales.

"Shapiro lured investors by falsely touting Capitol's securities as a risk-free investment with extraordinarily high returns," said Eric I. Bustillo, Director of the SEC's Miami Regional Office. "He used his prominence and prestige to gain investors' trust in funding Capitol's grocery diverting business, but behind their backs he diverted their money to enrich himself."

Grocery diverters like Capitol purchase lower-priced groceries in one region and resell them for a profit to another region where prices are higher. According to the SEC's complaint, filed in U.S. District Court for the Southern District of Florida, Shapiro used his business relationships and word-of-mouth to solicit investors and sell them short-term promissory notes.

According to the SEC's complaint, Capitol was operating at a loss by late 2004 and had virtually no operations by 2005 when, in a classic Ponzi scheme manner, Shapiro began using funds from new investors to pay principal and interest to earlier investors.

Among the alleged misrepresentations that Shapiro made to investors:

* He falsely told investors their funds would be used as short-term financing to purchase and resell groceries for Capitol's business.

* He falsely touted Capitol's financial success as well as his own.

* He falsely assured investors that their principal was secure because Capitol would not broker the sale of the goods without first obtaining a purchase order from a buyer.

* He falsely told investors that Capitol would pay the principal and interest from the profits it received when it resold the goods.

The SEC's complaint further alleges that Shapiro misappropriated at least $38 million of investor funds to enrich himself and finance outside business activities unrelated to the grocery business, including a sport representation business and real estate ventures. His lavish lifestyle includes a $5 million home in Miami Beach, a $1 million boat, luxury cars, expensive clothes, high-stakes gambling, and season tickets to premium sporting events. Shapiro additionally tapped approximately $13 million of investor funds to pay large undisclosed commissions to individuals who attracted other investors.

The SEC's complaint charges Shapiro with violating the antifraud provisions of the federal securities laws. The complaint seeks a permanent injunction, sworn accounting, disgorgement of ill-gotten gains, and financial penalties against Shapiro.

The SEC coordinated the filing of these civil charges with the U.S. Attorney's Office for the District of New Jersey, which today unsealed criminal charges against Shapiro, who surrendered to authorities this morning.

The SEC appreciates the assistance of the U.S. Attorney's Office for the District of New Jersey, the Federal Bureau of Investigation, and the Internal Revenue Service. The SEC's investigation is continuing.

Source: http://www.sec.gov/news/press/2010/2010-63.htm

Author Tip ➡ The SEC now offers RSS feeds for up-to-the-minute litigation news at www.sec.gov/rss/litigation/litreleases.xml. You may subscribe to receive these news feeds at the site.

Financial Industry Regulatory Authority (FINRA)

(Formerly the National Association of Securities Dealers - NASD)

According to FINRA's Web site (www.finra.org)—

> "The Financial Industry Regulatory Authority (FINRA) is the largest non-governmental regulator for all securities firms doing business in the United States. All told, FINRA oversees nearly 5,100 brokerage firms, about 173,000 branch offices and more than 665,000 registered securities representatives.
>
> Created in July 2007 through the consolidation of NASD and the member regulation, enforcement, and arbitration functions of the New York Stock Exchange, FINRA is dedicated to investor protection and market integrity through effective and efficient regulation and complementary compliance and technology-based services."

FINRA is important to investigators as a resource to check on brokers. The Web site allows name searching of an individual or a brokerage firm. This is a key resource when investigating any type of investment advisor. If the advisor or broker is registered in FINRA, the user can download an eight-page Adobe Acrobat PDF file that outlines the subject's history, including his employment history. Brokerage firms also are searchable for any disciplinary actions taken against a company, or brokers who are involved with arbitration awards, disciplinary and regulatory events.

National Futures Association (NFA)

According to NFA's Web site (www.nfa.futures.org)—

> "National Futures Association is the industry-wide, self-regulatory organization for the U.S. futures industry. We strive every day to develop rules, programs and services that safeguard market integrity, protect investors and help our Members meet their regulatory responsibilities."

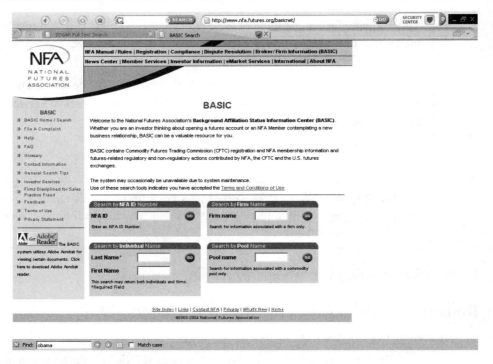

(Source: www.nfa.futures.org/basicnet)

Searching the futures database is very straightforward, offering basic searches that use an individual's name or a firm's name. Results give any arbitration or regulatory action filed against the individual or firm, if listed with the NFA.

In summary, each organization monitors public companies and brokers for impropriety, and oversees securities dealers, brokerage firms, and compliance requirements. Each has the authority to investigate and enforce regulatory actions.

North American Securities Administrators Association (NASAA)

Another excellent resource that merits attention is the North American Securities Administrators Association (NASAA). With members from the 50 states, the District of Columbia, Puerto Rico, the U.S. Virgin Islands, Canada, and Mexico, NASAA is devoted to investor protection.

NASAA members license firms and their agents, investigate violations of state and provincial law, file enforcement actions when appropriate, and educate the public about investment fraud.

NASAA members also participate in multi-state enforcement actions and information sharing. The NASAA Web site (www.nasaa.org) contains links to individual state, provincial, and territorial jurisdictions for securities laws, rules and regulations.

Central Registration Depository (CRD)

An important collaborative effort of NASAA, FINRA, and the SEC was their joint development of the Central Registration Depository (CRD). State securities regulators for NASAA, FINRA and the SEC realized that it was inefficient for each regulator to have their own filing systems to license broker-dealers and their agents, so they created the CRD for this purpose. The CRD reports are available through state regulatory authorities. A list of which can be located at the NASAA Web site.

Quick Scrambling

A longtime client called one day with the name of a company to investigate. The client was clear about the company name and asked me to conduct a due diligence investigation. I dutifully wrote the company name, and started the project. After pulling together a large report, highlighting all the key information concerning litigation, media, business filings, financials, and key principals, I reported my findings to the client.

The next day the client called and explained that he only wanted to locate the company's factory locations in South America, and was not interested in all the minutiae of details I had pulled together for his report. I asked him if he had checked the company's Web site. On the site was a Web page, under the "Locations" tab, with all the contact information for each of the factories.

Not all was lost though. In my research, I discovered media stories that mentioned there were talks of this company acquiring one of its competitors. The client was quite happy to receive that information.

The story demonstrates what is common in investigations. The investigator does a great job, but the client still is not impressed. Here is where the customer-service angle comes in. Always follow up with the client and ask him what he thought of your work. This is oftentimes avoided, because it can be very difficult to hear criticism.

Author Tip ➡ Business personalities, business types, and foreign entities, whether they are small, private companies or large, multinational, publicly traded corporations, will present unique challenges to the investigator. This is especially true for those new to the corporate world. Always remember that there is someone smarter than you out there, so do not be afraid to reach out and ask. Join associations and attend seminars that will offer you business and investigations training. Also, check community-college business classes. One semester in International Business 101 will broaden your horizons and give you a better understanding of the corporate world.

The U.S. Excluded Parties List

While the above legal entities are all useful when researching the legal history and filings of a company, there are many other sites that contain information on companies that have been cited for compliance problems or have regulatory violations that block them from doing business with the government.

One of the most important is the Excluded Parties List System (EPLS). EPLS contains information on individuals and firms excluded by over 85 federal government agencies from receiving federal contracts or federally approved subcontracts, and certain types of federal financial and non-financial assistance and benefits. To indicate the significance of the EPLS, the list of these 85 agencies that participate is shown in the Appendix. Note that individual agencies are responsible for the timely reporting, maintenance, and accuracy of their data. When reviewing this list, you realize the government generates this information from a variety of agencies that you may not be aware of, such as the Appalachian Regional Commission.

Searching the EPLS

You can search for the company-excluded parties on the EPLS site www.epls.gov. Easily search the list by full names, partial names, or even multiple names, by Social Security Numbers, and by federal employment identification numbers. Information shown may include names, addresses, DUNS numbers, Social Security numbers, employer identification numbers or other taxpayer identification numbers, if available and deemed appropriate and permissible to publish by the agency taking the action.

The example below is record from a partial name search using "ab . . . " (the names have been changed).

EPLS Record - as of 2007

Name	ABC Industrial Source Inc.
Classification	Firm
Exclusion Type	Reciprocal
Description	none
Address(es) --	
Address	104 Terrace Dr., Chicago IL, 55512
DUNS	186355555
CT Action(s) --	
Action Date	03-Jun-2003
Termination Date	Indef.
CT Code	B
Agency	AF
Action Status	Created (03-Jun-2003)
Action Date	03-Jun-2003
Termination Date	Indef.
CT Code	S
Agency	AF
Action Status	Created (03-Jun-2003)
Action Date	06-Oct-2006
Termination Date	Indef.
CT Code	A1
Agency	AF
Action Status	Created (03-Jun-2003)
Action Date	18-Dec-2006
Termination Date	02-Jun-2023

CT Code	A
Agency	AF
Action Status	Created (03-Jun-2003)

Cross Reference(s) --

Name	Action Date	Term Date	CT Code
1. Captiva, Rose A.	03-Jun-2003	Indef.	B
	03-Jun-2003	Indef.	S
	06-Oct-2006	Indef.	A1
	18-Dec-2006	02-Jun-2023	A
2. Lonne, Mark M.	03-Jun-2003	Indef.	B
	03-Jun-2003	Indef.	S
	06-Oct-2006	Indef.	A1
	18-Dec-2006	02-Jun-2008	A
3. Technical Systems, Inc.	03-Jun-2003	Indef.	B
	03-Jun-2003	Indef.	S
	06-Oct-2006	Indef.	A1
	18-Dec-2006	02-Jun-2023	A
4. Romeo, Ross M.	03-Jun-2003	Indef.	B
	03-Jun-2003	Indef.	S
	06-Oct-2006	Indef.	A1
	18-Dec-2006	02-Jun-2018	A
5. Shaver, Mary E.	03-Jun-2003	Indef.	B
	03-Jun-2003	Indef.	S
	06-Oct-2006	Indef.	A1
	18-Dec-2006	02-Jun-2008	A

The **CT column** gives the reason why a company is excluded. Refer to the URL below for a code list of the causes with explanations—

https://www.epls.gov/epls/jsp/CTCodes.jsp?type=recip

An important fact to keep in mind is that the agencies reporting to the EPLS also may have their own excluded party databases located on their Web sites. An example is the Department of Health and Human Services. Locating independent lists from EPLS is easy. Search google.com using the agency name and add, "excluded" (e.g. Department of Health and Human Services excluded).

The Department of Health and Human Services has an Office of Investigative General, with an excluded parties list at http://exclusions.oig.hhs.gov. Search by personal or company name. Results for individuals return the addresses, names, and dates of birth, as well as a box to verify the Social Security numbers, if you have them. Companies' results return the addresses, points of contact, and a box to verify federal employee identification numbers.

Each state and practice also will have its own excluded parties list. For example, in New Jersey, the Bureau of Securities (www.njconsumeraffairs.gov/bos/bosdisc.htm), part of the Division of Consumer Affairs, has a listing of enforcement actions taken against persons involved in securities fraud. Check with brbpub.com for a listing of each state's consumer affairs, or similar, agency and see what is available online. A phone call may be necessary, since not every agency has published its material on the Internet.

Other Federal Agency Watch Lists

This section examines specific watch lists from the Commerce Department, Labor Department, State Department, and Treasury Department. The text appearing in this section is an excerpt from the *Public Records Research Tips Book* by Facts on Demand Press.

Commerce Department

The Bureau of Industry and Security (BIS), at www.bis.doc.gov, provides lists relevant to import or export transactions.

Denied Persons List (www.bis.doc.gov/dpl/Default.shtm)

The purpose of the Denied Persons List is to prevent the illegal export of dual-use items before they occur and to investigate and assist in the prosecution of violators of the Export Administration Regulations.

Unverified List (www.bis.doc.gov/Enforcement/UnverifiedList/unverified_parties.html)

This is a list of parties whom BIS has been unable to verify the end use in prior transactions. The Unverified List includes names and countries of foreign persons who in the past were parties to a transaction with respect to which BIS could not conduct a pre-license check (PLC) or a post-shipment verification (PSV) for reasons outside of the U.S. Government's control. If you would like to be informed when changes occur to the Unverified List, consider subscribing to the BIS Email Notification Service.

Entity List (www.bis.doc.gov/Entities/Default.htm)

The Entity List, available in PDF or ASCII text format, is a list of parties whose presence in a transaction can trigger a license requirement under the Export Administration Regulations. The list specifies the license requirements that apply to each listed party. These license requirements are in addition to any license requirements imposed on the transaction by other provisions of the Export Administration Regulations.

Labor Department

The Office of Labor-Management Standards (OLMS) in the U.S. Department of Labor is the Federal agency responsible for administering and enforcing most provisions of the Labor-Management Reporting and Disclosure Act of 1959, as amended (LMRDA). The LMRDA is meant to ensure basic standards of democracy and fiscal responsibility in labor organizations representing employees in private industry, unions representing U.S. Postal Service employees and other Federal employee organizations. OLMS does not have jurisdiction over unions representing solely state, county, or municipal employees. OLMS responsibilities include—

- **Public Disclosure of Reports** - Labor unions, their officers and employees, employers, labor relations consultants, and surety companies, must file reports which are public information and available for disclosure at OLMS offices.

- **Compliance Audits** - OLMS has responsibility under the LMRDA to audit local unions for records review and to verify LMRDA compliance.

- **Investigations** - OLMS staff conduct investigations to determine if violations of the LMRDA provisions have occurred and to protect and safeguard union funds and assets. OLMS must refer information it uncovers regarding possible embezzlement violations by union officers or employees to the U.S. Attorney who decides if criminal prosecution is warranted.

- **Education and Compliance Assistance** - Among the services OLMS provides are education and compliance assistance programs to promote voluntary compliance and conducting seminars and workshops about the law in general or about specific areas per regulations by the LMRDA.

The OLMS Internet Public Disclosure Room web page enables users to 1) view and print reports filed by unions, union officers and employees, employers, and labor relations consultants for the year 2000 and after and reports filed by unions for trusts in which they have an interest, (2) order reports for the year 1999 and prior, and (3) search the union annual financial reports for the year 2000 and after and the trust reports for key data items. Also, searchers can generate a number of reports comparing data saved from multiple searches.

Visit the Disclosure Room at www.dol.gov/esa/regs/compliance/olms/rrlo/lmrda.htm or contact the U.S. Department of Labor, Statutory Programs, Washington, D.C. 20210 at 202-693-0126.

State Department

Debarred List (www.pmddtc.state.gov/compliance/debar.html)

A list compiled by the State Department of parties who are barred the International Traffic in Arms Regulations (ITAR) (22 CFR §127.7) from participating directly or indirectly in the export of defense articles, including technical data or in the furnishing of defense services for which a license or approval is required.

Nonproliferation Sanctions Lists (www.state.gov/t/isn/c15231.htm)

The State Department maintains lists of parties that have been sanctioned under various statutes and legal authority. Seven separate lists are found at the web page including Sanctions for the Transfer of Lethal Military Equipment and under Missile Sanctions laws.

Treasury Department

Specifically Designated Nationals (SDN) List (www.treas.gov/offices/enforcement/ofac/sdn/)

The U.S. Department the Treasury, Office of Foreign Assets Control (OFAC) publishes a list of individuals and companies owned or controlled by, or acting for or on behalf of, targeted foreign countries, terrorists, international narcotics traffickers and those engaged in activities related to the proliferation of weapons of mass destruction. The site also indicates individuals and entities that are not country-specific. Collectively, these individuals and companies are called "Specially Designated Nationals" or "SDN." Their assets are blocked and U.S. persons are generally prohibited from dealing with them.

In addition, the Export Administration Regulations require a license for exports or re-exports to any party in any entry on this list that contains any of the suffixes SDGT, SDT, FTO or IRAQ2. The OFAC's "Hotline" is 1-800-540-6322.

The Banded - Sanctions and Law Enforcement Resources

Being banded because of government sanctions is rather large on the scale of excluded lists. Terrorists, drug cartels, countries that have embargoes placed on them or break treatises are considered sanctionable. Sanctions focus primarily on the maintenance of international peace and security, but other issues include legality and corruption.

United Nations Security Council Committee (www.un.org/sc/committees)

The United Nations Security Council (UNSC) decides which countries and organizations to sanction. Sanctioning these entities indicates that a company is blacklisted. An embargo can be imposed because of the subject's involvement with known terrorists. The embargo prohibits any future arms deals, technical training, or technology transference.

The UNSC Resolutions can be viewed resolution by resolution in PDF format. All countries tied to the UNSC follow this list. It is a good place to begin.

The following country-sanction committees also abide by the UNSC resolutions[30]:

- Hong Kong Monetary Authority
- Commission de Surveillance du Secteur Financier, Luxembourg
- De Nederlandsche Bank, Netherlands
- Department of Foreign Affairs and Trade, Australia
- Monetary Authority of Singapore
- Office of the Superintendent of Financial Institutions, Canada
- Reserve Bank of Australia

England - HM Treasury (http://www.hm-treasury.gov.uk/financialsanctions)

The HM Treasury lists include those persons whose assets have been frozen in the U.K. The lists of sanctioned persons and organizations are in downloadable format and can be viewed online. A list of investment ban targets designated by the European Union under legislation relating to current financial sanctions regimes is available.

European Union Financial Sanctions

(www.ec.europa.eu/external_relations/cfsp/sanctions/list/consol-list.htm)

---

[30] Not a complete list.

The European Union (EU) Financial Sanctions list includes the European Banking Federation, the European Savings Banks Group, the European Association of Cooperative Banks, and the European Association of Public Banks (the EU Credit Sector Federations).

Office of Foreign Assets Control (OFAC), U.S. (www.ustreas.gov/offices/enforcement/ofac)

OFAC, and its predecessor, the Office of Foreign Funds Control, have been around since World War 2 following the German invasion of Norway in 1940. The enforcement list as developed by U.S. Department of Treasury consists of individuals and organizations that are suspected of being connected with terrorist and organized crime activities.

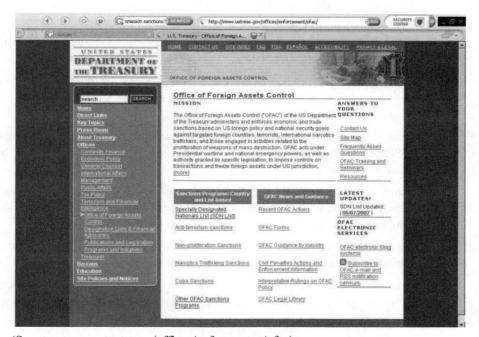

(Source: www.ustreas.gov/offices/enforcement/ofac)

Law Enforcement Resources and Most Wanted Lists

Searching the law enforcement sites for the most wanted is easier than searching for regulatory issues. Usually, a wanted list will be very clearly stated on a Web site, in press releases, or on wanted tear sheets. Each applicable federal agency and international body has a Web site with a most wanted list. The more popular agencies are listed below—.

- U.S. Federal Bureau of Investigation (www.fbi.gov/wanted.htm)
- U.S. Bureau of Alcohol, Tobacco, Firearms and Explosives (www.atf.gov/wanted/index.htm)
- U.S. Drug Enforcement Administration (www.usdoj.gov/dea/fugitives/fuglist.htm)
- Each state will also have a "Most Wanted" list.

Other International Sources

Check the Appendix for a list of key foreign regulatory bodies and law enforcement entities.

Cynthia's Key Chapter Points

♦ "Dirt" comes in many flavors. Investigators spend much time digging the dirt up the dirt from courts, disciplinary actions, watch lists, and other public and private sources.

♦ There is no comprehensive source for legal, civil, or criminal filings in the U.S.

♦ Discovering where to search for criminal, civil, and disciplinary actions is key. With subjects moving from location to location, at times a proper court search can become cost prohibitive. Often you still do not know if you checked every resource.

♦ If you are not an attorney, legal secretary or paralegal, or do not have an in-depth understanding of legal filings and the unique language uses, then be sure to quote your findings and list the citation, for reference.

♦ A handy U.S. resource for federal filings for bankruptcy and district court matters is PACER (www.pacer.uscourts.gov). PACER is inexpensive and easy to use, but make an effort to understand its limitations.

♦ Another great resource is the Stanford Law School of Securities Class Action Clearinghouse found at securities.standford.edu. For years this resource has been cataloging and updating U.S. class action lawsuits.

♦ Know that there are special circumstance court systems, such as Tribal Courts (Native American lands) and even Taxi court (New York City).

♦ Pilots, doctors, massage therapists, private investigators, securities regulators - just about every type of job or position, whether white or blue collared - has a state board who regulates and manages the members.

♦ Financial crimes are regulated by state and federal agencies primarily. It is important to know what kind of crime occurred in order to find the oversight group who would investigate and follow up on the matter.

♦ Federal government agencies as well agencies around the world, including the United Nations, have searchable Watch Lists for known terrorists and international criminals.

Chapter 7

Asset and Lien Searching

*If a rich man is proud of his wealth, he should not be praised
until it is known how he employs it.*

—Socrates

An asset is anything of economic value. The International Accounting Standards Board[31] defines
an asset as—

> "...a resource controlled by the enterprise as a result of past events and from which
> future economic benefits are expected to flow to the enterprise."

Locating the assets of a business can be incredibly difficult because assets can be held in many,
many ways. Some assets are out in the **open**, easily found in public records. Some are **intangible**
– they lack a physical presence and may be hard to place a value upon. And other assets may be
hidden – cleverly by choice to hide wealth, or hard to find because of government financial
protection laws.

Finding liens is an import part of a business asset search. To an investigator, assets and liens go
together like salt and pepper. Usually, liens are recorded as public record, and as any investigator
knows, finding liens will lead to finding assets, or to other liens which could lead to other assets.

This chapter examines the various reasons why a business asset search is performed, where to
find assets and liens, searching techniques, and some first-hand applications along the way.

Six Reasons for a Business Asset Search

Understanding the reasons why your client wants you to search for assets is a necessity.
Knowing the specific intent help focus the investigation, will keep you on target to find what
you are looking for and will make sure you perform your investigation in a legal manner.

1. Pre-assess Before Filing a Lawsuit

Your client has not been paid. Prior to filing a lawsuit against that party, you are asked to
research and locate the party's assets. In some cases, the outstanding debt may never be
collected because the debtor has nothing of real value, or has run out of funds and can no longer
sustain his own business. The client wants to know first, if filing a suit is a waste of time and
energy.

---

[31] See www.iasb.org/Home.htm

When conducting an asset investigation prior to a lawsuit, the Gramm, Leach, Bliley Act[32] and Fair Credit Reporting Act[33] restricts the investigator, because he cannot obtain credit histories, bank statements, or financial reports without the authorization of the party or debtor, in this case.

2. Collecting on a Judgment

If a lawsuit has occurred and a judgment has been issued, the creditor may place a lien on the assets identified in the lawsuit or, preferably, collect on the judgment. Finding assets of debtor party is one of the most common reasons in investigator is hired for an asset search.

Even lawsuits can have liens placed on them. A physician can place a lien on a pending lawsuit that involves an injury to his client. For example, if a carpenter is hurt while working on the job and sees a doctor, but he does not have the insurance or funds to pay the doctor, then the doctor can place a lien on the carpenter's pending lawsuit against his employer. When the case closes and the money is doled out, the attorney is paid first, the physician second, and the individual last.

3. Locating a Project's Funding Party or Mysterious New Investor

The third reason for asset location is tracking down the money behind the mission, the silent partner in a business deal, or the real owner of a company.

The silent partner in a business is the lead investor in the company. Sometimes this is as simple as a family member getting a second mortgage to assist a budding idea. However, this also can be large, hedge-funds investors, private money from overseas investors or fronts for shell companies.

4. Finding Prior Ownership

It is necessary to find the owner of an old asset, like a product or property, when the new investor needs to allocate a liability claim against the owner.

This is more likely to happen in property cases. If a company purchases a property from another, the purchasing company needs to search for all liens against the property to insure it is not buying bad debt.

The purchasing company also needs to conduct a geographic survey of the land because it could be getting more than it bargained for. Many early, industrial plants stationed near waterways, railroads, and major byways were unregulated polluters that created toxic-waste areas, now dubbed superfund sites. Today, the Environmental Protection Agency (EPA) forces the current land owner to clean up the area, resulting in millions of dollars of expenses that the owner may not have anticipated.

Another issue could come from an old product, such as a workman's tool. What if the product fails and someone is injured? Who is sued?

---

[32] See www.ftc.gov/privacy/glbact/glbsub1.htm
[33] A copy of the Fair Credit Reporting Act can be located on the Federal Trade Commission Web site at www.ftc.gov/os/statutes/031224fcra.pdf.

Both cases require asset searching. In the case of the failed product, the investigator needs to locate the manufacturer of the failed product so the attorneys know where to file suit. The historical property ownership is also an asset search for a current company that needs to know where to send the clean-up bill.

5. Employment Purposes

Pre-employment screening is often performed on applicant for key positions. Assessing the strength of an individual that may be placed in upper management or in a high-level accounting and financial position is a must. An individual's financial history is an indicator as to his fiscal responsibility. If a company is going to trust the new hire with its financial records, vehicles, and office equipment, it will want to insure that the person it is hiring is reasonably financially secure. That can be a long yardstick to measure with; however, indicators of a troubled worker will appear in a credit report, as collection-agency notices, bankruptcies, and severely late payments to vendors.

6. Investment Opportunity or New Business Venture.

When an entity is considering a business relationship with another entity, it is prudent to establish the strengths of that particular company or individual. Researching and assessing a corporation's financial strength is not much different from an individual's financial check. Corporate financial reports are published by D&B and Experian. They offer their own indicators as to a corporation's financial strength, based on the payment history submitted by vendors, annual sales and revenue reported, and risk indicators determined by the industry.

Investigating the financial strength of a company can be quantified by **SWOT Analysis**. **Strength**, **weakness**, **opportunity** and **threat,** the words that make up the acronym, are the indicators devised by observing and analyzing how a company fairs by itself, in its market and in comparison to similar companies.

For example a shoe manufacturer may demonstrate *strength* (particularly in cash flow) because of paying vendor invoices within 30 days, opposed to 120 days. A *weakness* can be noted if a company reports only $1.2 million in sales, when other shoe manufacturers of similar size are reporting $4 million and more. But if the end product is good, there is *opportunity* of acquisition. In other words, the company has the talent in place, but is not reaching the channels and market to the fullest extent. Finally, a *threat* can be seen if the shoe manufacturer has filed for bankruptcy, has been delisted, or has demonstrated poor financial health, such as extended credit problems.

Again, when looking for the money behind a person or a company, start with a public records search. Researching properties, liens, automobiles, and other such tangible goods will help create a financial profile of the person. If an individual is deliberately hiding property from either the government, as in a lien, or from a potential lawsuit, he will often register the deed in someone else's name.

Liens and Security Interests

Before examining the different asset categories and searching techniques, let's review the types of liens that are researched in a business background investigation.

With or Without Consent

Liens are secured on assets either by choice or not by choice. Examples of liens placed with the consent of the asset holder include mortgages or loans on balance sheet items such as equipment or accounts receivable. Liens placed without the consent of an asset holder include tax liens, mechanic's liens, and liens filed on assets as the result of judgments issued by courts.

Uniform Commercial Code (UCC) Filings

Uniform Commercial Code (UCC) filings are referenced a good deal in this chapter because a UCC is essentially a statement of business ownership of possessions. A UCC is a document that cites a business loan. That loan could be for new equipment, new property, or the acquisition of other assets. The filing will state the debtor, the creditor, the contact information, and what has been placed as collateral. Examples are computers and machinery, communication systems, air compressors and conditioners, and even non-tangible goods.

A UCC recording allows potential lenders to be notified that certain assets of a debtor are already used to secure a loan or lease. Therefore, examining UCC filings is an excellent way to find bank accounts, security interests, financiers, and other similar assets.

> **Author Tip** ➡ A significant change in UCC filing took effect in July 2001. Prior to that date UCC documents were recorded either at a centralized state agency or at a local recording office. At the time, there were over 4,200 locations in the U.S. that recorded UCCs. Revised Article 9 of the Code mandated effective July 2001 that all UCC documents were to be filed and recorded at a state level agency, with the exception of real estate filings such as farm-related real estate. According to the UCC Filing Guide, now less than 3% of filings are done so at the local level. However, there is a caveat – any existing UCC filings if previously filed locally can be renewed or extended at the local level, instead of being renewed at the state level.
>
> Although there are significant variations among state statutes, the state level is now the best starting place to uncover liens filed against an individual or business, but it is not the only place to search. Strict due diligence may require a local search also, depending on the state.

Non-Consensual Liens

Judgments

If a business fails to pay an attorney, a contractor, an engineer, etc., these parties have a right to file suit in court against the business. If the court finds in favor of the plaintiff, a judgment is issued. These judgments are generally found in the state court system at the county level, and liens will be recorded against assets (if any) of the defendant.

Tax Liens

Another typical non-consensual lien is one placed by a government agency for non-payment of taxes. The federal government and every state have some sort of taxes, such as sales, income, withholding, unemployment, and/or personal property. When these taxes go unpaid, the appropriate state agency can file a lien on the real or personal property of the subject. *Normally, the state agency that maintains UCC records also maintains tax liens.*

Tax liens filed against individuals are frequently maintained at separate locations from those liens filed against businesses. For example, a large number of states require liens filed against businesses to be filed at a central state location (i.e., Secretary of State's office) and liens against individuals to be filed at the county level (i.e., Recorder, Register of Deeds, Clerk of Court, etc.).

Liens on a company may not all be filed in the same location. A federal tax lien will not necessarily be filed (recorded) at the same location/jurisdiction as a lien filed by the state. This holds true for both individual liens and as well as business liens filed against personal property. Typically, state tax liens on personal property will be found where UCCs are filed. Tax liens on real property will be found where real property deeds are recorded, with few exceptions. Unsatisfied state and federal tax liens may be renewed if prescribed by individual state statutes. However, once satisfied, the time the record will remain in the repository before removal varies by jurisdiction.

More on Investigating Liens

Do not be surprised if a search for liens and UCCs turns up an odd, tax lien in a state where your subject company is not located. A big company, say based in New York City, might show a tax lien in Utah. This should be followed up, because it could mean there is a second location for that company.

If a lien has been placed by a private authority, and not a federal or state tax entity, then there is going to be a collection issue. For example, the creditor party wins in a lawsuit, but now has to wait for payment. So the business assets, personal home, property, or vehicles may be named in the judgment. As investigators, use these judgments, UCCs, and lien notices to help identify assets that are being outlined in the filings. Collecting on judgments is a unique talent that combines legal know-how with investigative ability. The judgment collector is well versed in the state laws and understands the involved ramifications. One such association, the California Association of Judgment Collectors (www.cajp.org), offers a beginner to continuing-education training on judgment collection.

Types of Assets Held by a Business

As mentioned, an asset can be **liquid** (cash or easily converted to cash), **intangible** (hard to find or evaluate), or **hidden** (tucked way so no one can find them). Typical assets controlled by a business include—

- **Real Property**
- **Personal Property**
- **Investments and Trusts (Financial Assets)**
- **Intellectual Property**
- **Subsidiaries and Spin-offs**

We will examine each asset type and gives examples on how to search and investigate.

Real Property

Real property refers to real estate. For many individuals, the first sign of wealth is taking on incredible debt, like a mortgage. In most instances, families own one home. However, it should not be assumed that is always the case. There are plenty of baby boomers with extensive investment money who have purchased summer homes, investment properties, or second homes for their extended families. They may also own undeveloped property, farmland, or open-space land

Businesses also own property, manufacturing plants, and office spaces. They may use all or part of the property for themselves, or rent several floors to other interests.

Where to Search

Researching these property deed or assessment record is a snap with the right sources. Property records are recorded and maintained by the county or parish or city in which that property resides. These local county[34] records are open to the public. Most of the populous counties usually found on the Internet through a variety of free and fee sources. Once again, the Web page at www.brbpub.com is a good starting place to locate county-by-county records. On the fee side, search LexisNexis, Westlaw, Accurint, IRBsearch, LocatePlus, Merlindata, and ChoicePoint.

A key point here is that there are many counties that do not share these public records online. These counties may maintain their records in an electronic index and have decided not to supply online service, or the records may be maintained in card files or microfiche. When this instance occurs, contact the county recorder's office and ask about the cost and turnaround time for a search within that county, or hire a local record retriever for an on-site search.

Finding a Stalker via Property Records

Although not directly related to business investigation, I received a call one afternoon from a concerned investigator in Washington. Apparently, her new client was being stalked by someone who had an inordinate amount of information on her, including the client's

---

[34] There are over 3,600 locations in the U.S. where property records can be recorded. When referring to county-level recorder, the author is also including reference to parish, city, and town locations where documents can be recorded.

nursing-school schedule, her visits to the library and her interests in kayaking and water sports. In fact, the stalker knew about her family's summer lodge deep in the mountains of Washington. He even went so far as to email her, saying that he would "love to visit you next time you and your brother go away to the lodge;" and then he gave the lodge's address.

Talk about frightening! The investigator hired me to trace the email and to coordinate with law enforcement on the technical issues. In the due course of the investigation, I located the vacation- property record, but found that the database did not exist. The property record was not available online. Hence, the stalker knew about the property either from hearsay or by following her.

The stalker was eventually identified and it was learned that he obtained the lodge's address by following her. And for the curious, he was also a nursing student. When I tracked the emails, I found that he was sending them to her from the same campus that she attended.

Personal Property

This category includes transportation vehicles, and business equipment like computer and machinery. Personal assets are classified as personal property.

Motor Vehicles and Vessels

Big companies will own some or all of these assets. The company car takes you to the company jet, and then you are flown to the company yacht for an important meeting. The company car might be something as simple as a fleet of work vans for a local contractor, or as imposing as limousines with their own dedicated drivers. Not every company will own an airplane but it certainly should be checked on. Do not discount the possibility that a company may not own its own airplane, but may participate in fractional jet service.

Small-business men may own vessels like luxury, weekend crafts or imposing yachts.

Motor vehicles searches usually depend on which state you are searching. Motor vehicle records that contain personal information, like an address or physical characteristics not public record. However, if you have permissible purpose, according to the Driver's Privacy Protection Act (DPPA)[35], you can look up title and registration records. For example, a look-up by plate number will give current owner information, or doing a name search can lead to vehicles registered or titled under that name. A permissible purpose includes enforcement of a judgment, an existing court case, or an investigation involving anticipated litigation. Of course it is up to the individual state to decide to adopt these allowable permissible uses.

---

[35] *Prohibition On Release And Use Of Certain Personal Information From State Motor Vehicle Records* is located at http://uscode.house.gov/download/pls/18C123.txt. See the act at www.mvrdecoder.com/default.aspx?pageid=10

You will find that many of the state agencies that oversee vehicle records also oversee vessel records and DPPA restrictions apply. However, a number of states have a different agency regulate and hold vessel records. These agencies usually oversee wildlife and outdoor activities, including the issuance of hunting and fishing licenses. The good news for investigators is that many of these agencies do not follow DPPA and records are open. An excellent reference book to find which states consider vessel records open is *The Public Records Research Tips Book* by Facts on Demand Press.

Many of the state agencies that oversee vehicle records offer online access to record indices and sometime even to record images. Generally a subscription is required. This is a good way to find records for current and historical automobiles and vessels. If you do not see any cars registered to the individual, check the spouse's name.

A great search technique that potentially offers more leads to assets is to conduct the search offline. Send a surveillance investigator to the home and workplace of the individual you are searching, or to the subject company's location, to see if there is a car or a fleet of vehicles. You can look up the plate numbers by state and get the owner's information as described above. In this way, if the individual has registered the vehicle under another name, or company name, this new lead may be the avenue to follow for other assets.

Vessels and watercraft that weigh more than five tons are registered with the U.S. Coast Guard, see www.st.nmfs.noaa.gov/st1/CoastGuard/. Another handy location to search for larger vessels, or to search by lien or title, is the Coast Guard's National Vessel Documentation Center, found at www.uscg.mil/hq/cg5/nvdc/.

For the very wealthy, if you are searching for yachts or luxury liners, it is very possible that the vessels have been registered in a foreign country, such as Bermuda. When checking for these large vessels as floating corporations, scan the business databases by the boat name. Also, search the Web with the boat name and any other indicators that you may have. It is possible that the company is selling or buying the boat, and is showing off photos of it online, with all of its statistics.

Finally, the vessel may be named in a UCC filing, and will have an insurance policy. Make sure to obtain all the UCC records for the company and individual.

Aircraft, Airlines, Pilots

The International Civil Aviation Organization (www.icao.int) maintains aircraft registration standards for participating countries. Each aircraft (over a certain weight) must be registered with a national aviation registration number. Different countries have different registration schemes. For example, the U.S. uses an "N" followed by 1 to 5 additional characters.

The main U.S. government information center regarding certification for pilots, airman, airlines, aircraft and for aircraft registration and ownership, and airports is the Federal Aviation Association (FAA). The website is www.faa.gov, the toll-free phone number is 866-835-5322.

One of the leading private information resource centers for searching flights, pilot certifications, and regulatory overviews is Albuquerque-based Landings.com. They can be reached at

702.920.8298. Visit www.landings.com for many excellent searching links and background information.

Another extremely in-depth source of aviation information of every kind is Jane's Information Group. Jane's reference, news and analysis information covers the areas of security, defense, aerospace, transport, public safety and law enforcement for not only aviation, but also for vessels and railroads. The North America office is located in Alexandria, VA. They can be reached at 800-824-0768 or visit www.janes.com to access many free searches. Offices are found throughout the world.

Another industry leader in aviation information collection, analysis and distribution is Cincinnati-based Aviation Research Group. Call them at 800.361.2216 or visit www.aviationresearch.com. They offer a free aircraft registration search on the web.

Search Canadian aircraft information at:

http://wwwapps2.tc.gc.ca/saf-sec-sur/2/CCARCS/aspscripts/en/menu.asp.

Computers and Machinery

Several assets may be overlooked because they seem like everyday objects, such as computers or construction or farm equipment. However, like automobiles, these are assets of value, depending on their depreciation and age.

UCCs will often list the major assets of a company because they are used as security for loans. Each state has a division of its Secretary of State office that handles UCC records, and records or at least the index can be searched directly from that agency's Web page. Finding these sites is easy using the public record database sources already mentioned. In addition, public record vendor Web-site services like www.iqdata.com, www.openonline.com, and www.knowx.com are handy for viewing UCC filings.

Financial Investments and Trusts

Financial assets are stocks, international stocks, currencies and commodities, bonds, and mutual funds. These financial assets are often considered the *golden egg* since they are can be more valuable than physical assets like cars or machinery. If you are judgment searching, use some of your database sources and if necessary legal process (process serving) to find bank accounts and 401K plans. However without a judgment in hand, there is little in the way beyond gum shoe tactics to finding these accounts. Depending on the state and city laws, trash pickups are still a viable way to find bank accounts. One hint I can offer is to pick up garbage when companies' boards are meeting and approving quarterly reports. These voluminous printed quarterlies usually get thrown out in whole. However this is not the method of choice, and privacy laws are tightening up even on trash runs. The following technical approaches make it easier, if not cleaner, to locate assets.

Searching for Investments and Other Financial Assets

If you own more than five percent of a stock, it is public record and can be searched in ChoicePoint and through SEC filings. However, most individuals do not own that much stock in company. One aspect to locating investments is to search legal filings. If the individual filed for a divorce, the assets listed in the divorce decree will offer a page-by-page account of all assets, including 401K retirement plans, stock options, and other key investment information. Trusts can be located by address. Search the individual's home address in a public-record database, and if trust accounts are registered to that location, you will see them. Without legal process, nothing else can be obtained on them; however, it is an indicator that assets are being stored under the trust.

Another trust finder is Dun & Bradstreet. Searching the free side of D&B is quite effective in tracking trusts under family names.

There are some excellent **industry news resources** that are incredible sources for venture capital and private equity research and alerts. These resources are on the high end of quality and offerings. Their subscription prices match the information they give allowing you to search by investor, find company reports, and help you understand what the status of funding is within a company.

- VentureSource, by Dow Jones, covers news in the venture-capital market for the US, and is a subscription service. www.venturesource.com

- Thomson Financial focuses on Canadian capital markets with its VCReporter service; found at www.canadavc.com.

- Another great, but expensive, source is Standard & Poor's Capital IQ. Capital IQ offers almost 10,000 profiles on private, capital firms worldwide. Information on companies, co-investors, individuals' biographies, and corporate portfolios can be found here. See www.capitaliq.com.

- Mergermarket Ltd., owned by the *Financial Times*, offers intelligence, reporting, tracking, and alerting for any merger moves or equity shifts. See www.mergermarket.com.

- To keep abreast of these markets without spending the entire database budget on one service, go to www.edgar-online.com, www.secinfo.com, or www.sec.gov.

If you are involved in a judgment collections case, there are additional sources available like MicroBilt's eFunds Debit Report Collections (www.microbilt.com/efunds_debit.asp).

A sample report is shown on the next page.

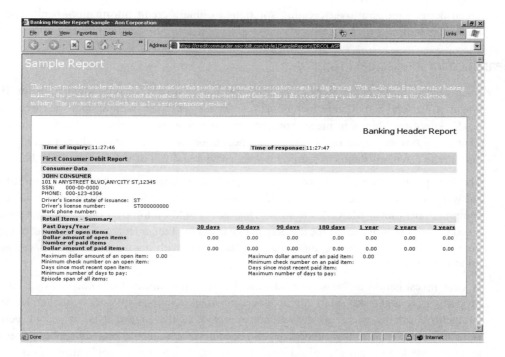

(Source: https://creditcommander.microbilt.com/style1/SampleReports/DRCOL.ASP)

Intellectual Property

There is a large amount of asset searching that gets missed when focusing only on cash in hand or capital investments. What about the untenable assets? I refer to this as **intellectual property**.

While flying back to Newark, New Jersey from Southern California, where I had spent some quality time training members of the California District Attorneys Association (CDAA), I reflected on what had transpired. The training was the conclusion of a three-day continuing education for prosecutors, paralegals, police officers, and detectives, and the topic was asset forfeiture. If the topic had been about breaching, accident reconstruction, or weapons tactics, I would not have been invited as the closing-session speaker.

These CDAA professionals track down the finances of fraudulent individuals and their companies, from drug traffickers, corporate raiders, and terrorists. The audience was a unique mix, from tattooed, sunglasses-wearing, thuggish-looking "narc" officers to librarian-looking soccer moms. Appearances, notwithstanding, they did have a keen sense of "looking under mattresses" or into family member accounts and other likely or unlikely places to track the assets of their subjects.

This audience also was equipped with resources not available to private investigators, such as access to a district attorney's office, the support of a full legal team, Experian credit reports, and subpoena power. With compliance of the Fair Credit Reporting Act in mind, private detectives spend hours agonizing over creating solutions to obtain credit information, bank reports, and financial details.

Searching for Intellectual Property

Imagine your target is the focus of an asset check for a divorce or pre-judgment claim. He has a house, a car, and a moderate income as a software developer with a small research firm. His 401K retirement plan is in place; however, it is not ripe for retirement for him or anyone else. That is a pretty dry asset list, but it is not uncommon. Most individuals do not hoard stashes of cash in the Cayman Islands or secretly warehouse garages full of vintage cars in Dubai.

The key phrase above is "software developer." The subject may be attached to patents for software, or ideas, registered in the U.S. This intangible asset maybe more valuable than a shipping yard full of Mercedes-Benzes. This asset could be the next operating system idea for YouTube or a security patch for the destructive program Trojan Horse. Your subject could be the next Bill Gates, and you are summing up your report with his most valuable asset equaling a 2004 Ford Taurus.

If your investigation is focused on identified new opportunities for a client, using intellectual property is a great way start an investigation track. Serious investors, market leaders, and competitive intelligence professionals are all aware of the edge that is created by getting the right information first. Researchers who specialize in certain markets subscribe to patent-alert services that keep them posted on new developments and patent applications from particular companies in certain sciences and fields. Nefarious individuals wishing to launder money look for good investments, perhaps by putting their trafficked money into something that results in laundered money with a profit.

Sources for Finding Intellectual Property

United States Patent and Trademark Office www.uspto.gov/main/patents.htm

This is the ultimate source. If you can spend some time learning to correctly search within the Web site, you will get the best results. Remember, when you are searching for a company, refer to it as "assignee." Separately, search the assignee or the town, if small or unique, (skip New York and Los Angeles), and search for the inventor by last name. Other reliable sources include—

- www.freepatentsonline.com – Indexes the full page, but does not give the full results.
- www.patentgenius.com – Excellent search capabilities but, unfortunately, the results are limited.
- www.google.com/patents – Does not index the full page.

If you specialize in patent research, work with an attorney who specializes in intellectual property or visit www.uspto.gov on a regular basis. Also, it pays to work with the professional tools, such as Thomson Derwent, that can be accessed through Dialog products.

Patents and Using Derwent

The following description of the Derwent World Patents Index (DWPI) is taken from the Dialog Bluesheets[36] —

> "Derwent World Patents Index (DWPI), produced by Thomson Scientific, provides access to information from more than 30 million patent documents and gives details of more than 14.8 million inventions. Each update, approximately 20,000 documents from 41 patent-issuing authorities, is added to DWPI.
>
> Each record in the database describes a single "patent family" that contains data from the first publication of an invention, known as the "basic patent," as well as any further published patents relating to that invention, known as "equivalents." The records contain bibliographic data, Thomson Scientific-assigned titles, abstracts, general indexing and in-depth chemical and polymer indexing. Additionally, electrical and engineering drawings are present in records dating back to 1988, and chemical structure drawings are present in records dating back to 1992.
>
> The records in DWPI have been enhanced further with original publication data, such as author name and address, document title, abstract, claims, and legal representative. The amount of this original publication data present in each record varies by publishing authority, patent kind, and time, as shown in the Sources section below."

Also, please see the bluesheets for Derwent World Patents Index First View, which provides fast-alerting access to new patent documents before the complete DWPI record is released; Derwent Chemistry Resource (DCR), which provides graphical, chemical-structure searching with a link to the DWPI records; and Patents Citation Index (PCI), which details examiner- and author-patent citations for patents from the six largest patent-issuing authorities.

Subject Coverage

DWPI covers pharmaceutical patents from 1963, agricultural patents from 1965, polymer and plastics patents from 1966, all chemical patents from 1970, and all patentable technology from 1974. Beginning in 2006, selected original publication data by authority is included. The table in the Sources section below provides a list of the authorities covered in the database and the original publication data included for that authority."

The sources for the 30 million patents found in the DWPI, per the Dialog Bluesheets, include data from 39 countries plus—

European Patent Office - Original titles since 1978; original abstracts since 1978 in English and since 2000 in French or German; first claim since 1991; inventor full name and associated address, and original patent assignee and associated address since 1978; agent and associated address since 1978.

Patent Cooperation Treaty - Original titles since 1978; original abstracts since 1978; inventor full name and associated address, and original patent assignee and associated address since 1978; agent and associated address since 1999.

---

[36] The Dialog guide pages are known as bluesheets because they used to be printed on blue paper.

International Technology Disclosures – TP (Ceased publication June 1994)

Research Disclosure (RD) www.researchdisclosure.com.

Trademarks and Marks

A trademark is a type of intellectual property, and typically comprises a name, word, phrase, logo, symbol, design, image, or a combination of these elements. It is used by an individual, business organization, or other legal entity to uniquely identify the source of its products and/or services to consumers, and to distinguish its products and/or services from those of other entities.

Simply put, if it is original, distinctive, and something you think others may value, then register it as a trademark.

One notable case of trademark infringement was the iPhone debacle. Years ago, CISCO registered the term "iPhone." Later, Apple began naming its products that started with an "i." Its newest creation is the iPhone. This prompted trademark infringement lawsuits between CISCO and Apple, since CISCO owned the term first. Obviously, the lawsuits were resolved, but the story illustrates the important point of trademarking your products and services.

Even more unusual was Harley-Davidson's bid to trademark the unique roar made by its motorcycle mufflers—

> THE MARK CONSISTS OF THE EXHAUST SOUND OF APPLICANT'S MOTORCYCLES, PRODUCED BY V-TWIN, COMMON CRANKPIN MOTORCYCLE ENGINES WHEN THE GOODS ARE IN USE.

Harley-Davidson Trademark Registration, U.S. Patent & Trademark Office, February 1, 1994.

(Source: http://tess2.uspto.gov/bin/showfield?f=doc&state=4007:9osacm.3.3)

Since trademarks are another form of intellectual property, you can visit the same Web sites and sources as patent searching.

Foreign Research for Patents, Trademarks and Other Intellectual Assets

Foreign research can be done country by country as well. The **World Intellectual Property Organization** (www.wipo.int) is one organization that oversees patent laws, litigation, and intellectual-property issues.

Also, to check European patents, visit the **European Patent Office** (EPO) Web sites at www.espacenet.com or www.epo.org. These sites offer some free searches and a subscriber-only section. Searches can be done in English, as well as the language of origin.

According to the EPO's Patent Information Centres Directory—

> "PATLIB is the name given to the network of patent information centres comprising the national patent offices of each member state and all regional patent information centres. In total, over 328 such centres in Europe can help you with information and competent advice.

"Patent information centres located throughout the Member States of the European Patent Convention provide the opportunity for the public to consult information on patents. This directory contains the addresses of patent information centres belonging to a selected list, provided by the appropriate national patent office. Where possible, the names of contact persons are given. The intention is not only that members of the public should be able to find their nearest patent information centre but also that the centres themselves will be able to contact their counterparts in different regions or even different countries."

(Source: www.epo.org/patents/patent-information/patlib/directory.html)

> **Author Tip** ➡ The Appendix contains an excellent resource list Web pages of foreign country government agencies that oversee the issuance of patents and trademarks in their respective countries.

Non-Conventional Marks and Ownership Identifications

There is also a range of non-conventional identifiers that, when examined, can lead to other forms of intellectual properties. Some of these non-conventional identifying marks are ISBN, UPC, and domain names.

Visit a U.S. Patent and Trademarks page at www.uspto.gov/main/profiles/otherid.htm. This informative page lists 36 identifiers. Many identifiers, like ZIP Codes, SSN, EIN, etc., are commonly used investigators. But there are some rather obscure identifiers that may be able to assist an investigation into assets. Some of these include—

- Bar Codes
- UPC – Universal product Codes (check out www.uc-council.org)
- ISBN - International Standard Book Number - for the publishing industry
- NAICS - North American Industry Classification Codes

Web Domains

Trademarks also can be searched in the form of Web domains. A big issue is using trademarked names as domain names. For example, I registered the domain name www.virtuallibrarian.com more than 10 years ago. Another librarian wrote me and said that I was violating her ownership of that domain name since she owned www.virtual-librarian.com. Neither of us had actually registered the trademark ownership or mark ownership with the www.upsto.gov. However, when I checked on who had registered the domain name first, I found that I had exceeded her by at least three months. When I emailed that fact to her, she backed off, knowing that I had first-use rights of "virtual librarian" as a domain name on the Internet, and thereby making the mark mine.

The Web site www.icann.org is the authority that oversees the disputes of domain name usage. There are many companies and individuals who have registered hundreds of key expressions, business names, or similar names to themselves, regardless of their actual needs or uses. These entities are called cyber-squatters. Like leaches on an organism, they squat on these domain names and hold them hostage until a company either disputes the issue with legal process, through the Internet Corporation for Assigned Names and Numbers (ICANN), or pays off the squatter. Considering that international cases can be very expensive, it is often cheaper to just pay off the squatter.

Copyright Issues

The U.S. Copyright Office, part of the Library of Congress, is the source for copyright ownership, publication, transfers and derivative works. Searches can be performed from the Copyright Office site at www.copyright.gov/records.

Generally, the reason to search copyright records is to find the current owner of a copyright. However, you can search to find if an older work is now in the public domain. Each of these reasons requires a search of different Copyright Office records.

To determine the copyright ownership of a work, search the "catalog" for records of registered books, music, art, and periodicals.

The Certificate of Registration indicates who originally registered the work. But just as important are Assignments which occur when copyright ownership is transferred.

(Source: www.copyright.gov/records/)

Subsidiaries and Spin-offs

Subsidiaries are sometimes the most valuable part of a business. Imagine that a very successful company starts to see a troublesome market and needs to consider preserving for future investment opportunities.

It spins off the assets as separate subsidiaries, and then lets them leave the corporate nest altogether, with the full intention of recouping these businesses at a later date.

Preposterous? No.

Consider that during the technology swing of the late 1990s, most "e" companies survived completely on venture capital, and did not generate revenue. They eventually folded and many individuals lost investment money, jobs, and interest in investing in technology stocks.

What happened to all that new technology? Did it just get left on the desktop? No, the intellectual property was moved to a subsidiary or spin-off company, and is probably in the technology we use today, e.g. Web 2.0.

Where to Search

Spin-offs and the creation of subsidiaries are newsworthy events that not only can be expensive, time consuming, but also can alter the legal and accounting lines of the parent company. As they say, any publicity is good publicity. When a subsidiary is created the parent company will generally send out a press release through PR Newswire (www.prnewswire.com) or the Associated Press (www.ap.org) announcing the change.

Eventually corporate record database vendors, like Dun & Bradstreet and Hoovers, will recognize and document the new subsidiary within the family tree section of these reports. You can also look into *Who owns Whom*, and other corporate database sources to see who is recognized as the parent company, or ultimate parent.

Finally, if the company is a publicly traded they have to list in their holdings, including subsidiaries in their annual reports which can be found on their own Web site, or through EDGAR on the SEC Web site.

How to Search for Hidden Assets

Using the Five W's

Locating hidden assets is important for fraud investigations, locating special interest monies (i.e. funding for organized crime and terrorism). Hiding assets from ex-spouses, business partners, debtors or others that are there to collect on open liens and judgments, is common practice. The investigator's challenge in finding assets will take them through the five W's.

1. With Whom

Individuals will hide their money under aliases, or with relatives, friends, and partners

2. Where

For cash accounts, which are nearly impossible to locate, funds could be stashed away in their home, or in a safe deposit box. Money can be kept in offshore and foreign accounts.

3. When Paid Ahead

Money could be reserved in overpayments to life insurance policy, credit cards, federal tax payments, or mortgage payments

4. As What

Cash could be turned into expensive physical assets as such automobiles, boats, planes, jewelry, and art. The asset can then be relocating to a brother, spouse, friend or other party to hold onto while being investigated.

5. Why Not For a Rainy Day

Keeping cash liquid for easy access could result in money being found as traveler's checks, savings bonds, money markets, or checking accounts filed under a different Social Security Number (a subsidiary corporate FEIN which is now defunct, or perhaps a child's SS #).

Use your imagination when looking for these assets; the following tips will help.

Search Tactics

Some tactics for tracking hidden properties when the address is unknown—

- Search under the spouse name.
- Search under the father, mother, or sibling name.
- Search under the business name.
- Search by trust name. (Usually the last name of the family)

Some tactics for tracking hidden properties when the address is known—

- Run the address and find the last owner. Contact that entity and request to see the sale documents. The attorney of note and purchaser should be two key pieces within that mountain of paperwork.
- Search the address in business databases. It can be an office location, and not a real home address.

For example, when I researched a well-to-do executive, I found that all his mail went to his office. Searching deeper, I noticed that his residential address was the same as his office. Finally, it dawned on me that he owned the building, a high-rise structure with most floors dedicated to business and the penthouse floor devoted to him personally.

Another key point on searching properties is the interaction you will have with individuals while researching them. Several of the fee-based resources will flag suspicious addresses when they match business post offices (UPS Store/Mail Boxes Etc.), prison addresses, campuses, or similar, shared locations.

Little used, but very effective, D&B allows you to run an address search. So, if the subject is running a fraudulent operation from any of those shared addresses, or actually has more than one business running out of his suite or office address, it will list all the businesses registered there. Other recommended sources for similar searches are the public-record databases mentioned earlier.

A Few Words on "Other" Assets

Assets are something that can be taken, possessed, sold and bartered over. But while you are investigating assets, keep in mind to look for a bigger picture – what the assets mean to the individual or the company. If you are not sure what I mean by this, walk into any old established bar and look above the cash register. You will most likely see the first currency that they bar received, framed and signed. That first dollar carries more emotional weight to the owner than the entire register to the owner. If it is still not clear, ask a woman who has been married for 30+ years what is her favorite piece of jewelry. She will most likely tell you about jewelry her children gave her, any anniversary or sentimental pieces, or her wedding ring.

Companies do not have the same sense of loyalty or emotion attached to the assets, unless the asset is their brand name or patented technology. In some cases, companies realize their greatest asset is in the intellectual capacity of their employees. Years ago, large firms like IBM used to refer to their employees as "family" and would never consider reducing staff in order to maintain profitability. Today, companies are now faced with foreign markets and improved technology from competitors. Holding onto a dinosaur staff is no longer an option. The expression "family" was changed to "team." As in you make the cut, or you don't. But the fact is, the team can still be a company asset.

The point of this is that **not all assets are material, or property based.** When researching a company, check the staff size and see if it has risen or shrunk in the last few years. Massive hiring and firing will give an indicator as to the company strength and weakness. What you want to find is a steady stream of progressive growth, not erratic ups and downs. The rollercoaster rides can be indicators of market trouble, poor management and leadership that you can factor into your investigation

Assets come in many facets, property, intellectual property, human capital and in financial vehicles. Keep your mind open when searching for anything of value; you will be surprised what is considered valuable and where it can be hidden.

Six Examples of Business Asset Searching

Pre-assess Before Filing a Lawsuit

Looking for assets can be a costly endeavor for clients, depending on how hidden they may be. This story tells one way to find assets prior to filing a lawsuit.

The Video Store

I received a call one Friday afternoon from a longtime client for whom I had performed quite a bit of due diligence in the past. He was "fuming mad" about a renter of his who leased about 10,000 square feet of mini-mall space for a video business. Apparently the renter was behind three months rent, which was unusual because he normally paid on time. When my client would call the renter, he would be continually put off by someone in the store, saying that the owner was not available.

The client was planning to hire his attorney to draft a letter threatening a lawsuit if the rent was not made up in short notice. Feeling bold I told the client not only would I be able to recover the unpaid rent, but would do so for less cost than the attorney's fees.

I began by running a D&B report. It appeared this small independent video store had been very successful with a steady stream of loyal customers for three years. His D&B showed increased revenues for the last two years, but there was a red flag in the vendor payments section, with an over 90-day payment history on several accounts. It was obvious that the landlord was not the only creditor not getting paid.

To determine if an event occurred three months prior that might have played a factor in the business problems, I searched local newspapers. I found that a month prior to start of the payment problems a large video chain store opened a few blocks away and was attracting the community with special offers, fancy lights, more current movies always available, etc.

Figuring this explained why the business might be struggling, I visited the small video store and in a discreet casual chat with the clerk found out the following.

Me: "I see that new video chain moved in around the corner. Have you checked it out yet?"

Clerk: "Yea they opened a few months ago. I checked them out when they opened and they are awesome! They have video games as well as the recent videos."

Me: "No kidding. Maybe I should go there (laughs) but I like small shops, you get better customer service. But how are you guys staying alive with such a heavy competitor around the corner."

Clerk: "Just barely, this store will probably close when the boss gets back and we'll move our stuff over to his other store in [next town over]."

Me: "Oh good… you have another store [We didn't know this!]. Where is it, just in case I need to return these videos and I'm late?"

The clerk gave me the other store address, which I research later for the client.

Me: "When do you think you'll close, should I watch these tonight, will you be open tomorrow?" The clerk laughing told me that the boss would be back in two weeks after returning from India. He was there the entire summer; his father was dying and he was coping with his family overseas and his family in the US.

Returning to the office, I researched the second video store and found it was indeed owned by the same man was in much better financial shape. After reporting this news to my client, he took an interesting plan of attack. When the owner returned three weeks later, my client visited the store. The client showed surprise when the store owner told him about the death of his father, the long trip home, two families, two cultures, the competition moving in, and his mistake in using his nephew to manage the store while he was away. Since we had already provided this information, the client was prepared. So he smiled, told him he understood and gave him two months to make up the back payment of rent. There was no threat, no lawyers, no anger, just an understanding landlord who emphasized with family issues and competing markets. But he also did mention "Well you can always rely on your other store to carry you over during the hard times." This let the store owner know that our client did his research.

Within two months, our client collected all of his back rent. He also talked the store owner into relocating his shop to another location, away from the competition, but still within the territory and on our client's books.

Not only did the client not have to sue, create judgments and liens on this fellow, costing him attorney fees and headaches, he maintained a valuable client relationship.

Unfortunately not all pre-searches result in happy endings. Most result in handing the claimant a list of assets and potential assets to be attached if they end up going to court.

2. Collecting on a Judgment

Once a judgment is put in place, it is up to the claimant to keep an eye on collection. There may be a judgment outstanding on an individual, but meanwhile the debtor may be acquiring extra property, cars, boats, and making investments. The claimant can sell the judgment to a judgment collector who then has the legal right to attach the debtor's assets and go after them themselves. However, "be careful for what you wish for." Assets do not always mean cold cash, but you could be leaving with physical assets.

Put Another Log on the Fire

Swapping stories one night with a group of judgment collectors, we were lamenting about the funniest, scariest and oddest things recovered. One judgment collector told a story a visit with a fellow who owed about $5,000 on a judgment she was trying to collect. She met him on his property in northern California, an older log cabin in the back woods, and did not see anything of value. Figuring that collecting $5,000 from this fellow was as likely as getting water from a stone, she asked him his occupation. He mentioned landscaping, tree maintenance and selling wood during the winter months. She then realized his asset was wood, and the sale of wood. For her part, she lived in the same winter cold months and had a fireplace. So she told him; she would take his payment in wood split for her fireplace.

A week later a dump truck dropped 10 cords of wood on her driveway, and that was only half the payment!

3. Locating a Project's Funding Party or Mysterious New Investor

Sometimes an asset investigation involves trying to find the money guy or the idea guy of a new entity.

Who Are Those Guys?

A software company in a very specific transportation niche kept hearing the buzz about a new competitor in the market. As the market-share leader, the software company was used to small competitors. But this new development firm seemed to have come out of nowhere and was quickly generating a lot of talk. The software company hired me to find out who was behind the mysterious new company.

I located the Web site for the new company and saw that it was partnering with other competitors, but it was not clear who the owner was. The corporate reports were all registered with the seemingly legitimate, new officers. Did the officers come from another industry and decide to create transportation software? As I was about to start looking deeper in the officers history, it dawned on me to check one other source.

Using the URL or Web address of the competitor company, I visited Network Solutions at www.networksolutions.com, and ran the address through its WHOIS search. WHOIS gave me the registration information for the competitor's Web site. The Web site was registered to a former employee of my client's software company. My client immediately sent a cease-and-desist letter to the former employee, because the former employee was in violation of a signed non-compete clause.

The mysterious competition was a former employee re-creating my client's software. Checking the competition's asset – a Web site – led to the identity of the competitor. However, the real asset in the story was the intellectual property, and my task was asset protection.

Small Companies, Big Ideas, and Borrowed Money

A common trait of new companies is trying to make themselves look bigger than they really are, to show potential clients they are established and prepared to take on new business. Setting up an office requires space, supplies, marketing materials, staff sometimes, advertisements, and technology. In other words, money! A new company must rely on initial capital that can come from personal funds, private equity, and/or another company.

If you are asked to investigate a company, look for this situation. Sometimes these "big" companies are really just business fronts in rented, temporary offices and are not legitimate. If possible, visit the office to get a sense of how long the company has been at that location. The first thing to look for is the company's nameplate on the building directory. Also, research the office address at www.google.com. Try searching for the address you have, "12 Main Street, New York City," to see if there are any matches to temporary offices, virtual offices, or by-the-hour offices.

Look at All Those Gold Albums!

A gentleman called me regarding a new contract he was considering with a musical production company. He had met the producers in their Manhattan office and was very impressed by the gold albums on the wall, their plush office, and the professional décor of the building. He thought they seemed legitimate, but wanted to conduct some basic due diligence on the producers before proceeding.

At the outset of my investigation, I searched online for the producers' business address and found that the suite used was a temporary office. Also, the phone and fax numbers went to an office-rental company, not the producers' office. I called their phone number and talked to a "floor receptionist." When I asked about the producers, she said they were no longer renting. Then I asked how long they had rented the space, and she said it was for only one day, and they had been asked to leave because they had damaged the walls when they hung their gold albums.

The producers were part of a shell scam, set up for a day's worth of meetings to worm money out of unsuspecting investors.

Investigating this further, I contacted the furniture office-rental company and inquired about the producers' identities and their method of payment for the suite. Normally a company would be hesitant to share this information, but, in this case, was interested in legally pursuing the producers for damaging the walls. The suite was secured with a credit card, using the name of a woman who was not one of the producers. It became apparent that she was the sister of one of the likely producers and was the money behind the scam. She and the producers were reported to the police for fraudulent behavior.

In following the money trail, there was obviously a lack of real funds behind the fraudulent producers, as the real money came from the sister's credit card. If this seems like an odd example, keep in mind that many companies set up shell corporations to hide their identities and their assets. They also set up companies with liabilities in mind. They may transfer assets or liabilities to a new company and then sell it.

4. Finding Prior Ownership

It is sometimes necessary to find a prior owner of an asset, especially when the current owner is facing certain liability claims.

The Smelter Search

Some time ago, my company client had moved into a plant that was situated in an urban area. Ten years later, the EPA inspected the grounds and declared the property a superfund site. The current manufacturer was producing a non-toxic product. Historical research on the building showed that the original factory was used as a smelting factory. All the burn-off of the metals leeched into the ground and poisoned the ground water. The company hired me to locate the owners of the original plant.

A deed search was straightforward enough to see who owned the property. But, the deed owners were companies that changed hands year after year, and the assets and liabilities were split. The original firm was Jersey Smelting from the 1860s. It was sold to a large, publicly traded firm that merged, split, and was bought and sold more than a half dozen times because the company kept shifting and growing.

Two sources really were instrumental in the search for this company's ownership. Moody's Investor Services, found at the local library usually in microfilm, listed the company's assets within its reports on publicly traded companies, and considered property an asset. The other tool was the local newspapers. I spent many hours sitting in front of the microfiche and microfilm machines, spooling through issue after issue of newspapers for any mention of the building location, or any fires, events, sales, etc.

In fact, one piece really jumped out and helped clear up something the attorney presumed as a truth. The attorney found a history book on the manufacturers in that city in the mid-1800s. She quoted a bit of text that stated Jersey Smelting was sold to Paterson Smelting. That lead sent the attorney on a day's worth of tracking information from state archives. Nowhere could she find that a sale had occurred. And the article I found contradicted her version.

In scanning the original newspapers, I discovered the book's author was incorrect in saying the company was sold. The newspaper stated that the Jersey Smelting factory was leased to Paterson Smelting, but not sold. Hence, the assets were still with Jersey Smelting until it merged with a completely different company, which later sold its smelting practice to a foreign corporation.

5. Employment Purposes

Investigating for employment purposes is not limited to only FICA-Medicare employees. This type of investigation can include many "employee-employer relationships."

Whom Do You Trust

Usually when friends and family ask me to conduct an investigation or "do a little research" I pass them over to another investigator. However a friend called to complain that his accountant had misfiled his last two years of taxes and that he now owed almost $10,000 dollars to the IRS. Understandably and justified in being upset, I told him I would see what I could find on the fellow.

In less than twenty minutes I called back to verify the spelling of his name. Correct in my spelling, I told my cheated friend that his accountant was not licensed in his state of practice. The state consumer affairs office did not have his name listed in their database and a phone call to their customer service elaborated that his license was revoked. When I asked for the cause the friendly representative stated, "Oh... felons can't obtain their license without going through a panel review first." Felons?! While I was on the phone with my friend, I did a name search on the Bureau of Prisons Web site (www.bop.gov). Sure enough there was a match. His accountant had been convicted on drug possession charges and served almost 12 months. Later I following up with media and located a story about an arrest of three men charged with possession and intent to sell cocaine within a school district.

Unfortunately this did not get help with the IRS bill, but my unfortunate friend learned to vet the people he does business with, for no matter how polished they seem, they could be fraudulent.

6. Investment Opportunity or New Business Venture.

When an entity is considering a business relationship with another entity or investor, it is prudent to research and assess establish the financial strengths of the other party.

Some Got It, Some Don't

A new client asked that I vet out a potential investor. During the course of my interview with the client, I learned his firm was contacted via email from an overseas investor and offered a few million dollars to buy into a partnership with the client company. My gut reaction was to tell him this was a spam email, a fishing expedition for anyone who would reply. But he was adamant that I take the case. There was limited information about the other party. The person making the offer was from Pakistan and supposedly was part of a multi-national firm involved in petroleum, automobiles, technology and financial industries. The firm claimed to have almost 17,000 employees and 1.7 billion in revenue.

First, checking through Bureau van Dijk, then Skyminder, D&B, and other databases, I could not locate the company. This immediately raised an alarm because any company of that size and profitability would have a credit history and business reports. Further research on the company name in the news did not reveal any matches. Finally using one of my Web resources, I found the company name appearing on a listing of known spammers.

Some ventures are real though. In the same week, I was hired to research the background of a small company interested in investing in a new venture my client was spinning off. He asked that I check the credentials of the potential investor, which I did. To my surprise the "little venture company" was a side practice for the Berkshire Hathaway Group. My client doubled the amount of money he was going to request from the venture firm after learning the firm was a big player and could afford larger risks.

Author Tip ➡   For a list of state Web pages that offer free access to UCC filing records, go to pages 257-258 in **Appendix 2**.

Cynthia's Key Chapter Points

- ◆ Assets, whether financial or physical, are open, intangible, or hidden.

- ◆ There are a number of reasons to conduct an asset investigation, some amount to assessing someone's wealth before conducting business or suing them. Other reasons include discerning ownership of an asset, employment matters, or collecting on a judgment.

- ◆ Uniform Commercial Code (UCC) filings point to assets pledged used to secure financial loans. Tax liens may point to additional assets.

- ◆ Businesses hold several types of assets including as property, investments, intellectual property, and subsidiaries or spin-offs.

- ◆ Personal property such as boats, cars, houses, equipment, and other tangible goods can add up quickly.

- ◆ Intellectual property is often missed in an asset investigation. Intellectual property of a company or individual can be greater in value than the tangible and investment assets combined.

- ◆ Use the five W's for finding hidden assets. Remember to rely upon your imagination.

- ◆ Search for assets under defunct company names, new company names, spouses, kids, parents and close relations.

- ◆ Look for recent "pricey" or personally valuable purchases by the individual being investigated. Consider the person's hobbies and interests when looking for these valuable purchases.

- ◆ Use open social networks to see if the individual is bragging about recent expensive vacations or purchases.

Chapter 8

Researching Affiliation Resources

*God, grant me the senility to forget the people I never
liked anyway, the good fortune to run into the ones I do,
and the eyesight to tell the difference.*

—Unknown

This chapter examines the many possible affiliations and relationships that a business will develop and maintain over the years. These affiliations include *personal* relationships with vendors, customers, investors, or employees, and *required* relationships with government vendors or contractors. Any or all of these relationships can be critical points of reference within an investigation.

Vendor Relationships

People judge you by those with whom you associate, and the association a business has with vendors is significant. ABC Company may make a business decision that it will only buy services from a few specific vendors. Those vendors have been approved by the procurement department and an account has been established. The fact that you might be able to buy the same product more cheaply from a non-preferred vendor is not as important as using the approved vendor. Why? Vendor relationships form because of necessity, bias, desire, or convenience.

Recognize Relationships Based on Necessity

Some companies select their vendors based on necessity. For example, it is necessary that a company produces a certain number of widgets on short notice. If only one vendor can supply the widget raw material in the manner that the company requires, then it becomes the vendor of choice.

Supply chain analysis, as discussed in Chapter 3, teaches you to recognize weaknesses within the product development lifecycle. One slowdown in development or a weak link in the chain will affect the entire product development. Analysis of this situation tells you that the company has vulnerability when relying on only one vendor, and if anything unforeseen should happen to that vendor, the supply chain would collapse.

When analyzing a competitor and identifying a relationship based on necessity, understand that the competition is going to think 'opportunity.' The company being examined will be looking for alternatives to the widget single source, or will be considering bringing that development in-house. Depending on the type of product and complexity, it might be an impossible task; however, no company likes to be told that its supply chain is limited, and then forced into an arrangement it does not desire. In other words, companies, like people, want choices.

Recognize Relationships Based on Bias or Desire

Many times collusion, kickbacks, and fraud can be traced to a relationship based on greed, bias, friends or family. Laws, such as the Foreign Corrupt Practices Act (FCPA) were passed to protect stockholders, by preventing persons and companies from enjoying kickbacks after vendors were overpaid.

Investigating and analyzing biased-based vendor relationships will require analysis of the following questions—

- Does the vendor produce the product to specifications?
- Is the vendor stable, consistent, and prepared for a catastrophe?
- Do the price points match up and are they competitive?

The reason a company should pick a specific vendor is because the vendor can produce the product at the level and speed needed and for a fair price.

Check the marketplace to find who else is selling the same services. If the vendor's prices are higher than its competition, consider this a red flag. If a company is seduced by free giveaways like lunches, ballgames and other perks from a vendor, there is a possibility that the company also may be receiving kickbacks or participating in collusion. Rather than hide the collusion, some participants prefer to enjoy it.

One specific area where many companies seem to slip in their "friendly" vendors under the radar is customer service. A company representative might say, "Oh that vendor has terrific customer service! When I have a problem, I call the vice president and he takes care of it himself." An inquirer might retort, "No kidding, but the vice president is your spouse!"

In examining the vendor relationships through the supply chain analysis, be cognizant of who is the purchaser. In large companies, there is always a procurement person. This executive authorizes invoices and purchase orders. Also, there is an executive who initially orders products or services. Both employees should be examined to see if there is any relationship between them and the seller. Another avenue to investigate is if an outside person or company negotiated the contract. Look for ties that may produce evidence of kickbacks or collusion.

Find Ties That Spawn Fraudulent Practices

There are some typical relationship ties between a corporate individual and a vendor to examine, if there is suspicion of fraud or collusion.

1. **Past Relationship**. The procurer may have purchased products or services from the vendor prior to the relationship he has with his current company.

2. **Regional**. The seller and buyer may live in the same community, and their kids may go to the same school or attend the same college.

3. **Family**. Maybe the two parties are related through blood or marriage.

4. **Idealism**. Perhaps the two parties attend the same church, or both belong to the same organization outside of work.

5. **Infidelity**. There might be a personal or sexual relationship between the two parties that is deemed inappropriate.

When investigating parties that are suspected of any of the aforementioned relationships, be sure to scan addresses, affiliations, and family members. The tie between the two parties may be found in a shared address. Or one of the spouses may have had a different last name, a name that matches your current vendor.

Other Types of Bias

A vendor relationship may spring from a shared bias against racism, sexism, and localism.

Racism and sexism seem obvious enough, but it is important to look at both sides. The president of a company may be a chauvinistic racist and not want to work with women or minorities. However, on the flip side of the coin, his company may be required to conduct a certain volume of business each year with females and minorities.

Localism is when a company wants to conduct business with only regionally specific persons. The attitude of "buy American" is a type of localism, as is supporting local companies like contractors, store owners or farmers. Unions in the U.S. also enjoy a strong amount of support, and the mentality of "support one of us" is pervasive. Additionally, buying green or environmentally conscious products made by indigenous persons shows a bias in the purchaser.

The buying habits of a company are not too different from the buying habits of an individual. When given a choice, how does a company decide which two producers to choose? Corporate procurement rules create standards to abide by; however, there is always room for personal preference. If that is the case, then the choice between two options at the same price, supply, and value may be made on local preference.

The Role of Politics

Local, state, and federal politics often play a role in the management decisions of corporations. Gaining favor with a particular political party may assist a firm in securing contracts or jobs with government agencies. For example, if John Smith's company headquarters is located in a Democratic stronghold, John or his company might support local community projects, sponsor Democratic-agenda items, or pay for expensive campaign dinners. But, when he is not wearing his business-owner's hat, he may be a Republican at heart.

The point is, do not discount someone's personal preference for a political party when investigating business support. Righteous idealism always takes a back seat to billable work.

Chapter 5 on political affiliations discusses searching for the personal, political leanings of an executive or employee.

Discovering the Investors

Silent partners can be difficult to pin down. Below are five investigative tracks that help identify investors.

1. **Secure and read annual reports**. Depending on which state a company has its headquarters, the annual reports and available data will vary. Some states offer extensive details about the company, the partners, and the owners. Florida is a great state for gathering information on company shareholders. Whereas other states like Delaware and New Jersey, the information can be weak, oftentimes excluding the officers.

2. Investors can be identified through a few **online services**. Check business reports from D&B and Experian. The best source for this type of search is Capital IQ from Standard & Poor's.

3. Check **legal histories**. If the company, whether large or small, has been sued in the past, all the investors, major shareholders, and partners should be listed as defendants. Also, conduct legal searches on any identified chief officers. Perhaps the company you are searching for has not been sued directly; but if one of its officers has, it may be because of his connection with a prior company. That prior company may share the same investors and shareholders as the current company. Look for connections in the UCC filings, as discussed in Chapter 7.

4. Thoroughly examine the **company's Web site**. Look for links to "Partners, Management, and Investors." Some companies list their business partners as board members or advisors. Also, if the company maintains press releases, read them for leads.

5. Check media resources. Look for press announcements of partnerships or similar types of events. Even finding past corporate affiliations will open up leads.

The necessary diligence in reporting information should lead the investigator to writing a history for each person found. As the biographies are written, cross connections can be established.

The Obscure Connection

Years ago, I took a case that went from complicated to chaotic.

My client's company was on the verge of making an announcement that would cause a dramatic increase in his company's stock price. But before the information was made public, the company owner became aware of recent investors who had developed a sudden interest in the company in a big way, each investing a minimum of $50,000. The owner suspected an internal leak and asked me to investigate connections to these investors.

At face value, the only common issue among the eight investors was that they were all men. Other than that fact, all were from different regions of the country, were of varying ages, had different religious backgrounds, and were not related.

As I investigated each man separately, outlining the highlights of each life, eight very different social and economic backgrounds emerged. None of their spouses were related and they had no common political connection.

Then, drawing out a map of their lives, one avenue made itself obvious. Each man attended the same Midwest university. With ages ranging from 28 to 67 years, the educational affiliation was not obvious at first, because the university had changed its name 30 years ago. The lead formed in two of the online biographies I located during the investigation. I noticed that the two men mentioned the same school and fraternity. Since it was a connection, I traced it back further and found out that this fraternity was affiliated with the university since the late 1920s. Given this new lead, I checked the educational background of the remaining men, and found four more with the same school and fraternity link.

Next, I searched my client's company Web site for any biographies that listed education. Listed on the site were the biographies for all the key officers and managers. I discovered one manager also was a Midwest university alumnus and fraternity member of the same university and fraternity as the investors.

An examination of the manager's email showed he was an active "poster" in the fraternity listserv, with his most recent posting advising his fellow fraternity brothers that his company was on the brink of a major shift and that the investment time was ripe.

There is a lot to be gained by drawing long biographies, with key aspects highlighted per person, per investigation. Sometimes seeing the history of a person will help pinpoint the lead that you have been looking for. For very large cases, a software program like *i2 Analyst's Notebook* by i2 Inc. will help to organize information visually. As data is entered into the program, connections are cross-checked and the indicators for each person are compared to each other, with a visual map showing lines between connecting points.

Programs like i2 are expensive and take some talent to learn. However, for continuing investigations, these resources are indispensable. But for the occasional user, do not underestimate the traditional "white board," as seen on TV cop shows. I am a strong believer in the white erasable board. Cases often are illustrated on the board, with the leads springing out of the center like an art project. The visual is very helpful, though, when looking at a person's life in sections. You might exclaim, "Here is education! Here is employment history! Here are family relations and bank accounts!"

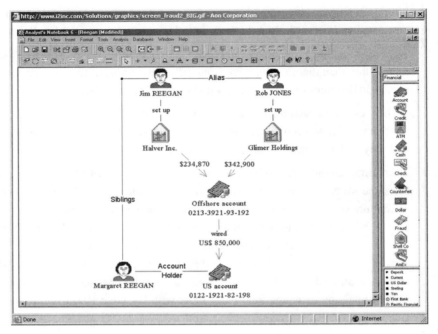

(Source: www.i2inc.com)

Finding Their Clients

Digging into a subject company to find clients (as well as employees or vendors) will expand the association and affiliation leads for interviews, trend watching, and corporate intelligence. Also, discovery of clients is very valuable when establishing the size, scope, and capabilities of the company being evaluated.

Clients are not usually hidden. In fact, some companies like to share their client lists to show that their companies are busy and successful. However in some cases, client lists will be dissolved from company names to preserve client privacy.

There are several other areas to check that may lead to finding clients.

- Read company **press releases** to find out about potential business partnerships.
- Look for **recent events** as leads to follow up. If the company has sponsored any golf outings or charitable events, try to locate the attendees and fellow sponsors. Also, check with the vendors who worked the event. They may remember who attended and who were clients of the company.
- Key clients are often listed in a company's **annual report**.
- Review **marketing material**. Ask for handouts that may have this information listed.

Finding Their Employees

Locating employees of a company is big business. Finding the right employee, either current or not, employee can blow an intelligence or due diligence investigation case wide open. Gaining an interview gives an investigator access to primary, first hand experience, all of which are valuable in any case.

Several information brokers claim to sell internal corporate directories of companies. Older, but valuable, sources of corporate directory data are the published phone directories that the companies printed and passed out to their employees. All the info broker had to do was to somehow obtain a copy. Now with the advent of searchable company Intranets, these paper lists are less likely to be produced.

Once again, visit the company Web site to locate, at the very least, the company's top officers and managers. Try searching the Web, using www.google.com and other search engines, to find any mention of employees using expressions like "work for" or "employed by," and coupled with the company name.

Example: IBM + "work for"

Another method to checking on an employee is to call his company's phone number after regular business hours. Chances are the phone directory will offer a menagerie of choices, one of which will be to dial by the last name.

Two Recommended Online Resources

Zoominfo

Probably the best, free online tool to search for people listed by company is www.zoominfo.com.

The trick to obtaining names for free from www.zoominfo.com is how you go about conducting the search. If you initially search by company and then request to see "other employees," the list will be sent to you without the names. At this point, you can pay to join, or take advantage of the three-day trial period. However, if you can locate just one employee's name at that company and search that person, you will see down the Web page's left-hand side a network of individuals listed by name and company.

See the example on the next page.

(Source:

www.zoominfo.com)

Accurint

One of the best offerings from Accurint, that sets it apart from other public record vendors, is its People at Work program. Using People at Work, you can search by name, address, phone number, Social Security Number, and company name.

The results seem to be based on a variety of aggregated sources, such as secretary of state filings, business registrations, domain name registrations, and probable matches from www.zoominfo.com.

For example, I searched my name, Cynthia Hetherington, at both Zoominfo and Accurint. Each returned the phrase "Recurring Columnist for *PI Magazine*." True, I have had a few articles published in *PI Magazine*, but I am far from a recurring columnist and, at this writing, have not submitted an article in more than a year.

The point is to fact check all the results you retrieve when using fee and free online services.

A screen sample of Accurint is shown on the next page.

Besides the two services mentioned below, there are other database services like D&B, Hoovers, and LexisNexis which offer searchable directories for individuals as well.

Remember to utilize the Web, and the company Web site, as much as possible when trying to locate connections between individuals, affiliates, and employees, or when trying to create a customer or partner list.

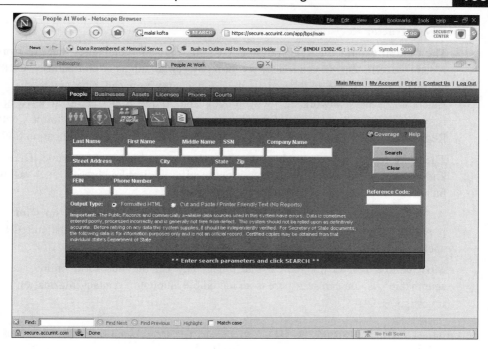

(Source: www.accurint.com)

Finding Government Vendors and Contractors

There are no limitations to what the U.S. government will build, study, report on, or get involved with. The "Feds" build bridges, study rodent populations, help small businesses grow, educate, and facilitate.

The amount of money moving between private industry and government is beyond imagination. To get a sense of how deeply the federal government is involved with the nation's economy as an employer, visit the government search engine www.usa.gov and browse the topic areas. The Federal Business Opportunities Web page at www.fedbizopps.gov gives instructions and requirements to companies that are interested in doing business with the federal government. Business entities must be properly registered with the government before they can bid on providing services or products.

There are several essential Web pages to examine when investigating business entities and their possible connections to government contracts.

Web Resources to Find Government Vendors and Contractors

Two excellent starting points for investigators to find vendor data are the Central Contractor Registration (CCR) and the Online Representations and Certifications Application (ORCA).

Central Contractor Registration (CCR)

The Central Contractor Registration (CCR) site registers companies that are working with the federal government. If you visit www.bpn.gov/ccr/default.aspx and choose "CRR Search" you automatically will be redirected to the proper site. You can also get to the page from the Business Partner Network at www.bpn.gov and Acquisition Central at www.acquisition.gov. Look for links on the left side of the Web page and you will be directed to the Central Contractor Registration (CCR) and Online Representations and Certifications Application (ORCA).

There are four ways to search at this important page: by company name; D&B number (also known as DUNS number); address; or specific indicators/phrases, such as woman-owned business.

An example search is on the next page. I used my name and came up with a match to my previous company, Hetherington Information Services, Inc. The details, edited for brevity, are spelled out in the CCR registration.

Most contractors do not realize that when they fill out this form online, the data becomes searchable. As you can see, there is an incredible amount of contact information available for the investigator.

Current Registration Status:	Active in CCR; Registration valid until 05/28/2008.
DUNS:	116321555
DUNS PLUS4:	
CAGE/NCAGE:	41MM7
Legal Business Name:	HETHERINGTON INFORMATION SERVICES LLC
Doing Business As (DBA):	
Physical Street Address 1:	PO Box 123
Physical City:	ANYTOWN
Physical State:	NJ
Physical Zip/Postal Code:	07555-0123
Physical Country:	USA
Mailing Name:	HETHERINGTON INFORMATION SERVICES
Mailing Street Address 1:	PO BOX 123
Mailing City:	ANYTOWN
Mailing State:	NJ
Mailing Zip/Postal Code:	07555-0123
Mailing Country:	USA
Business Start Date:	10/01/1994

CORPORATE INFORMATION

Type of Organization: Other
Business Types/Grants: VN - Contracts

GOODS / SERVICES

North American Industry Classification System (NAICS): 541990 - ALL OTHER PROFESSIONAL, SCIENTIFIC, AND TECHNICAL SERVICES
Standard Industrial Classification (SIC) :   8999 - SERVICES, NEC

SMALL BUSINESS TYPES

SDB, 8A and HubZone certifications come from the Small Business Administration and are not editable by CCR vendors.

North American Industry Classification System (NAICS)			
The small business size status is derived from the revenues and/or number of employees entered by the vendor during the registration process.			
NAICS Code	Description	Small Business	Emerging Small Business
541990	ALL OTHER PROFESSIONAL, SCIENTIFIC, AND TECHNICAL SERVICES	No	No

POINTS OF CONTACT

Government Business Primary POC		Government Business Alternate POC	
Name:	HETHERINGTON INFORMATION SERVICES	Name:	HETHERINGTON INFORMATION SERVICES
Address Line 1:	PO BOX 123	Address Line 1:	PO BOX 123
City:	ANYTOWN	City:	ANYTOWN
State:	NJ	State:	NJ
Zip/Postal Code:	07555-0123	Zip/Postal Code:	07555-0123
Country:	USA	Country:	USA
U.S. Phone:	973-555-1234	U.S. Phone:	973-555-1234
Non-U.S. Phone:		Non-U.S. Phone:	
Fax:	973-555-1235	Fax:	973-555-1235

Electronic Business Primary POC		Electronic Business Alternate POC	
Name:	HETHERINGTON INFORMATION SERVICES	Name:	HETHERINGTON INFORMATION SERVICES
Address Line 1:	PO BOX 123	Address Line 1:	PO BOX 123
City:	ANYTOWN	City:	ANYTOWN
State:	NJ	State:	NJ
Zip/Postal Code:	07555-0123	Zip/Postal Code:	07555-0123
Country:	USA	Country:	USA
U.S. Phone:	973-555-1234	U.S. Phone:	973-555-1234
Fax:	973-555-1235	Fax:	973-555-1235

Online Representations and Certifications Application (ORCA)

The purpose of the ORCA system is so "…a contractor can enter their Reps and Certs information once for use on all Federal contracts. This site not only benefits the contractor by allowing them to maintain an accurate and complete record but also the Contracting Officer as they can view every record, including archives." ORCA is found at https://orca.bpn.gov. The link is also accessible from www.bpn.gov, www.orca.bpn.gov, or www.acquisition.gov.

Searching ORCA requires knowing the subject's DUNS number. This can be found using the CCR search. In the case of Hetherington Information Service, Inc., the DUNS number is 116321555.

The information that ORCA provides hits on many minority-opportunity and fair-trade issues, such as NAFTA, African-American colleges, and trade-agreement compliance.

When trying to establish income and revenue of a company, one section that stands out and can be very helpful is "Offeror Representations and Certifications – Commercial Items." The following is an example under this section—

State   Eligible Labor Surplus: Civil Jurisdictions Included:

And under this is...

(ii)   Offeror represents as follows:
    (A)   Offeror's number of employees for the past 12 months (check the Employees column if size standard stated in the solicitation is expressed in terms of number of employees); or
    (B)   Offeror's average annual gross revenue for the last 3 fiscal years (check the Average Annual Gross Number of Revenues column if size standard stated in the solicitation is expressed in terms of annual receipts).(Check one of the following):

Number of Employees	Average Annual Gross Revenues
☒ 50 or fewer	☒ $1 million or less
☐ 51-100	☐ $1,000,001-$2 million
☐ 101-250	☐ $2,000,001-$3.5 million
☐ 251-500	☐ $3,500,001-$5 million
☐ 501-750	☐ $5,000,001-$10 million
☐ 751-1,000	☐ $10,000,001-$17 million
☐ Over 1,000	☐ Over $17 million

As you can see, Hetherington Information Services stated it had less than 50 employees and less than $1 million in gross revenue.

At the bottom of this long document, there is a button that you can click to download the entire record in a PDF format.

Cynthia's Key Chapter Points

♦ The point to remember when researching companies is that their associations through vendors, clients, employees, partnerships and sponsorships are all indicative of the direction and reputation of the company.

♦ In CARA analysis, the entire gathering in a metrics analysis is based on what is found in affiliations and associations.

♦ Relationships between clients and their vendors are based on necessity or bias.

♦ These relationships could be intrinsically fraudulent or ethically questionable, in addition to being financially beneficial to one or both sides.

♦ Politics, family or friend relationships, kick-backs all can be questionable means to gain favor from outside a company, into it.

♦ Silent partners could be traditional investors or fraudulent parties who want a return on investment, but no recognition.

♦ To discover silent partners, obtain annual reports and publicly-filed corporate records and registrations.

♦ Read the company's Web site for mentions of strategic partners (usually in technology companies) or investors listed as board members.

♦ Check news stories on the company. Do online searches for any mention of the principals. Search blogs for musings posted by current employees

♦ Legal research discovers any cases filed by or against the company. Review these cases to find the names of the parties bringing the suit or parties being sued.

♦ Finding employees is easy with irbsearch.com, social network sites like linkedin.com, and specialized search engines like zoominfo.com.

♦ Company Web sites often list their top customers, providing they have permission to do so.

Chapter 9

Researching Industry-Focused Sources

Taking Research to a Deeper Level

To this point, I have examined investigative research with the array of sources that investigators are accustomed to using. For a case in hand, an investigator might analyze corporate business reports from Dun & Bradstreet, obtain court records from PACER, and review articles from the media giant Factiva. (See Chapter 10 about using the media.)

These are all good, generic resources. I would encourage the researcher to use them, along with the subject company's Web site, as a starting point to ferret out the makeup, size, span, and function of a company.

One easy method to reach all these generic sources at once and produce an overall report is to use www.hoovers.com. Hoovers, a D&B product, is one of several resources where you can find this generic data for free or for a few dollars. Hoovers conducts its own analysis by combining basic research, press releases, data from Hoovers' proprietary database, and from the subject company's Web site to create its reports. The information is helpful, and the overview section is insightful. You also get a sense that the person writing the short piece is purposely not projecting dry, confusing, Wall Street-type jargon that could leave readers wondering what the point was.

The point to all this is, if your client can as easily purchase a Hoovers' report as you can, and if your investigative reports offer the same generic information, then why should the client continue to use you? In other words, what can you do to make your investigative reports more comprehensive and stand out?

The answer is to be more specific in your approach, more in-depth in your research, and more analytical in your report. Consider the following:

- Be specific about answering the questions the client has, and insure that the information you return has been verified and is accurate.

- Be in-depth about the sources you are checking and where your information comes from.

- Use SWOT or a similar strategy in your report preparation.

This chapter examines where to find the in-depth research sources that specialize in specific industries.

Examples of Finding Industry Resources

There are plenty of industry sources and services, not necessarily known as available investigative tools, which are available to research. These sources primarily serve the industries they cater to.

For example, publishers specializing in specific markets can be as small as magazine publishers of a single, monthly monograph, or as large as *Medical Economics*, which produces volumes of journals, magazines, resource books, databases, and services specific to the healthcare industry.

Publications may be born from need or the lack of printed information for a particular group. These small, print publications may start as newsletters and eventually grow into magazines that take on a life of their own.

A good example is *Artilleryman* (www.civilwarnews.com). There is probably a healthy interest in Civil War cannons and other artillery, but not a great deal of literature for casually interested readers. Related article topics, found in this or similar magazines, could include recent sales, purchases, or destruction of collections, how cannons were instrumental in certain battles, or the dates of upcoming battle reenactments. Why ramble on about Civil War cannons? Because if an accident occurred involving one, perhaps during a reenactment or during a school ceremony, an authority probably would be needed to testify whether the cannon was used properly or not.

Bing Bang Theory

A unique bar in Key West, Florida is known for owning a large clipper ship, with crew, that its patrons can rent for parties, weddings, and pretend skullduggery. One of the perks to sailing on this vessel is that you can fire a flintlock and shoot the old cannon. I was involved on a case where one unfortunate fellow had a mishap – the flint from the cannon blew up in his face, burning him. He sued the restaurant, claiming medical and psychological damages as well as loss of income because he was incapacitated from his injuries.

My task was to vet the experts on behalf of the claimant's attorneys, as well as research the background of the defendant's experts. These experts were said to be well versed and respected as authorities in Civil War artillery. These experts turned out to be collectors and reenactment fans of the famous Civil War battles of the civil war. With such a small pool of experience in civil war artillery expertise, both claimant and defendant experts knew each other. The claimant's expert, whom we were bringing to court, was able to discount the defense based on former articles written, based on several inaccuracies. Odd though it may seem, he had debunked him in literature years prior, and used that to show how he was quick to judge munitions but not as clear on verifying the facts. It turned out to be a reputation blow to the defense expert. The end result was for the claimant. With the help of our expert's testimony, the court decided the claimant should not have been given access to firearms (no matter how old they are) in his state of inebriation and that the owner of the clipper ship should have demonstrated more responsibility in passing out liquor and guns to his guests.

Sometimes the research takes you in unusual directions, as demonstrated in the Big Bang Theory story. I would have never thought to be interested in Civil War reenactments. However, if the case takes you there, you have to learn to be interested! Yet, sometimes it is not the expertise that is the unique aspect of the investigation, but where you find it. In the next example an historical reference led to information necessary for our case.

Which Side Are You On?

This investigation focused on evaluating the credentials of a physician who had studied diet drugs, including a combination of fenfluramine and phentermine known as fen-phen. The attorney's directions were to review any articles written by the opposing counsel's expert physician to a) Locate the funding sponsor of the article, b) Establish if he was pro or anti in any of his theories, and c.) See if any of his articles were refuted in follow-up editorials or studies.

All of these issues were in relation to bias on the doctor's part. Was he writing articles in showing bias and support of his own funding source, such as a pharmaceutical company?

Research was located in articles written ten years earlier by the physician and funded by Wyeth Pharmaceuticals through its subsidiary, American Home Products. Wyeth was the leading producer of dexfenfluramine, used in fen-phen. The release of the physician's article and research conclusions coincided at the same time fen-phen was being re-evaluated by the FDA for causing strokes in women. After the FDA article was released, the physician was widely criticized for his findings. He then began to write "new studies" which were no longer funded by Wyeth, but were part of a teaching hospital study. These new articles were critical of fen-phen and its effectiveness. Thus, he completely changed his opinion from one study to the next.

Essentially, the attorney has found bias in the original study, since it was funded by the producer of fen-phen combination dexfenfluramine, and the physician changed his stand on the particular use of the drug after he left Wyeth. Neither issue is a big concern by itself; however, your research should uncover turn these events up before using a witness as an expert. Our attorneys researched the specific medical databases for articles on fen-phen and anything the physician had written or was recorded saying about fen-phen, and this resulted in huge embarrassment for the other party and their attorneys.

These two examples demonstrate how intricacies of specific information can lead a case into information sources which are unfamiliar and maybe out of your comfort zone. The important lesson here is that for each and every profession, hobby, and interest there will be magazines, Web sites, blogs, and perhaps entire publishing houses to examine and conduct research against. In these two examples, our research led us to magazines and trade journals.

Using Blogs

A relatively new investigative resource to find industry-specific sources and experts is a **blog**. Blogs (short for Web logs) are a relatively new interactive forum where individuals can create a presence on the world wide web in five minutes with no programming skills. Anyone with access to the Internet can visit free services such as www.myspace.com, www.livejournal.com or www.blog.com and create an online presence. There is no authority weighing on quality of content, verifying information, or even gauging the inane amount of drivel that people will write, just because they can. However, in the midst of thousands of teenage MySpace profiles and the banter that passes for writing, there are several valuable uses of this new communication vehicle.

Using information taken from blogs, you can locate company employees complaining about their jobs, offices, co-workers and bosses. Without intention, blogs also reveal trade secrets and intellectual property. The same employees posting on blogs will also talk about events they are planning to attend, up coming meetings and other pending events. There are also candid discussions on just about every topic imaginable, from household cleaning tips to financial and investment advice. There are blogs dedicated to tracking companies, products, lawsuits and trends. Two search engines specifically designed for searching blogs are www.technorati.com and www.icerocket.com.

> **Author Tip ➡** Blogs are helpful in investigations and intelligence. BUT always remember to VERIFY THE INFORMATION. Blogs are rampant with misinformation because it is so easy to anonymously post data.

Searching with www.technorati.com or www.icerocket.com for a topic specific to an industry or hobby will result in at least a few online authorities to tap into for insight. Just be prepared to vet the resources and the people who are posting the information. Blogs are very biased, even if they purport not to be.

The next portion of this chapter examines specific industries and the best fee-based and free resources to use when conducting an investigation within that industry.

Healthcare Industry Resources

In the case of the physician expert discussed earlier, how did I know where to start my search? Certainly an examination of the standard sources for any articles published on the physician would be undertaken. If results in the New York Times or other general press newspapers and magazines were found, I would read and analyze to decide if the information was relevant should be and included in my report. However, when targeting an expert, the goal is to find that expert's writings or things written about him, and to disclose any anomalies or opinions. To do this, you must research in the specific industry territory of the target individual. In the case of the expert physician, I needed to become familiar with the resources that physicians use themselves, in this case medical and healthcare information.

The direction to take on healthcare research will depend on the type of disease or health topic the case involves, along with a common-sense approach. To start, I imagine the types of magazines and Web sites would my expert would use. What does he subscribe to and how does he they keep up with the latest news in the profession? Yes, this tactic should be used in all professions, and not just healthcare, but it certainly resounds the loudest in the physical sciences. For example, with the topic regarding in the concern of fen-phen use, I focused on journals with a main theme of obesity and anorexia nervosa.

National Library of Medicine

One of the best resources available for a starting point in medicine and health research is the National Library of Medicine, sponsored by the U.S. National Institutes of Health (NIH). The NIH (www.nlm.nih.gov) offers a compendium of information cataloged under its own subject headlines, such as AIDS, influenza, and toxic chemicals.

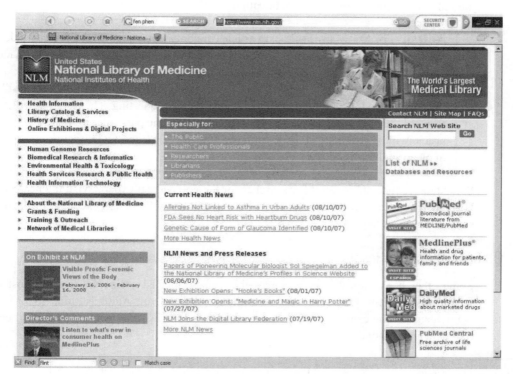

(Source: www.nlm.nih.gov)

Since the NIH Web site is so overwhelming, it helps to know specifically where to begin digging to find the searchable databases that will help educate you on a condition, or give you a source to look for concerning your expert's writings and testimonies.

In my opinion, the best starting point is MEDLINE, found at PubMed[37] by going to www.ncbi.nlm.nih.gov/sites/entrez?db=pubmed.

MEDLINE offers searching by topic, author, or journal. Also, I advise using the help sheets. The results of a name search will lead to abstracts, which describe each article published and where it can be located. The material and writing may seem foreign to most individuals, since the scientific nature of each article is very technical. For example, a search of "caffeine" returned more than 21,000 hits. Using one of the top-listed results produced the following—

> Aguilar-Roblero R, Mercado C, Alamilla J, Laville A, Diaz-Munoz M.
> *Ryanodine receptor Ca(2+)-release channels are an output pathway for the circadian clock in the rat suprachiasmatic nuclei.*
> Eur J Neurosci. 2007 Aug;26(3):575-82.
> PMID: 17686038 [PubMed - in process]

More likely, you will be searching by author, so performing an additional search of "Alamilla J" will result in finding this article and others.

Medical articles found in PubMed and similar high-end industry sources are considered refereed. In other words, a panel of experts, usually the Board of Advisors, must review them before the journal will accept the articles for publication.

> **Author Tip** ➡ Many healthcare articles are only referenced on the World Wide Web, but are not freely available for a download with a citation to the abstract made available. In this instance one of the fastest and least expensive ways to retrieve these articles is to visit your local library and ask for an "inter-library loan request" to be conducted. Print out the exact citation you are requesting. The librarian will forward the request to the nearest library that carries the particular journal. The article will be sent back to the librarian as a photocopy from the journal or perhaps in electronic form.

For extensive medical research, or searches for topical medical experts, visit the nearest teaching hospital. The library attached to the hospital most likely will contain excellent medical research sources pertinent to your subject matter.

Other Government Resources

Some other healthcare database sources that can be located online for free are hosted by the federal government. One such service is the Food and Drug Administration (FDA), found at www.fda.gov. The example to follow shows how the site hosts an entire directory of cell-phone radiation and safety data.

---

[37] PubMed is a service of the U.S. National Library of Medicine that includes over 17 million citations from MEDLINE and other life science journals for biomedical articles back to the 1950s. PubMed includes links to full text articles and other related resources.

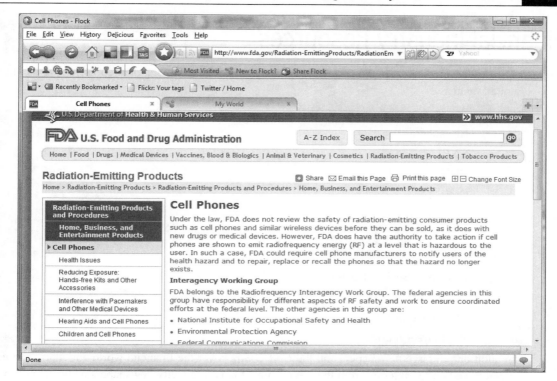

(Source: http://www.fda.gov/)

FDA can be involved in everything from food contamination, bioterrorism, drug recalls, and livestock concerns to cell-phone effects. For example, teaming with the National Academy of Science, the FDA conducts investigations into claims that cell phones can harm individuals. In the last few years, claims have surfaced that cell phones are responsible for the honeybee population demise, the sterility of men, and brain tumors in humans.

Fee-Based Resources

Perhaps the best place to find fee-based resource services for the healthcare industry is Dialog (www.dialog.com). Researchers may do a single search, subscribe monthly, or pay an in-house researcher to search within the databases for you. Dialog aggregates the majority of pharmaceutical pipeline sources, and chemical, medical, and scientific sources. Its sources range from PsychINFO® to diverse topics, such as Meteorological and Geoastrophysical Abstracts. Keep in mind that these are collected or aggregated sources on Dialog, so each service also is available independently. A researcher can access PsychINFO® through Dialog or directly at www.psycinfo.apa.org/psycinfo. The benefit to using Dialog is one-stop shopping.

Financial Industry Resources

The general media covers the finance world very well. The following is a representative list, but not all inclusive—

> Barron's
>
> Bloomberg
>
> CNBC
>
> CNN
>
> Crain's
>
> Financial Times
>
> Forbes
>
> Fortune
>
> Investor's Business Daily
>
> Morningstar
>
> The Economist
>
> Wall Street Journal

In addition, all large newspapers and the *USA Today* cover the financial world and many stories are archived on the Internet from their Web sites. Many large, city newspapers dedicate pull-out sections to covering world, national, and local finance issues. Much like medical and health research, finance is too broad a term to be narrowed to just a few specific topics. Finance issues can touch on economics, investments, banking, currency, regulatory issues, and a country's domestic concerns.

Of course, the first step is to focus on the resources for the type of financial issue you are investigating. This will help you focus on the sources you need. For example, if you are conducting a background investigation on a broker and you are looking for regulatory actions against the broker, begin with the Web sites for—

- Securities and Exchange Commission (SEC)
- Financial Industry Regulatory Authority (FINRA) – *Formerly the National Association of Securities Dealers – (NASD)*
- National Futures Association (NFA)
- North American Securities Administrators Association (NASAA).

The Web pages and a profile of each of these organizations, including how to use them for investigations, are found in Chapter 6.

But, if you are conducting a background on a new investor, or potential investment, the direction of the investigation should involve business database aggregators, like DialogWeb, or InfoTrac's General Business File ASAP, or the Business & Company Resource Center. All three products are in the Thomson family of services. Thomson Dialog and Thomson Gale are the actual subsidiary firms.

Thomson Resources

Each of the three sources listed below is valuable to the business researcher. Articles found through these aggregators often are not located in other directories. The Gale sources are listed on its Web site at www.gale.cengage.com/title_lists/.

DialogSelect Business Index (Thomson Dialog)

Using the research link at www.dialogselect.com/business/index.html, search these specific groupings:

- Advertisers and Agencies
- Imports and Exports
- Investment Research
- Management Studies
- Market Research
- Mergers and Acquisitions
- Tax, Accounting

General Business File ASAP (Thomson Gale)

Analyze company performance and activity, industry events, and trends, as well as the latest in management, economics, and politics. Access a combination of broker research reports, trade publications, newspapers, journals, and company-directory listings, with full text and images available.

Business & Company Resource Center (Thomson Gale)

Business & Company Resource Center is a fully integrated resource, bringing together company profiles, brand information, rankings, investment reports, company histories, chronologies, and periodicals. Search this database to find detailed company and industry news and information.

As mentioned in the previous section on healthcare, there is a very good chance you can access some of these business database sources through your own public library. All you need is a current library card, and you have access to thousands of resources from your home computer.

DialogSelect, however, is a subscription-based service that is not usually shared through an open network, like Gale does with libraries. DialogSelect services can be pricey; however, they do offer some easy interfaces and reasonable prices for some searching needs.

What investigators must realize is that subscriptions to general, newspaper databases, such as Factiva and LexisNexis, are not enough. While they do capture a good deal of business sources, no one aggregator can capture it all. With their focus strictly on business, DialogSelect and Gale have the means to help you zero in on the narrow approach that investigations often need to take. Researching the *New York Times* for all stories related to a company will certainly return results. However, using sources like *The Wall Street Journal*, *Crain's*, or *Barron's* will offer more insight and greater amounts of information, because they assume the reader understands the basic business language, and they report specifics that the *Times* does not cover.

Keep in mind that generic services do not cover the same depth as specific finance journals.

He had it All, He Thought

Five years ago, an investor wished to learn more about an opportunity he was offered. A good friend referred him to a group of ambitious young men who were looking for early investors in their hedge fund. The investor knew little about the group, and before he was to meet face-to-face with the men, he hired me to perform due diligence research on the team.

According to the group's Web site, the five men were involved with the hedge fund. While Web-site pictures of the men portrayed their youthfulness, the site itself was slick and very professional in appearance. It had all the right buzzwords and promoted a plan that sounded like the road to success.

To start, I located very little in the generic news sources on any of the players, and nothing on the new company. While searching through Business Files ASAP, an article from a hedge-fund magazine, *Buyside*, offered some insight. In a year-old issue, I found a story that profiled the principal of the fund.

In the story, the principal discussed the engagement to his fiancé and the "big ring" he bought her. He told how he grew up on the family olive grove, but was really more interested in the investment world. He bragged that his fiancé's father was a key investor in his new fund. Finally, he mentioned that the group of young men, who started the company with him, all were former college roommates.

These were all interesting tidbits to consider, as I started comparing the past with the current situation. Of the five men on the Web site, only two were part of the original college group. Researching the original names, I located the other three working as investment managers for other firms. Also, when I looked for news of the engagement or wedding, I located a legal filing (suit) that involved the future father-in-law and the hedge fund.

While this information was not an indication that the fund was bad, or the intent was misleading, nonetheless, the group was not the solid set of seasoned investors that it projected on its Web site. They were actually in business less than one year, and did not hold veteran experience of someone with multiple years and funds behind him. The CRD reports on these young investors were also very slim, just registration information, but they did not offer much in the way of experience.

Today, as I reach back to research this story for this book, I find that the hedge fund group is closed. However, the young man I was investigating is still very vocal on the Web, sponsoring a comical blog, and still offering too much information.

Telecommunications and Technology Resources

If any industry has built its own directory of resources, it is this one. Telecommunications and technology are the most readily available topics on the Internet.

The CorpTech Directories

One of the largest directories for technology companies is CorpTech (www.corptech.com).

CorpTech, now primarily focused on creating targeted marketing lists, has an astounding amount of historical data. Its large, silver volumes still are found on library shelves and offer a good deal of insight into each company it profiles. They have aggregated information from a network of resources, similar to other database providers. In addition their business lists and new business leads are derived from press releases, industry trade organizations and magazines, directories, web sites, customers, economic development organizations and competitive intelligence.[38]

The industries CorpTech covers go beyond technology; however, that is its strength. The list below indicates the areas of available research:

- Advanced Materials
- Biotechnology
- Chemicals
- Computer Hardware
- Computer Software
- Defense
- Energy
- Environmental
- Factory Automation
- Holding Companies
- Manufacturing Equipment
- Medical
- Pharmaceuticals
- Photonics
- Subassemblies and Components
- Telecommunications and the Internet
- Test and Measurement
- Transportation

---

[38] www.corptech.com/business-information/methodology.php

CorpTech comes in a variety of platforms, direct subscription, a per-use basis, and through Dialog. Depending on how much you will need them, which may be often or once in a while, I would recommend using this service through Dialog, or trying out their free week offer.

ZIFF Davis

With their colorful, glossy covers and techno-speak language, technology magazines portray themselves as incredibly diverse and complicated. You would think a multitude of publishers was competing for magazine shelf space. The truth is that most of the largest and respected magazines in this market are all published by Ziff Davis (www.ziffdavis.com). Ziff Davis covers all geek needs from *CIO Insight* to *Extreme iPod.*

Each magazine offers a search engine directly on its Web site for searching by topic, author, or business.

International Data Group

International Data Group (www.idg.com) is the other major player in technology news publications. Magazines like *PC World*, *Computerworld*, and *LinuxWorld* are staples in the technology market. However, these are only three of the nearly three hundred print and online sources that IDG manages and publishes.

Manufacturing and Construction-Related Resources

Thomas Global

The major source for information in this category is the Thomas Global directory of 700,000 manufacturers and distributors from 28 countries, classified by 11,000 products and services categories. Formerly known, and probably still best known as the Thomas Register of Manufacturers, this directory gives detailed product and company information in nine languages at www.thomasglobal.com. A search of "Tata" at this site revealed almost 50 company-name matches, from Tata Steel Tubes to Tata Telecom.

Using Trade Journals and the Blue Book

Primary resources of manufacturing and industrial knowledge are trade journals and periodicals associated with the specific industries. Contractors advertise, read and keep up with their industry through trade magazines. Trade associations publish many of these sources, such as *Scrap* magazine (www.scrap.org), published by the Institute of Scrap Recycling Industries, Inc. (www.isri.org). Other trade magazines are produced by for profit entities, such as *Architectural Record* by McGraw-Hill found at:

http://archrecord.construction.com/Default.asp.

A great overall resource of building trade data is the **Blue Book of Building and Construction** at www.thebluebook.com/. This site has many, many features including a links list of trade organizations, trade journals, journals, and up-coming trade shows.

The **Appendix** contains a list of the trade journals I have found to be very beneficial.

Resources of Market Research

Market Research Profound (www.marketresearch.com) houses over 250,000 global research reports produced by experts specific to every industry, from telecommunications to hospitality.

They collect and index each report, making them available for purchase. Using this service on an as needed basis, you can search for free against their vast resources and then select either the total report (which is often thousands of dollars) or take advantage of purchasing only sections of the report. Sometime a paragraph with the right information is all you need. Searching Marketresearch.com is very easy, but can be hit and miss at times. Searching with a "term" will result in several possible matches. When you select a term, an abstract, which may or may not make sense, is followed by the word you searched for. It tells you the page number the word shows up on in the report, and gives you some reference to the sentence where found. This technique is called the keyword in context (KWIC) view. While not providing a full set of data report, it does give you a sense of what may possibly be in that portion of the full report. You then must decide to purchase that section or continue searching for a better match.

The government also produces and funds a great deal of market research resources. In fact, government depository libraries are filled with free and valuable information on every industry possible, company type, whether profit, non-profit, defense oriented or horticulture, historical or futuristic. Check out the **government search engine www.usa.gov** for a great head start on finding free reports produced by the government.

Government documents research is a difficult process and not everything is available online. My third recommendation is to visit the **nearest government repository** in person and ask the government documents librarian for assistance. To find the closest depository, visit www.gpoaccess.gov/libraries.html.

Conclusion

Industry searching can be very uncomfortable because as an investigator you are stretching your intelligence to understand someone else's profession. Some investigators become incredibly specialized in certain types of investigations because they have investigated so many cases within the specialty area that industry is second nature to them. This is especially true for environmental investigators, financial investigators, and insurance claims investigators.

But, if you have a case that involves an industry that is unfamiliar to you, my recommendation is to consult with a professional who knows the industry. This professional may be a practitioner or even an investigator that specializes in those particular cases. The approach is to ask these experts what sources they consult, what magazines they read, the Web sites visited, and news and media preferences.

The next tip for learning about industry sources is to read everything! I grab and read magazines for computers, science, finance, health, home – you name it, I will read it. There may be a snippet about a new Web site specifically for some industry purpose, like a directory of manufactures of steel-related products. I will check the site to see if it provides inside information that I might need later, in this example if I have case involving steel parts and the owners behind certain products. My top three publishers are BRB Publications, Information Today and *PI Magazine*. These publishers of books, manuals, and periodicals are constantly releasing new sources of information.

The key point is to reach out to experts when applicable and not to slow down your self-learning. Collecting data resources by topic may give you an advantage when you have a case dropped on your desk a few weeks later.

Cynthia's Key Chapter Points

♦ Due to the variety of industries you are researching, most investigations will challenge the investigator. No one is an expert on all areas and topics. It's the investigators' challenge to *get smart* on any involved industry.

♦ In order to *get smart* in an industry, find an industry expert, read everything they have written and been interviewed on. If possible, contact them for assistance.

♦ Social networks, Zoominfo.com, linkedin.com are all freely available sources for finding industry experts, as well as searching for associations where experts congregate.

♦ The healthcare and financial industries are two good examples where organizations have many unique specialty associations and opportunities to locate experts.

♦ Technology and telecommunication experts are easily found online.

♦ Manufacturing groups should be researched amongst unions, and organized laborers.

♦ Market research sites like marketresearch.com offer very specific information about particular products and services, or industry reports comparing products.

♦ Industry specific resources may be readily available at the local library. Librarian can be very helpful in the identification process.

♦ Use intellectual property registrars such as the US Patent and Trademark office (uspto.gov) to search for experts who have created and developed specific methods. They can be consulted on competitors' products.

♦ Do not get tunnel vision in your reading habits! Read magazines, Web sites, blogs and similar on topics to familiarize yourself. Occasionally a professional or helpful topic will reveal itself to be useful for a later investigation.

Chapter 10

Using Media Resources

It was while making newspaper deliveries, trying to miss the bushes and hit the porch, that I first learned the importance of accuracy in journalism.

—Charles Osgood

If one morning I walked on top of the water across the Potomac River, the headline that afternoon would read: "President Can't Swim."

—Lyndon B. Johnson

There are two expressions that if followed would prevent many embarrassing or often damaging moments—.

"Do not write it down if you do not want to see it on the 6 O'clock news!"

"15 minutes of your fame will save me hours of research."

People's use of the media, whether it is an opportunity to see themselves on camera or press their views through an editorial, gives the investigator something concrete to discover in an investigation. Using the news to discover more about your target will lead to the possibilities of finding affiliations, business plans and strategies, trouble within the company, assets, etc. Anything and everything is possible in news and media searches. By examining the various news avenues available to an investigator, you will discover how old, current and future news can help make your case.

The News

With 24-hour news, press releases, videos, interviews, Web releases, and company announcements, almost everyone seems to get his or her chance at 15 minutes of fame, and that translates into hours of saved research time. Researching news in databases, through paper indexes or by instant alerts, is a skill that is different from traditional investigations. Many investigators do not delve deep enough into the news for relevant stories or potential connections. Yet, the news is exactly where to find many leads.

Recently, I had a case involving asset research for a firm based in the Cayman Islands, with its principals located in California. Investigations are costly when you have to enlist the assistance of a regional expert and add the expense of obtaining business reports and asset searches. I found an interview article in a local library database that provided new information. Not only were the principals involved in their own firm, but also they had mutual interests in other California-based operations. The article gave me so much detail about the lead principal's personal life that I even discovered the size of diamond he had selected for his fiancé.

> **Author Tip** ➡ I often tie business principals not by business reports, but to the media. In another case, I found an old article in the San Francisco Examiner that reported on an individual I was reviewing. He was accused of arms dealing with Iraq in the mid-1990s. As it turned out, he was a principal in a company with which my client was considering merging.
>
> The trick is to get these news clippings and follow up on the reports. Frequently, I have found misreported stories. Follow up on all the details you read, and if possible, contact the journalist to found out what information was edited.

Where to start? Which news service to use?

With so many sources to search for news, you will wonder which one to use. It is difficult to tout one service over another. They all offer general sources in common as well as specialty sources applicable for different reasons at different times. Perhaps the best scenario is to subscribe to them all. A suggestion for a frugal investigator is to try them all and see which one(s) works for your information needs, budget, and customer services. You are cutting your research short, however, if you use only one database.

Professional researchers subscribe to services such as Factiva, LexisNexis, Dialog, Dow Jones Interactive, EBSCO, ProQuest, Information Access Company and Thomson Gale. Each publisher has its own news vendor. You will find the New York Times in Dialog, but only for the past 10 years in full text; for 20-year coverage, use ProQuest. If you want to include The Wall Street Journal, use Dow Jones Interactive, and so on. Database aggregators change often, so stay informed about your subscribed services.

Using Current News

Current news is the handiest source for tracking press releases, changes within corporate structure, mergers and acquisitions and evaluations of new product releases.

I can recommend a number of available sources, both free and fee-based, for current-news research.

Fee-Based

For in-depth local news at an inexpensive cost, LexisNexis and Factiva lead the way for investigative uses. The earliest results are from 1970, and matches from 1980 are usually in full text. Anything prior to 1980 tends to be a citation or an abstract.

Dow Jones Factiva (www.factiva.com)

Web-based business and information tool offering access to a collection of nearly 8,000 global news and business publications, 10,000 Web sites and photo feeds from both Reuters and The McClatchy Company, formerly Knight Ridder. This is a definite subscription package. Once, I searched "Ronald Reagan" and found an abstract in the New York Times from January 4, 1971.

LexisNexis (www.nexis.com/research)

Offers 20 years of archived newspapers (1,302 at last count), including the New York Times, Washington Post, Chicago Tribune, Los Angeles Times, and other regional newspapers and newswires. You can access the Nexis news service on a pay-as-you-go basis by visiting the above link, if questions, call them at 800-927-4908.

Fee-Based for Free

The following are fee-based resources, but they are usually offered for free in local public and academic libraries. Visit your library's Web site to see which databases are available. You can subscribe to them directly, but you have probably already paid for the resource with your city tax dollars.

Keep copyright laws in mind. You are not allowed to cut and paste an article that you have not paid for without written permission from the publisher.

Each of the following providers is actually aggregators. So, for instance, a subscription to InfoTrac usually means you get five+ databases, not just one.

EBSCO (www.ebsco.com)

EBSCO provides subject-specific databases that index newspapers, magazines and books.

Master File Premier provides full text for nearly 1,950 general-reference publications, with full-text information dating back to 1975. Business Source Elite, dating back to 1985, offers full text for more than 1,100 scholarly business journals, including full text for more than 450 peer-reviewed business publications.

Newspaper Source is a full-text selection of more than 180 U.S. newspapers, international newspapers, newswires, newspaper columns and other sources, as well as indexing and abstracts for national newspapers. Specifically, *Regional Business News* provides comprehensive full-text coverage for regional business publications, incorporating coverage of 75 business journals, newspapers and newswires from all metropolitan and rural areas within the United States.

InfoTrac (www.infotrac.com)

Services include magazines, newspapers and books about business, health, literature, biography and general reference. Each database begins in the 1980s and continues to the present.

Two specific database selections are *General Business File ASAP* and *Business & Company Resource Center*. Each offers access to a combination of broker-research reports, trade publications, newspapers, journals and company-directory listings with full text and images available. They compile company profiles, brand information, rankings, investment reports, company histories, chronologies and periodicals.

ProQuest (www.proquest.com)

This giant offers more than 1,800 periodicals on a wide range of topics, including the arts, business, humanities, health, social sciences and other sciences. ProQuest offers newspapers such as the *New York Times*, *USA Today*, *The Wall Street Journal*, and *Barron's*.

Free News

Web sites that offer free access to news stories usually allow searching by either topic or by location. Here are five sites that I feel are excellent for investigations.

The two sites below are organized **by topic**.

- **Newspaper Directory** (www.newspaperarchive.com)

  This is not exactly free, but it is an inexpensive directory.

- **Google News** (www.news.google.com)

  Offers current news (within 30 days), and is an excellent source for local news, with approximately 4,500 news sources worldwide.

These three sites below are organized **by location**.

- **NewsLibrary.com** (www.newslibrary.com)

  Search by location and by available news on a specific topic.

- **Newspapers.com** (www.newspapers.com)

  Includes international locations.

- **Thepaperboy** (www.paperboy.com)

  Also includes international locations.

Searching Old News

Most aggregators offer news from the late 1970s to the present. Real full-text news starts in the early 1980s, with late '70s leads as just title and abstract.

It is not far-fetched to consider that you probably covered most bases by using a few aggregators to capture the bulk of your material. The difference between a good investigator and a great one is that a great one knows the information he is seeking cannot be found in just one database.

Old News is Good News

Indexing and abstracting are tools familiar to a librarian, especially one who attended library school before the 1990s, when the Internet started to change information-gathering methods. Librarians are trained to know which indexes would answer the questions, where to locate these indexes and how to use them.

Remember the story of the *Smelt Search* in Chapter 7? That story is a perfect example of using an old news index to help find a prior owner of an asset, when the current owner is facing certain liability claims.

Using Vertical Files

Vertical files are file cabinets with paper resources. They are treasure troves of local lore on any community. Any library worth its salt has kept a clipping file on its local history since the first librarian took the job. These files can be quite valuable. You can locate town maps, dating back to the town's inception; find personal histories of notorious or famous individuals who were born in the town or who lived there; and find an index for any local newspaper that is not big enough to merit a database entry.

Check with the reference librarian about the vertical file, and do not be afraid to ask for help when navigating it. More than likely, you will not be left alone with the collection, as you are usually looking at the only copy of the local history piece. Some libraries go beyond this, and have entire local-history rooms, but this is not the same. You cannot catalog an article or photograph into your library system, so there will be a vertical file!

Indexes of older news, commonly found in large and small, local and academic libraries, will vary. It all comes down to the size of the library's budget and the size of the collection. These periodical indexes are immense, so you may only find one or two popular ones, such as *Reader's Guide to Periodical Literature* and the *New York Times*. When you are searching old news, it pays to visit a local university library with a larger collection of indexes and abstracts.

Here are a few suggested resources. You will find many of them through Dialog or other aggregators, especially for material produced from 1980 to the present. For researching older news and accessing these rarely used gems, I recommend visiting the local library and availing yourself to their paper collections.

Reader's Guide to Periodical Literature

The Reader's Guide to Periodical Literature is one of the most widely used, generalist indices of the most popular news and magazines with non-technical articles. *The Reader's Guide* covers more than 180 well-read magazines and newspapers from 1900 to today, indexed by subject and author. Book reviews are in a separate section arranged under book author.

Business Periodicals Index

Since 1958, this is one of the best indexes for overall coverage for almost 350 business periodicals. Every subject, from accounting to paper and pulp, is organized by subject and author.

New York Times Index

New York Times may seem regionally specific. However, as a large, internationally respected newspaper, its coverage extends far beyond the city limits. Any major global event will be indexed in the *Times*. It is a great resource for obituaries, too. There is also a *New York Times* Obituary Index, and I would recommend checking both. People are listed alphabetically by last name.

The Wall Street Journal Index

The Wall Street Journal, very respected in the business world, is really a journal and not a newspaper. However, this does not prevent it from indexing and abstracting itself as one. The focus here is business news and industry happenings.

Others

Other indexes of note for investigations are the Humanities Index, Social Science Index, Predicast F & S (Business), National Newspaper Index and PAIS (Public Affairs). In addition to this list, there are dozens of other indexes that can be used.

The rule to remember is to **focus on your subject**. If the person you are searching for was in law enforcement, then you will need to find the law-enforcement index that will take you to Criminal Justice Index and Abstracts.

Using News Alerts

Being able to locate leads from 1950s news indexes will earn you the right to claim your favorite chair in the reference section of your local library. However, you need to understand today's technology and how it quickly brings breaking news to your attention. This is especially important because you can not underestimate the value of news for investigations. So many cases are handled in a short time because of what is reported in the media.

How News Alerts Help Investigators

Staying on top of the news helps investigators in many ways. Perhaps a political, social, or tragic story will help you discern describe relationships between individuals, their businesses and their interests. The stories may tell you about a targeted individual's involvement in events, be it personal or attendance at a conference. I have found hints of pump and dump schemes, upcoming bankrupticies, fall-outs and firings and subtle changes to product lines that have lead me to a new direction in an investigation.

Unfortunately, once the newsman has given his report, it is old news. Television has taken this hint, however, and now every news channel offers a scrolling line of text for a multi-tasking society. You are listening to the weather forecast, while you are reading the latest sports scores as they scroll past; or watching *Inside Politics* on the top half of your TV and reading the Dow Jones numbers at the bottom.

And yet, more, much more research is really needed.

For example, while looking up the assets of a now-defunct company in Moody's microfiche, I stopped to check email on my PDA (pocket or portable digital assistant, such as a BlackBerry or Palm Pilot). One of my news alerts popped up reporting that a client's competitor had been cited by the SEC for backdating stock options. I forwarded the piece to my client and asked, "Would you like me to find out more?" Not only was he impressed with the speed in which I received and conveyed the news, but also I picked up several hours worth of research and kept track of what was happening to the competitor as news was breaking.

> **Author Tip** ➡ The television in my office is always on a news channel while I work during the day. My PC browser window opens to CNN, MSNBC or other network sites, so I can stay current on world events. Needing to know everything all the time keeps me tuned in.
>
> The business benefit, of course, is staying competitive by keeping pace with business changes as they happen. And, it is also convenient when I want to know sports scores or the latest investment tickers.

But Hearing or Seeing the News This Way is Usually Too Late

Getting your news via the television is one of the last places you want to hear NEW news. By the time television journalists report a story, the information already has been written and disseminated across the wires. Wire news is quickly disseminated, getting to the finish line first with the breaking story. Associated Press (AP) reporters and photographers are fast-paced professionals and experts in their field.

Competitive intelligence agents try desperately to get the news before it even gets to the wire. However, they do pay heed to the wire services. Slight fluctuations in financial news can be catastrophic to the company they are watching. If in doubt, watch the closing bell on television at the end of the day. Networks will mention that trade lines fluctuated due to the news that another corporate official pleaded guilty to an indictment. Bad weather in Florida means a price increase in the citrus and fresh produce market. An earthquake in Asia means computer chip prices are going up. And war in the Middle East creates a slowdown in petroleum production and higher gas prices.

Staying in tune with the obvious is not so difficult, and a million Web pages will offer you this news for free at the click of a mouse. The trick is predicting and focusing on your news needs. If you are interested in the linen-rental business in Chicago, will an uprising in the silk industry in China have any bearing on your market?

Stories about high-powered executives reading news blogs to gain an advantage are not uncommon. Richard Rainwater of Rainwater Inc. has revealed in interviews that he watches doomsday-like blogs to predict the next Honeywell or Disney purchase.

If an investigator only uses one news service, such as Reuters, AP, Financial Times, etc., the focus is too narrow. Only an aggregator can gather and present news in one place well enough so that you can quickly ascertain what you need. Even so, that could still result in several hundred sources to skim on a regular basis.

So, how do you stay ahead? **News Alerting Services**!

News Alerting Services

What old school investigators would call a *clipping service* we now address as an *alerting service*. These alert services are fabulous for capturing news as it is being released on the press wires. The free services are a bonus; however, the fee based services can be really massaged to give you better results, because they have more delimitating capabilities. The fee-based services can be purchased separately. However, they are tools you would normally have access to with the complete subscription to any of the named databases below.

The following free and fee sources are great resources to alert you to the news as soon as it hits the wires and the Web. With these alerts, you can continue working on other projects. But when a story of interest hits, you are alerted by email, Intranet or wireless device.

Free News-Alerting Services

News Alerts by Google (www.news.google.com)

Offers approximately 4,500 news sources worldwide, with 30-day archive; you must specify your country of interest. Google.com introduced news.google.com for current headlines and news-alerting services. If you visit the Web site, on the left-hand side of the page, you will see "News Alerts." Here you can type your search terms, such as a person's name, place or object. The alert can be sent to your email as it occurs or just once a day, in digest mode. For a little more sophistication, you can use the advanced search feature to set up your news stories. Search "democrats" and you will find 32,000+ matches, but search "democrats–john," and the results are narrowed down to 19,000+ matches.

Yahoo Alerts (http://beta.alerts.yahoo.com)

Offers email, Yahoo Messenger or mobile-device delivery of current news items. Much like News.Google, you can add words to your search to make certain specific words do not appear in the story.

Fee-Based News-Alerting Services

Dialog NewsRoom Plus (http://newsroom.dialog.com/)

Coverage to 9,000 global news and business information services, 35 million hours of video and 20 billion Web documents.

Much of the same information and sources that are found in the free services are found here as well. Yet the customization is much more sophisticated. Most noticeable is the premium content of business and trade sources, which offers expert and precise analysis.

Dow Jones Factiva (www.factiva.com)

My recent favorite news database is worth its weight in subscription rates. My membership with Association of Independent Information Professionals allows me a special rate, so my costs are low, but Factiva offers a variety of packages for independent users and offices. Factiva offers nearly 9,000 sources from 118 countries in 22 languages, including more than 120 continuously updated newswires. More than 900 sources are available on or before the date of publication. You can set up a search query to fetch all stories related to your topic, and have them placed directly on your corporate intranet, portal application, Web browser or emailed to a client.

LexisNexis (www.nexis.com)

LexisNexis offers alerting services from several of its product lines. For example, you can purchase just The Wall Street Journal alerts or newsfeed. However, a more comprehensive alert service is available directly through its Nexis product. With more than 2,300 global newspapers, it is easy to track issues internationally.

BLOG Alerts

Google.com (http://blogsearch.google.com)

The buzz often hits the Web before it gets to print. Being alerted to the latest chatter in blogs is equally useful to those who want to stay ahead in the game. Google.com offers a blog-alert feature.

Wireless Updates

Each of the publishing houses offers news-update feeds for your wireless devices. This application is common among sports fans who need updates on the scores throughout the day. However, the tool is equally impressive for specific companies you are tracking, people's names you want to know about as soon as they are mentioned or any industry news that matters to you.

Because these news feeds are all in Extensible Markup Language (XML), it is only a matter of time before the Application Programming Interface (API) is refined to push news directly to your BlackBerry. With that type of common and accepted open-source language, coupled with valuable content, news probably will be fed to us faster than we can act upon in just a few years.

Currently, the larger aggregators have "publisher" products that allow companies to massage data into Intranet sites. That said, the next phase is BlackBerries.

The two big players here are—

- LexisNexis Publisher for Current Awareness (**www.nexis.com**)

  Offers law librarians and other legal professionals the ability to access LexisNexis content throughout the firm via email, intranet, portal BlackBerry wireless handheld, Really Simple Syndication (RSS) or the Internet. Get daily access to articles from 20,000+ news sources, including *The Wall Street Journal*, Dow Jones and 4,000+ legal sources. Monitor daily legal and law-firm news, client-company news and much more.

- Factiva Wireless Beta (**www.factiva.com**)

  Presently, Factiva is working on wireless-push services. However, the Factiva Wireless product, similar to LexisNexis, is available now with more than 10,000 sources in 22 languages.

International News

If you speak the language of the country you are searching, then you will be more qualified than an English speaker trying his best at French.

For news from 1980 to the present, utilize the same services mentioned earlier, such as LexisNexis, Dialog and Factiva. All have excellent coverage abroad and in multiple languages. Another source for a broad perspective, especially in business, is Financial Times.

Financial Times (www.ft.com)

> Offers news alerts, through RSS feeds, and also is available in print. Known for its non-U.S. perspective on global business and events, Financial Times is equally noticeable for the salmon-pink paper it is printed on.

Finally, when it comes to researching foreign news sources in an unfamiliar language, I recommend checking out the **American University's library in that country**. Look at the library's Web site to see which newspapers are identified as regionally significant, and which ones are accessible. Perhaps an email to the reference or periodicals librarian requesting assistance will be answered with enthusiasm.

With so many specific countries to mention, this is a great place to talk about Sheri Lanza's work, "International Business Information on the Web."[39] Lanza itemizes, by country, each of the various Web-available sources, including news.

Television News and Broadcasts

Television news does not offer the written perspective and thought out content as written news, but it does offer several unique and important features. A picture being worth a thousand words, television news offers us body language, tonal inflections, stammering and a face to associate to the story, and usually in real time.

Who would forget Tom Cruise picking fights with Matt Lauer on the Today Show…or how bad Richard Nixon looked on TV during the Nixon-Kennedy debates before the 1960 election? Try searching both incidents at http://images.google.com and see the photos that are available.

Searching for old news and television is difficult because, oddly enough, not everything recorded is saved for all posterity.

Past, Present and Future Video

Locating old television shows and news previously broadcast is difficult. The chances to find newer shows are better today with new technologies available such as TIVO, YouTube, and DVD collections of many of the favorite sitcoms and serials. It is possible to purchase broadcasts of old shows direct from the publisher, or to capture partial or total video from video Web sites. There may even be videos being sold on EBAY. But all of these sources are hit and miss.

---

[39] CyberAge Books, ISBN 0-910965-46-3

Fortunately, there are few reliable sources available for investigators that need to research past, present and future video.

If you are looking for old shows that may be on tape, check with both www.netflix.com and www.blockbuster.com. Also try visiting video stores. If the subject appeared on a game or television show, perhaps a special, a copy of the program may be available as a rental.

Re-Running Reruns

A client wished to locate a long lost family member. The last time anyone saw him was as a game show contestant on TV in the late '70's.

First, I needed to establish what game shows were playing at the time and present the list to the client. From here she picked out *The Gong Show*, and the hunt was on.

It was a tireless effort, checking first with the production company, then with available Web sites for old video collections available. However, in the end we did locate an individual who the client claimed was her missing uncle.

Television of the Past

Searching for television of the past is a sticky and complicated search. There are a few resources help investigators in this search as well as some really key places to start when digging for all types of celluloid.

Vanderbilt University (http://tvnews.vanderbilt.edu)

According to Vanderbilt Television News Archive's Web site at http://tvnews.vanderbilt.edu, "The Television News Archive collection at Vanderbilt University is the world's most extensive and complete archive of television news. The collection holds more than 30,000 individual network evening news broadcasts from the major U.S. national broadcast networks: ABC, CBS, NBC, and CNN, and more than 9,000 hours of special news-related programming including ABC's *Nightline* since 1989. These special reports and periodic news broadcasts cover presidential conferences and political campaign coverage, and national and international events such as the Watergate hearings, the plight of American hostages in Iran, the Persian Gulf War, and the terrorist attack on the United States on September 11, 2001.

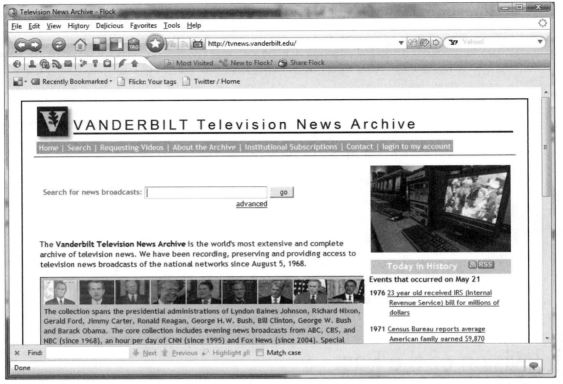

(Source: http://tvnews.vanderbilt.edu/)

National news programs from August 1968 to the present are in the archive collection. But news magazine programs, like ABC's 20/20, and local news programs are not part of the collection. Creating a free account, the investigator can search through the archives and request entire news programs to be duplicated for a minimal cost, with a three-day turnaround time for the VHS tape to be sent.

CNN Broadcasts

So much is seen on CNN and there are several resources and options for ordering tapes and transcripts of CNN news or broadcasts.

- Go to www.cnn.com/video/. CNN will send VHS or BetaSP upon request for a fee.

- Viewers can read transcripts from all transcribed shows by visiting the transcripts page at http://transcripts.cnn.com/TRANSCRIPTS/

- You can order programming aired on CNN and CNNfn by contacting the Federal Document Clearing House (FDCH). It archives CNN footage from 1996 to the present. You can contact the vendor by calling or by checking the FDCH Web site. Note that CNN shut down CNNfn in 2004. www.fdch.com; 800-CNN-NEWS

CNN International/CNN Headline News tapes and transcripts can be obtained by contacting Video Monitoring Service.

- **Video Monitoring Service** (www.vmsinfo.com); (212) 736-2010; CNN (United States), CNNfn, CNN Headline News, CNN International, European feed: Two months

- **Broadcast Monitors** (London, England): 011.44.207.247.1166

- **Tellex Monitors** (London, England): 011.44.208.247.1166; CNN International European feed: Two months

- **Monitoring and Analysis** (Mexico City, Mexico): 52.5.566.0454; CNN en Español: One month

If you are still unable to locate footage after contacting the broadcast monitoring services, or if you need CNN footage from 1980-1995, call the CNN ViewerSource Library at 404-827-1335.

Television News Present and Future

Researching present television news is rather easy. Keeping tabs on future events can not only be a great way to keep an eye on the assignment at hand, but also develop leads to clients you have served in the past.

For those with an unlimited budget, **Burrelles*Luce*** is the go-to source for news monitoring. Burrelles*Luce* requires you to establish an account and indicate what you wish to track (i.e. all episodes NBC's Today Show). You can also use a Tivo, or other pre-recording system. When tracking the mention of brand, like Poland Spring Water as captured by the news or specific shows, Burrelles*Luce* will monitor the news and television channels and report all findings. The key point to remember is that the time to use Burrelles*Luce* is when you have time to plan ahead.

However, if in retrospect you realize you missed planning, try contacting Burrelles*Luce* at www.burrellesluce.com/Media_Monitoring. If you speak with Burrelles*Luce*, be sure to ask about the video library in New York City

If you are looking for the actual words spoken on a newscast, in either text or video, take a look at **Teletrax** (www.teletrax.tv).

Another service is **ShadowTV** (www.shadowtv.com). This service offers real-time, keyword searching of video, using voice-recognition technology, from all the major news networks and local stations in about four or five major markets, like New York, Los Angeles, and Chicago. Even more interesting is that you not only read the transcript, but then you watch the video on your computer.

In other words, if your name is mentioned on CNBC at 8:02 A.M., you will be able to search then view the video online around 8:05 A.M. This services costs about $40 a month. ShadowTV will even send you an email alert notifying you that the words were spoken on the air.

Another key resource is **TVEyes** (www.tveyes.com). You can set up your searches in advance by keywords, make cluster searches, target channels, and search 30-days' worth of archives.

TVEyes covers most national broadcast networks and stations, like BLOOM (short for Bloomberg Television), CNBC, CNN, Comedy Central, CSPAN, CSPAN2, Discovery Channel, E! Entertainment, ESPN, Fox News, FX, Headline News, MSNBC, National Public Radio, SPEED, and TNT, not to mention the many, many ABC, NBC, CBS and FOX outlets. You can subscribe for $500.00 a month, or buy a week-long subscription for $250.00 when you need it. The customer service is excellent and friendly.

If you have a single company to monitor, you should set up news watch lists for references to a company name, the principals, the competitors, and product lines. If this sounds familiar, you are probably comparing this to a clipping service.

Web Video

Finally, search engines are offering a new venue for free and easy-to-find news and television shows, through **Google's Video Search** (www.video.google.com) and **YouTube** (www.youtube.com).

For an example, a search of "Puerto Rico police" returned 32 matches. There was a police shooting in Puerto Rico and a man's name was mentioned in the news. At least 6 of the 32 matches were video images captured by a bystander.

It is amazing what self-capture videos offer. From parodies to plunders, individuals with too much time on their hands and those with real talent can post their home movies on Youtube.com. Some legitimate news is also captured on random web video as well. Be sure to check on your company and principals when conducting any search. Imagine finding a training video for a company, or from a conference or similar event for a company you are investigating.

Cynthia's Key Chapter Points

- Use media resources. Investigators typically underuse these services and discount the value of newspaper and online media services.

- News services are fickle, especially free ones found online. Keep up with favorite free or publicly available services, but subscribe to at least one reliable fee-based news service.

- Web search engines, such as google.com and yahoo.com are good for current news, but weak for anything historical.

- For historical news from the 1980's forward it is best to use a fee-based service. Anything prior to the 1980's will require onsite library research.

- The public library is the best place to conduct news and press research. See what the local library offers online through their Web connections.

- Use News Alerts will give you the advantage of learning of something as it happens.

- International news resources could offer a strong bias. Check their publishing agents, who could be a foreign government.

- Television, video and audio news is readily available on the Internet and via cell phones. Historical video can still be obtained through the publisher or special library archives.

- Research industry-specific news channels should be researched. Channels and topics can appear online via video archive or in traditional print resources.

Chapter 10.5

Advanced Strategies Using Internet Resources

The mutual and universal dependence of individuals who remain indifferent to one another constitutes the social network that binds them together.

—Karl Marx

The Internet has certainly erupted into a major means of conducting business globally. With over 1.5 billion users and hundreds of millions of social-networking registrants – Facebook had 400 million active members as of June 1, 2010 – the web can be a terrific starting point for many investigations. Knowing a few tricks definitely helps investigators.

This chapter examines how to make use of social networking and auction sites in an investigation and some of the more robust features of Google.

Social Networks and Web 2.0

Growing fiercely on the World Wide Web are next generation websites known as Web 2.0 social networks. The most popular social networks are Facebook.com, Myspace.com, and Twitter.com.

Web 2.0

Wikipedia (a Web 2.0 phenomenon) defines Web 2.0 as follows–

"'Web 2.0'" refers to a perceived second generation of Web development and design that facilitates communication, secure information sharing, interoperability, and collaboration on the World Wide Web. Web 2.0 concepts have led to the development and evolution of web-based communities, hosted services, and applications; such as social-networking sites, video-sharing sites, wikis, blogs, and folksonomies." (en.wikipedia.org/wiki/WEB_2.0)

The underpinning of Web 2.0 is XML. This eXtended Markup Language brings a strong foundation as a true programming language and makes up for the many gaffs that HTML has permitted for years. Browsers like Internet Explorer and Netscape have been very forgiving of badly coded HTML pages.

By design XML is a respected and repeated markup language that is consistently used throughout all developing projects. XML remains constant, so we can confidently search across multiple venues and get descent results. Tags within the source code like <meta name="keywords"> do not change from site to site like they did with HTML. Since Meta Tags are a staple of XML pages, sites are better indexed and cataloged by search engines.

The improvements gained in this new environment are coupled by how seamless it appears to the user. The Everyday Joe doesn't notice that he is surfing, shopping and communicating in an entirely new environment. Plus, because of the Web 2.0 developments he is now able to communicate and create his own presence on the Web. For example, if Everyday Joe was HTML challenged, or didn't know how to create a website in the past, he can now easily sign up for free at Linkedin.com or Blog.com and have his thoughts and opinions shared with the world in fewer than five minutes.

Today it seems everyone is sharing their lives openly with anyone willing to loginand read. For example this morning I see fourteen of my fellow high school alumni are drinking coffee. Thanks to the simplified architecture of Web 2.0 social networks and blogs anyone can create a profile and start sharing their thoughts, ideas and rants with the world.

The fact that you do not have programming experience or even common sense to post on these social networking sites makes them simultaneously simple yet dangerous to those who are exposing their lives in a public forum.

Finding Subjects on Social Networks

Locating your subject online is doable using straightforward, easy to follow methods and resources. Each social network has a search box for locating members. You can search by name, phone number, or email address. A login is needed to search for members, but searches can be done anonymously. For example, MySpace's default settings allow any member to openly view another member's information.

However, what you see will vary. If a profile is set to "private," then you will only get a snapshot of the information. Facebook.com and the professional network Linkedin.com require you to *connect* with the other party in order to view their profile. Many private profiles are set up to avoid specific people. Either "She" does not want her boyfriend to see her online activity, or "He" is thwarting ex-girlfriends from contacting him. If you want to view a private profile, try to create a compelling, attractive, simple profile of yourself, then ask to be invited into your subject's network. I am not saying to create a false identity, and definitely DO NOT use someone else's identity! But if you are interesting enough, good looking enough, or just savvy enough, you will probably be accepted into their network. I created an obviously false identity as Jane Doe on several networks, and just listed my true graduating year and schools. It did not seem to matter that no one could recall "Jane Doe" from the class of 1992. They saw me as fellow alumni and invited me into their networks.

If you wish to broaden your reach and see where else your subject may be located, then the following sources may be of use.

Resources for a Search and Track

Trackle.com

This resource offers tools to guide you on the first search, then track under multiple topic headings. A *tracklet* can be set up to follow any number of items. Tracklets for following names in blogs and on Web sites are very useable for observing behavior online, seeing changes, or mentions of people, brands or topics.

The premium sources are worth the minimal cost for subscription. Premium includes Boolean logic queries, and advanced searching and tracking options. It is now possible to conduct brand searching, personal name tracking, get alerts on sites that make edits which you need as soon as they occur. Trackle.com is the single most impactful online resource offered since Google.com.

Spokeo

Spokeo.com is the search engine designed specifically to locate online profiles within social networks and track them. This very direct site allows you to search by a person's name, their email address, a phone number. You can also paste the actual URL for a MySpace.com or similar profile, then set it up for tracking.

Investigators and researchers will find this is an incredible tool that helps track down subject information in a way Google.com never did. One of the great features for Spokeo, is that as they are adding partner sites to search queries, and tracking those members. For example, you may view a subject's profile in not only Facebook.com and MySpace.com, but also in Hi5.com Xanga? Did you even know what Xanga was? One of the great features for Spokeo, is that they are adding partner sites for search queries, thus makes users aware of new sites. For example Wretch.com is a Chinese social network and Hi5.com is rather popular in India.

You can search and track the first handful of email addresses or names for free; thereafter you will be required to pay about $24 per year, or $2 per month. The free resource area also offers open source address searches and minimal public record information.

Resources for Strictly Searching

YoName

Yoname.com is very similar to Spokeo.com, searching eighteen of the same services as provided by Spokeo.com. However, many of the social networks found in their archives are unique to YoName.com. While YoName.com is free, know that the results are a bit random. As a test, I use will run a search by email or name of someone I know who has a social profile, often it does not appear at YoName. Spokeo.com has a better return rate on its searches.

Important to note with YoName.com: If you search by a user's email address, the user will receive a notification email stating someone was looking up "yo name" in YoName.com. The email does not contain the searcher's information, but this tip could be enough to alert a suspected fraudster.

Technorati

Technorati.com is the "Google" of blog search engines, meaning it is the market-share leader, at least for now. Use Technorati.com is the search engine for websites like YouTube.com, mySpace.com, blog.com, xanga.com, etcetera. This rich search engine covers almost 100 million blogs daily and enables searchers to efficiently narrow down a results list.

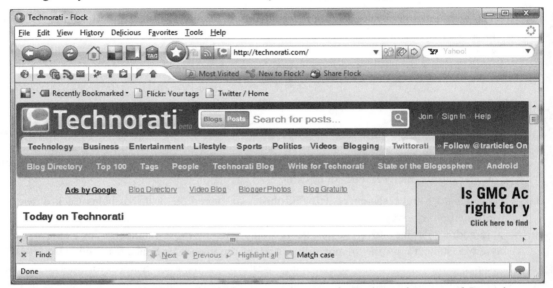

To search on a particular topic, it is a must to search Technorati.com *and* Icerocket.com (following this) to perform a thorough search through the Web and social-network world. Using the *Advanced Search* option your search can be narrowed to a particular blog, perhaps to search for the one or two times a topic is mentioned by a single blogger. Also, one may search by tags (explained further in Icerocket.com) to sites that are linked to a particular blog, and by the standard phrase or single-word search methods.

Icerocket

Icerocket.com offers a unique array of tools for bloggers and researchers. Backed by Mark Cuban, owner of the Dallas Mavericks and avid blogger himself (see *www.blogmaverick.com*), this resource was created to track *what people search for*. Icerocket.com focuses primarily on blog sites, using meta-tagging to categorize and index their content. A search can be conducted by a keyword which also captures any relevant matches found on a site, but will prioritize matches marked as tagged searches.

For example, say a blog is written about places to eat in Seattle. The blog names several Italian, Spanish, and French restaurants by design, such as Seattle Italian restaurants:

- La Trattatoria

- Seattle Spanish Restaurants
- Papi's Cocina

The words will be captured by the search robot (bot) and indexed. However, if the writer tags or self indexes their post as Italian restaurants, Spanish restaurants, etc., it will move up in rank in our search results.

The real benefit to using Icerocket.com is its search engine. Icerocket.com searches through blogs, image directories, and importantly Twitter and MySpace. Even though you can search directly in MySpace, using the Icerocket.com search engine tool for your MySpace searches often presents a more comfortable search environment, since Icerocket uses more traditional searching operators. Its advanced search link uses search operator categories or options such as title, author, and tag. Hence using a search of **title:"public records"** would show results that require the words "public records" show in the title. Another example is **author:"Cynthia Hetherington"** will return all mentions in Icerocket about written by "Cynthia Hetherington." A search using **tag:Yankees** will return all posts tagged "Yankees."

Also, advanced search features can be combined. Search for **title:"Public Records" author:"Cynthia Hetherington"** to locate all blog posts by Cynthia Hetherington with public records in the title.

Twitter.com

In 144 characters or less you can blast your thoughts, opinions, and ideas – or absolute nonsense – to the world via Twitter.com. Although many are quick to discredit the value of Twitter for investigative uses, the truth is that this service is probably one of the best resources to arrive since Google. When someone decides it is a good time to complain about their job, their boss, their spouse, they may do this openly on Twitter. Perhaps a Tweet stems from an incident such as an accident, or pandemonium erupting (workplace and school violence). Those tweets are all archived and searchable.

You can search directly in Twitter via search.twitter.com. What is key about Twitter? The content is real time – and so are search results. Potentially you can find information posted within seconds.

Other Twitter Search Engines:

Icerocket - Icerocket is a perfect way to search Twitter if your company firewall will not let you access Twitter directly.

Monitter - Monitter.com offers you three simultaneous searches on Twitter.com posts

Oneriot.com, **Scoopler.com**, **CrowdEye.com**, **Addictomatic.com**, and **Collecta.com**

Each of the above sites tracks RSS feeds, blog posts, Twitter, Flickr, other social networking sites, and news. However, you will not locate the historical information shown from a traditional search engine.

Finding Other Network Resources, Sites, and Search Engines

For an ever-expanding list of resources and for locating social networks that focus on individual cultures, social groups, and country specific blogs, visit Wikipedia.org at http://en.wikipedia.org/wiki/List_of_social_networking_websites.

Craigslist Searching

The site www.craigslist.org is an online emporium or a flea market, depending on your perspective. The large want-ad listings include products, garage-sale items, rental properties, houses for sale, services, and personal ads. The catch to correctly searching Craigslist is its geographic restriction. If you are interested in San Francisco items, that is the only geographic location you can search under; example is http://sfbay.craigslist.org. Craigslist will not allow you to search multiple jurisdictions as one. To expand your search, you have to specify Northern California or name another area. Or you can use SearchTempest.com.

Searchtempest

Tired of hunting around Craigslist for your suspect's posts, stolen goods, or to see if your hard-to-find sports memorabilia is anywhere to be found? Craigslist itself does not offer a way to search across the board, much to our frustration when conducting investigations. Lo and behold a search engine comes to the rescue, www.Craigshelper.com, now known as www.Searchtempest.com. You may search by distance in miles to a zip code, pick multiple cities, type of sale, and even if you want eBay results or not. A search on Dukes of Hazard from New Jersey brought up results as far as Monterey Bay, California.

Getting the Most Out of Google

Let's switch gears. As the market-share leader of free search tools on the Internet, Google certainly gets a good deal of use. Already we have reviewed certain Google features such as image searching, news searching, books, maps, products, and translations.

However, I believe Google is probably one of the most underappreciated search engines available, and not fully understood by many investigators.

There are numerous enhancements that go well beyond merely pushing words through and clicking "Google Search" or "I'm feeling lucky." An accomplished investigator should know how to use the advanced-search feature, operators, and how to take advantage of the advanced search feature settings.

Google Operators

Using Google operators will smarten a search and enable you to find the right link faster. Look in the first column in the table below for the bolded characters known as operators. They help define or narrow a search.

This Search	Operator	Finds Pages Containing ...
cooking Italian	none	With both the words cooking and Italian, but not together or in order
vegetarian **OR** vegan	**OR**	Information on vegetarian or vegan
"Can I get a witness"	""	The exact phrase "Can I get a witness"
Henry +8 Great Britain	+	Information about Henry the Eighth (8), weeding out other kings of Great Britain
automobiles ~glossary	~	Glossaries about automobiles, as well as dictionaries, lists of terms, terminology, etc.
salsa -dance	-	The word "salsa" but NOT the word "dance" (note the space before the hyphen)
salsa-dancer	-	All forms of the term, whether spelled as a single word, a phrase, or hyphenated (note the lack of a space)
define:congo	**define:**	Definitions of the word "congo" from the Web
site:virtuallibrarian.com	**site:**	Searches only one website for expression, in this case virtuallibrarian.com
filetype:doc	**filetype:**	Find documents of the specified type, in this case MS Word documents
link:virtuallibrarian.com	**link:**	Find linked pages, i.e. show pages that point to the URL

Google operators can also be combined. Follow the example below:

site:hp.com filetype:pdf "5010 LaserJet" printer FAQ

This search is directed to the Hewlett Packard website, looking for an Adobe Acrobat PDF file of frequently asked questions regarding the 5010 LaserJet printer.

Also available on Google are the common mathematical operators. The following symbols between any two numbers will automatically perform a math function.

Symbol Function

+   Addition

-       Subtraction

*   Multiplication

/   Division

To locate other advanced Google operators, use the Advanced Search Page, or you can perform the advancing searching right in the search box.

There are dozens more operators and search techniques for beginners and experts alike. A great resource for search help is www.googleguide.com.

Using the Preferred Results Feature

One option can save time and help insure not to miss vital hits is to simply set the number of results from 10 (the default) to 100. To do this, go to the first screen of Google.com, click on *Search Settings*, which is a link on the upper right of the screen, and then slide down to "Number of Results." You will see a pull-down menu that should be displaying "10" in the box. Change that to "100" and click the "Save Preferences" button at the bottom right of the page. Now every time you use Google.com on that computer, you will receive 100 results per page.

The *Preferences* option also allows you to specify the default tolerance for "safe searching filtering." Google's SafeSearch blocks Web pages containing explicit sexual content from appearing in search results. The filter options are:

- Use strict filtering (filter both explicit text and explicit images)
- Use moderate filtering (filter explicit images only—default behavior)
- Do not filter my search results.

Google Proximity Searching Feature

When an asterisk "*" is used between words or expressions, Google offers a very rich proximity searching feature. Used between two expressions, proximity will return results that are within 15 words of each other.

For example, a search for *"cynthia hetherington" investigator* returned 755 matches in Google. Whereas, the search *"cynthia hetherington" * "investigator"* resulted in 24 matches.

Hence, the expression "cynthia hetheington" did appear on the same Web page as "investigator" 755 times, but it only occurred in close proximity to "investigator" 24 times out of the 755 matches.

Another example is *"Tampa Bay" * "Devil Rays"* which will return results when "Tampa Bay" appears within 15 words of "Devil Rays."

Common Phrase Searching

For English-language searches, consider using the common expressions people use in everyday language. With email, text messaging, and other basic-device communications, writing has turned into an extension of speaking. Many people no longer think about what they are writing; as far as grammar is concerned, they tend to write like they speak. Shorthand and expressions are common. Below are common expressions that can be used for creative phrase searching.

- I hate XXX (my job, my mom, my school, my employer)
- Better than XXX (<restaurant>, <product>, <any proper noun>)

- I love XXX (my job, my mom, my school, my employer)
- XXX was the nicest (<geography/location>, <company or person>)
- XXX was the worst
- XXX was off the charts
- XXX was off the hook
- XXX was off the map
- XXX was such a jerk/babe/<expletive>
- XXX was so hot/stupid/boring

An example search using "Better than Disney" returned hits on such pages as:

- Is Disney Land better than Disney World?
- Nick [Nickelodeon's children's network] is slightly better than Disney

The key to using common phrase searching is to be inventive. Consider how you would describe a similar topic, then run your searches in the same style using quotes to contain the phrases.

Google Alerts

As mentioned in the previous chapter, **Google Alerts** is one of the handiest tools that Google offers for investigators. The Google Alerts tool sends emails automatically when new Google results match your pre-submitted list of search terms. These results are culled from Google News, Web, Blogs, Video, and Groups.

The easiest way to use the Alerts feature is to start at google.com/alerts. Here you set up your customized alert list that will email you as an event is found. Preferences may be set to alert you on a as-it-happens, or once-a-day, or even once-a-month basis. Type in your search query or key words—such as a proper name, expression, or phrase search—then use the pull-down menu to select what you want to track for your personalized alerts.

You will want to use a return email address specifically set up to capture heavy traffic. Use the same type of account you would when signing up to various websites and social networks.

Google Images

Image searching in Google can offer a host of interesting results. Using the same type of search queries, you can look up a personal name, company, or idea. The Advanced Image Search offers limiters by image type (such as black and white, color, and drawings) and has a search feature for finding only faces and only news content. Filtering with the "faces only" feature will narrow down large result matches. The "news content" feature is terrific considering the image search happens within media and press-oriented websites. Normally news and media searches are conducted on databases such as LexisNexis or Factiva, where images have been stripped out of stories. For more information, go to www.google.com/advanced_image_search

Google Video

Google owns YouTube.com. YouTube is a tremendous resource for obtaining video footage of people in action, inside pictures of facilities, and location/geography snapshots. For those investigating insurance fraud, YouTube.com is a must for checking if the disabled claimant has posted any videos of himself doing heroic feats. Visit video.google.com or YouTube.com to search.

Google Maps

The Google Maps tool is quite useful for needs beyond the well-known driving directions and the "where is?" feature. Search an area with familiarity to see the variety and tools that go beyond directions of east to west. The My Maps tab offers a variety of features and tools where you customize your searches and zero in on certain geographic aspects.

Searches can be narrowed to show real estate listings, user-contributed photos with Picasa Web Album or Panoramio, and places of interest. Use the distance measurement tool to establish the length between two map points. Various measurement results are offered. For example, the distance between Minneapolis and St. Paul, Minnesota, is 8.73084 mi or 128.052 football fields, 13.1711 верста, 281.019 pools, and so on.

Bing.com

Just when you thought all cool single-word expressions were taken, Microsoft introduced Bing. Bing is the latest search engine to take on the formidable Google.com and Yahoo.com. Bing focuses on four key areas: shopping, local, travel, and health.

A number of features and benefits of this new search engine are reviewed below. It is worth mentioning that the interface is rather pleasant with a photo backdrop, which is fine on a computer with no bandwidth issues. However, large image files are always a burden when you are strictly looking for content, not bells and whistles. The PDA version – accessible by Blackberry, iPhone, and similar devices – opens with a plain-text screen.

Bing Search Features and Settings

Go straight to Preferences in the right-hand corner and change the settings for *Results* from 10 to 50 (unfortunately the highest number). While you are there, note the obvious similarity to Google's preferences page with a few noticeable add-ons. Bing identifies your physical location based on your ISP location. My ISP is in Oakland, New Jersey, and it says so in the preferences. You can change this, but I imagine Bing is trying to use a location to determine the best marketing material to attach to my searches. You have the option to turn on (default) and off the suggestions box. It can be annoying when you start typing an expression and the Bing tries to finish your words.

The search box takes up to 150 characters, including spaces. The standard stop words ("a," "the," "and," etc.) can be included in your search if used in quoted phrases, e.g., "The Di Vinci Code".

One odd feature was the increase of results when searching with quotes against a name. A search without quotes on *Cynthia Hetherington* returned 60,500 results, whereas the search with the quotes returned 179,000 results.

Although, the algorithm is not clear, it is possible Bing uses a proximity command as a default when searching one or more expressions. This would make sense to limit bad results such as a document that lists "Cynthia Nixon" at the top of the page and "Hetherington Smith LLP" six pages later. A nice feature brought back to use in database searching is the Boolean terms "or" and "not." By default, search engines tend to assume the "and" (e.g., chocolate "and" cake), and the "not," which can also be represented as a "−" (minus) in the query. Although the "or" (represented as "|") gets a little lost in the advanced features, it is good to see Bing highlighting this little-used but resourceful feature.

Bing has brought back parentheses to allow you to combine expressions to be included or not. This is great for intelligence investigators who suffer due to popular names flooding their results. For example, Bill Gates returns 24 million hits. Add (Gates Foundation) to the search and you are limited to 700,000 results. If you subtract (or NOT Gates Foundation), the results jump back up, but the results will be significantly less than the original 24 million.

Bing maintains an ongoing history of your searches in the left-hand column. Avid researchers and investigators have ways of remembering what they looked up and in what order, but this list takes the questions out of doubtful searches. For example, in all my Bill Gates searches, did I ever try searching him as William Gates? A quick look to the left gives me that answer.

Also down the left-hand column are related queries and recommendations.

On the right-hand side of the results page, if you mouse over the returned links, you will see your search expression as it appears within the context of the website that was found. Other links offered on that page are also shown.

Bing includes many of the same resources we find in other popular engines that focus on the consumer market. There are searches specific to travel, video, pictures (images), and maps. The pictures searches are easier to manage because you see more images on the results screen as compared to only 10 per page on Google's results screen. Narrow down your search by "head and shoulders" shots and "just faces" shots. Also, the type, size, and color of the picture can modify your search and are offered to the left of the screen.

The features for Bing are very well designed, even if they target a consumer market. I tried the cashback option and saved more than $5 and received free shipping on a new purchase through one of their vendors.

Given the popularity of Google, Bing is going to have a challenge gaining market share, but it returned surprisingly better results on traditional search queries and photo searches. The mapping queries were easier to run. Bing is a new Data2know.com top-ten choice!

Other Worthy Search Engines

Throughout this book, a number of other traditional search engines have been mentioned for their products and unique features. If you frequent one of the search engines mentioned below, I strongly urge to take time and to check out all their available features and searching tips.

- Alltheweb.com
- Altavista.com
- Ask.com
- Yahoo.com

Cynthia's Key Chapter Points

- Social Networks and other Web 2.0 applications create an exciting new prospect for investigating subjects. The sudden vastness and availability to the everyday individual, has created an unprecedented amount of online confessions, mental pondering and random musings.

- Using and applying Social Network findings into your cases is going to become as common as conducting records checks, interviews and other consistently applied investigative techniques.

- Embrace the new medium, but remember to use it with responsibility and verify all of your findings. Most importantly, stay on top of the latest sites and services.

Section 3

Putting It All Together

The purpose of this book is to help make you successful not only as an investigator, but also as a business person.

As part of this endeavor, this section will scrutinize four key functions in the relationship you establish with your clientele—

1. Taking the Order

2. Client Agreements

3. Creating the Report for the Client

4. Analyzing Your Costs and Billing Your Services

Chapter 11

Taking the order and Client Agreements

It takes twenty years to make an overnight success.
—Eddie Cantor
Success is simply a matter of luck. Ask any failure.
—Earl Wilson

Taking the Order

This topic was discussed briefly in Chapter 2, which outlined the importance of communicating with the client to establish criteria and expectations. I cannot emphasize enough that the expectations between the client and the investigator must be made clear at the outset of a case. This starts with how you take the order or accept the case.

The rest of this subsection has been adapted from a chapter in *Public Record Retrieval Industry Standards Manual*, written for members of the Public Record Retriever Network (PRRN). The Network's co-director, Carl Ernst, wrote the original article. This article really hits home on explaining the nuances to consider when taking a client order. I sincerely thank Mr. Ernst and PRRN for allowing me to modify the article and to place it in this book.

How Do You Take an Order?

Generating a great report, while protecting your firm from complaints and litigation, starts with the manner in which you take the original order.

If you get your client's search instructions in writing, either by mail, fax, or email, your chances of making a mistake in the execution of the order is minimized, although you must still be careful that the instructions are legible and complete, as discussed below.

If, on the other hand, you take an order by telephone, you must be extremely diligent to follow a set of written, standard procedures in taking the order, not only to insure that you took it correctly, but also to be able to convince a disgruntled client later that you did not mishear any part of the order. The reason you should commit your telephone-order procedure to writing will become clear momentarily.

The Six Essential Questions

Procedure is one thing; content is another. If you do not ask all of the essential questions needed for you to complete the investigation exactly as your client wishes it to be completed, you can still get in serious trouble. Remember the old saying that to ASSUME makes an ASS out of U and ME. Ask all the questions. Make sure both you and the client are clear about the objectives in doing the search.

Here are six questions that are essential to include in standard, written procedures. Ask the question, record the answer.

1. What is the Purpose of the Investigation?

You must always be crystal clear about what information your client wants. Do not let your client give vague instructions. The purpose of the investigation will determine what you investigate and research. Remember the discussion in Chapter 1: If your client says, "I would like to know more about ABC Company." The investigator's follow-up questions should be, "What do you want to know about ABC Company? Is it a competitor, a potential acquisition, or a defaulted company?"

2. What is the Subject's Name?

If the Subject is a Business Entity . . .

Your client may ask you to find a corporate name. Would your client also like you to search LLC and limited partnership records, trademarks, or fictitious names?

Whatever the type of search, it is best to tell your client the options she has, and then let her choose from them. If the client wants less than what you would consider a full search, make the restriction clear in your report.

If the Subject is an Individual . . .

The procedure followed by a national UCC search firm is to read back the subject's name letter by letter, using a version of the "Able, Baker" alphabet. A check mark is placed above each letter as it is confirmed. Then the location to be searched is repeated, and a check mark is placed over it when it is confirmed.

In the event a client later complained that you got the name wrong, you could produce the original order, point out the check marks, and show a copy of your procedures manual to affirm what the check marks meant. I can assure you that this procedure has quickly stopped a lot of complaints.

You also should use certain standards to determine if the subject name you are given is complete for your purposes. An individual's name, like "Carl Ernst," may be adequate for your purposes, or you may want to ask whether the middle initial is known, especially if the name is common. "C. Alexander Ernst" may create real search problems for you if you don't know what the "C" stands for.

In addition, if the subject is an individual, you must determine the purpose of the investigation or search to avoid running afoul of federal or state laws with respect to personal information privacy, such as the Fair Credit Reporting Act. If the stated purpose is, for example, employment related, you must be aware of the rules that govern the responsibilities of you and your client as a credit reporting agency or retriever.

3. What Results do You Anticipate?

A business investigation is not a test. Your job is to try to find anything that is on the records, but only within the constraints placed by your client, by the government office, and by your standard search practices. You are not Superman or Superwoman. You may be expected to find common variations of the subject name, but you cannot, nor are you responsible to, determine all the weird variations that a keypuncher might inflict on a name.

Therefore, it always helps to know whether your client is aware of any records that now exist on the subject. This is especially helpful when a filing office charges a lot for copies, and makes them for all searches automatically. If your client knows the subject has hundreds of filings, you may be able to advise her of more cost-efficient ways to search the records without incurring substantial copy charges.

Occasionally, your client may say, "That's none of your business; you do the investigating." In that case, your client may be testing you, and that is OK. But you should take the opportunity to explain that part of your investigation will involve searching public records, and these records are frequently mis-indexed by the clerks or filing officers. So you would usually extend your search procedures beyond your usual thorough methods, if you did not get a hit when one was anticipated.

If your client asks for a UCC search, does she mean to include tax liens, and if so, just federal, or federal and state tax liens? What about judgments or judgment liens? If the search is in a former dual-filing state, is only a central office search being requested, or should a local, filing office search also be conducted? Is your client aware of the different types of search methods necessary to overcome the limitations of searches, under Revised Article 9 of the UCC, in most central filing offices?

If the investigation involves real estate searches, a client needs to know if a subject owns any property in another county, and she might want to know if any properties are mortgaged.

4. What is the Time Period to Investigate?

When using online systems, you will need to be careful that the computerized data goes back as far as the client wants. Otherwise, you will need to perform a separate, manual search of the older records. You will need to know how far back to search many public records.

5. What Documents Do You Want to Obtain?

I am not going to dwell on this aspect of the order, except to say that it can be really costly if you order or copy 500 UCC filings, and then find out that your client doesn't want them and won't pay for them. If, however, you have no choice but to obtain documents as part of a search, you should inform your client of the possibility of excessive copy costs before performing the search.

6. How Do You Want the Results?

This question has two parts. First, when does your client need the results? If the client needs the information in four weeks, you say OK, but produce the results in two days. Then, you will look like a hero, which is good for your marketing. On the other hand, if your client has an unreasonable time expectation, you might as well deal with the problem up front to avoid the disgruntled phone call later.

Second, what is the form of delivery for reporting the results? Does your client want the report by email, fax, phone, express mail, or just standard mail?

Creating the Agreement

There are three types of documents to consider when establishing an agreement with a client.

1. **A Letter of Agreement** specifically outlines what the investigator is hired to do and how to prepare the results, and it gives at least an outline of the anticipated charges and fees.

2. **A Contract** is generally used for ongoing work with a client, spelling out the work and expectations.

3. You and your client should sign a **Non-Disclosure Agreement**. This document protects you and your client from the loss of trade secrets or sensitive information.

The tradition in many client/investigator relationships is to rely on a mostly verbal agreement, with a small, written component that is stated on the search report and/or on the invoice for services. However, the lack of a written agreement or contract can prove to be a mistake for both the investigator and the client. It is a mistake for the investigator because the responsibilities are never clearly stated, and perhaps, not well understood. It is a mistake for the client because she is never required to thoroughly think about what she should expect, and not expect, of the investigator.

Letters of Agreement

Many investigators think requiring a written agreement will get in the way of doing business. This is not true. You can use a standard-form document that allows you to enter the specifics about the case and about the client. Or you can simply use company stationery. The information should include:

- Your company's name, address, and contact information
- Your client's name, address, and contact information
- Date and time order was placed
- Client instructions
- Any agreed upon specifics, like turnaround time or pricing
- Anticipated results, if applicable

A sample Letter of Agreement is found in **Appendix 1**.

Contracts

If your written contract needs to be negotiated, then use this is an opportunity to educate your client about the real world where disclaimers are necessary, because of the vagaries of resources, public records, and the artfulness of the search process.

There are multiple styles and formats for writing a contract. They should include financial terms, timeline expectations, expected deliverables, and legal jurisdiction.

> **Author Tip** ➡ Nolo Press offers many contracts for sale via its Web site at www.nolo.com. You also can inquire within a state or national investigator association for any samples or templates from other investigators.

Hiring an attorney to help set up some basic paperwork templates for your office also is possible, and will give you better peace of mind.

Non-Disclosure Agreement

A Non-Disclosure Agreement (NDA) should be a standard item, signed by both parties when an investigator takes on a new client. In fact, every new client should ask you to sign his own NDA. If the client does not suggest this, then offer one of your own. The NDA can be part of a package for the new client, with the Letter of Agreement or the Contract. An NDA is especially important for compliance with the federal regulations mentioned previously, such as SOX and HIPPA, and should be an expected requirement from all clients because of the sensitive nature of investigative work.

A sample NDA is in **Appendix 1**.

Chapter 12

Preparing the Report

The Investigative Report on a Principal

As discussed earlier, while there are many styles used to write reports, using a format that is simple, clean, and professional is a definite must. An excellent reference for report writing is what I have called my go-to guide since college, *The Publication Manual of the American Psychological Association* also known as the *APA Style Manual*. Although using this reference may seem like overkill for some reports, keep in mind that your report *could* be read by attorneys and judges. By using a format commonly used in graduate schools, your client will understand the style and appreciate your attention to detail. That said, not everything I do is applicable to this style guide.

Depending on the type of investigation you are conducting, SWOT and CARA are interchangeable in many ways. SWOT is probably the most widely used analytical tool, so I have used CARA and Supply Chain Analysis in the sample reports to follow.

A Sample Report on a Principle

The following is an example of a report style for a standard due diligence check on an individual with an emphasis on using the CARA method of analysis. This example has instructional text mixed in with sample, reporting language, which is in italics. Although presented on a bullet-list basis, a numeric-list presentation is also very acceptable.

Cover Page

The cover sheet should include your company's name, the client's name, the date, and the name of the report.

Also on the cover page, place the words *Privileged and Confidential*. If you are working with an attorney, place the words *Attorney Work Product*.

Summary Analysis

If the report exceeds 30 pages, create a table of contents. If not, then just continue to the next point.

- **The Objective**

Stating the basics of who hired you and why is sufficient, but you can expand on this as well.

ABC Company has engaged XYZ Investigative Services, Inc. to conduct a personal due diligence/background check on Joseph Smith. This investigation was conducted utilizing public records, legal filings, media sources, and discreet interviews.

- **Executive Summary**

Summarize the individual's background and highlight any key issues. Also make recommendations and follow-ups. Draw out key findings from documents you have analyzed so that the client reads these first. You do not want to force the client to find out about the subject's criminal history ten pages into your report. Very clearly itemize what is important in your summary, and what needs to be done.

- **CARA Analysis**

Here, state any very notable CARA indicators that developed during the course of your investigation. This text also may be incorporated into the summary statement.

Characteristics give a sense of the subject's personality. Look at his rank or position and the type of car he drives. Is he litigious? Has he been convicted of any crimes or rewarded for any heroic acts?

Military records indicate John Smith spent 20 years in the United States Army and retired honorably with Purple Heart and Meritorious Service Medals.

Associations with other people, either professional or personal, help in understanding the socio-economic position of the subject, whether he is wealthy, an average worker, or a criminal.

A marriage announcement, located from ten years ago, [put the actual date in] states that John Smith married Antoinette Vanderbilt of the Vanderbilt Estates, a wealthy and well-established family.

Reputation searches present the best opportunities to hear what people say about the person and his affiliates.

According to interviews with former subordinates, Smith was considered a fair commander, a brave soldier, and lived very much by the book. However, an interview with a female former staff sergeant who served under his command, revealed that Smith held a bias against women in the military, and was opposed to females in combat. And although he never publicly stated as such, he "showed a bias against known homosexual military personnel."

Affiliations with certain companies, organizations, associations, and educational facilities are very telling.

Currently, Smith is connected to the Republican Party and it is rumored that he is considering running for public office. Local media have asked him if he is considering entering the race for the U.S. Senate, but he will neither confirm nor deny this speculation.

Body of Report

- **Vital Information**

Public records reveal the subject's full name and his date of birth, as well as his spouse's full name (need maiden name) and her date of birth.

The couple reside at 170 Dryer Road, Swisstown, in Morris County, New Jersey 07524, since June 1993. The telephone number listed to both is (908) 555-4567. He is listed as having five children, with their names and ages also listed.

- **Professional History**

Discuss the type of professional business career your subject has had and note if there are any discrepancies in his employment dates. If the subject does not have any companies listed for two years and you cannot fill that gap, make sure you mention that fact. It might be an indicator that the subject was out of the country or in prison.

If any questionable information turns up, you should write it directly at the beginning of this section. Otherwise, list the following in descending order:

- Years of service
- Company that employed the subject
- Subject's job title
- Short definition of the company's practice

For example; *Here is information that was located on the subject, listed in descending order:*

1994 to 1996

DEF Group L.P.

Limited Partner

Capital investment group with major investments in emerging markets, petroleum, and generic pharmaceuticals.

- **Board Positions**

Chapter 5 goes into depth on why board positions are so important. This section of the report should be presented in the same itemized style as the professional history. Again, highlight any incongruence or possible collusion issues directly at the beginning of this section.

Subject has sat on several boards, but one of note is Reliance Hospital. This might seem inappropriate, as the subject is also the lead developing contractor for the new wing of Reliance Hospital. Recommend further research into this matter to insure no collusion or favoritism was bestowed on the subject, considering his role as a board member.

1996 to present

IBM

Board Member

Chair of Compliance

- **Political Affiliations**

Political affiliations will enlighten you on where the subject spends his money, and how he feels about hot-button issues, like stem cell research and the environment. However, do not judge too quickly because many corporate executives play both sides of the political race to get the best advantage for their company.

If the subject is active in politics, explain that here. Mention any donations to campaigns. If you locate his voter registration information, mention it.

- **Charitable Works**

If your subject sits on the board of a charitable organization, take note of who else is a board member. Many corporate people sign up for feel-good projects because it is great networking. They like to attend swanky annual fundraisers and mix with the rich and famous. Keep in mind though, if they are dedicating a good deal of their time to charities, or if you are reading a lot about their activities, then they may have real reasons to be involved. People often join children's health charities because of personal interests regarding their own children or a friend's children.

Mention any notes regarding the subject's personal interest versus professional interest; mention any donations to charities; describe charitable works, projects and activities; and list any charity board seats.

> *Subject is a board member for the United Way of Greater New York. Also on this board are several corporate CEOs* [name a few]. *Subject also is active in the Children's Diabetes Foundation. A New York City metro newspaper article, published on January 5, 1999, talked about the subject's involvement with the Children's Diabetes Foundation because of his "son's severe diabetic condition."*

- **Academic Credentials and Special Licenses**

If your subject attended college or trade school and has received special certifications in his profession, highlight the achievements here. But, you should verify these claims. Education is one of the most frequently exaggerated sections of a report.

I'm Working on It

Hired to verify the resume of an environmental engineer who had testified in numerous environmental cases throughout his career, I did not expect to find much inconsistency. After all, I thought that another investigator or law firm would have found any holes in his resume before it got to me. Not so! When I contacted his stated university to verify that he was really working toward his master's degree in environmental science, I learned that he was stretching the truth a bit. The engineer claimed on his resume that the degree was "pending." There is no exact timetable for "pending," but I thought it at least meant that he was attending class and was close to getting his degree. However, I learned that he had not attended class since 1979! So yes, it was "pending," but it was not exactly the same as current students on the class rolls.

Once the information is collected and vetted, report it in a manner that is consistent with section on board positions.

The following academic records information can be verified by contacting the records departments for each school:

- Level of education
- Year graduated
- University, college, or trade school
- Certifications, if any

Elaborate on certifications if they are pertinent to the case.

- **Identified Assets**

Physical assets such as properties, automobiles, luxury boats, vacation or investments homes, business licenses, and significant shareholder wealth should be identified in this section. This works as a great pull-out section for the reader to get to the bottom dollar. Many times these background checks are performed to see if the subject is worth going after in court. A prejudgment search to identify any assets, prior to litigating, might help the client collect on his debts.

Types of assets are indicated below:

Real Property

Subject is the registered owner of 170 Dryer Road, Swisstown, in Morris County, New Jersey 07062. The property was purchased on January 15, 1999 for $8,000,000.

Previous and unverified addresses include:

123 5th Avenue, Floor 15, New York, New York 10017

101 Knights Palace, Bronx, New York 10468

Physical Assets (Note: motor vehicles, vessels, airplanes, etc.)

Subject is the registered driver of a 2007 Mercedes-Benz Coupe. Mercedes-Benz Credit Leasing, Inc. is listed as the registered owner. There is also luxury watercraft listed for the subject, a 2004 Sea Ray 390 Motor Yacht.

Financial Assets

Financial assets are certainly an indicator of wealth. If your subject has a trust account named for him, he may come from a wealthy lineage. If not, he may be protecting his assets. Indicate the investigation results for the following items:

- Trusts
- Significant shareholders
- Recipients of any judgments
- UCCs
- Intellectual Properties

One of the most valuable items that could be in your subject's coffer is any patent that he may hold. Make sure you report these items correctly. A corporate scientist may be the patent creator, but his company is the patent holder. In terms of intellectual property, I always grab a PDF copy of the stated asset and append it to my report. And, in this particular case, I would mention that the subject was shown to have 12 registered patents under his name, in what appeared to be a fuel-processing methodology.

Copyrights and trademarks are much more straightforward. For instance, in the example above, I would report that the subject has had several copyrighted works published on fuel processing and that he owned the trademark to the mark fuel methods.

Following the APA Style Manual in citing works for papers, I use the same style guide for professional reports. See the following examples.

Sample text using fonts from APA Style Manual:

- Copyrights
  - Smith, J. (1999). *Fuel: Processing Methods.* Chicago, IL: CCR Publishing.
- Patents
  - Smith, J. (1995). U.S. Patent No. 123,434. Washington, D.C.: U.S. Patent and Trademark Office.
- Trademarks
  - Smith, J. (1995). *Fuel Methods.* Washington, D.C.: U.S. Patent and Trademark Office.

- **Legal Findings**

Civil and criminal matters should be cited clearly and separately in this portion of the report. Report criminal matters first. Make sure you know the search variables of the sources you used so that you can accurately report what was and was not searched. For example, many states only offer convictions history and do not indicate arrests without dispositions.

Example:

For the last seven years in [State]*, there were no convictions, misdemeanors, or felonies located.*

A domestic dispute charge was filed in [County] *on 12/24/1999.*

Then list the details.

There are two format methods to use to report civil cases. The first example is reported as follows:

Case name

Date filed

Date terminated

Office

Nature of suit

Cause

Plaintiff

Defendant

If you notice names or further content in the dockets or summary, continue your listing with a short narrative.

The second example is:

> *On January 15, 1999, ABC Company filed a breach-of-contract claim against the Smith Group in New York County Supreme Court. Defendants named, in addition to the Smith Group, were Kathy and John Smith. The case was voluntarily dismissed on June 9, 1999.*

- **Regulatory, Sanction, and Disciplinary Issues**

Chapter 6 discusses how to investigate regulatory and disciplinary issues. Below is how to report the findings. Use the headings as shown in the sample text below:

Reporting Regulatory Issues

> *Online searches, through various U.S. regulatory agencies like the Office of Foreign Asset Control, the Central Contractors Registry, and the Excluded Parties Database, did not reveal any matches to the subject.*

Reporting Disciplinary Issues

> *A search in the Health and Human Services Office of Inspector General did not reveal any matches to the subject. Nor were any matches located in the State of Florida Disciplinary Actions database for physicians.*

- **Financial Troubles**

Liens and debts, caused by lawsuits and bankruptcies, are straightforward for reporting purposes. Below is sample text:

Tax Liens – Judgments

> *Subject is seen to have an unsatisfied federal tax lien of $10,000 from 1998, registered in the state of Montana.*

> *Subject has an unsatisfied judgment/lien for $5,000, resulting from a lawsuit filed in 1999 by the ABC Company.*

Bankruptcies

> *Subject filed for Chapter 7 bankruptcy protection on August 2, 1998. Bankruptcy was granted and a list of his debts and creditors can be provided, if requested.*

You can list the creditors and the money owed, but appending or offering for further information later is better, unless you see something significant in the creditor's report.

- **Media**

The media findings should be reported in descending order. There are two schools of thought on how to report media issues, and both are certainly acceptable.

You can summarize the story for brevity sake, which is a more professional approach to report writing. Sample:

- *Date – Source – Title*
  - *Truncated article, italicized, justified, and indented .5 on each side.*

Or you can include key portions of the article, quoting it entirely or paraphrasing the report. In some cases, this is necessary because the subject material may be beyond your comprehension of the topic, and the paraphrasing could turn out to be inaccurate. Sample:

- *Summary of article as follows:*

  - *On June 2, 1996, the* New York Times *reported that Bob Smith was found guilty of racketeering.*

The Investigative Report on a Company

Much of the company reporting style is the same as the principal's style just outlined. In this sample breakdown report on a company, the supply chain method of analysis will be demonstrated. A bullet-list method is used below for presentation. Again, sample text is shown in italics.

A Sample Report on a Company

Cover Page

The cover sheet should include your company's name, the client's name, the date, and the name of the report.

Also on the cover page, place the words *Privileged and Confidential*. If you are working with an attorney, place the words *Attorney Work Product*.

Summary Analysis

If the report exceeds 30 pages, create a table of contents. If not, then just continue to the next point.

- **The Objective**

Stating the basics of who hired you and why is sufficient, but you can expand on this as well.

ABC Company has engaged XYZ Investigative Services, Inc. to conduct a corporate due diligence/background check on Stated Company. This investigation was conducted utilizing public records, legal filings, media sources, and discreet interviews.

- **Executive Summary**

Summarize the corporate location, key managers, and history. Bring to light any current and important issues that may have been revealed in recent media reports or through your research and analysis. Make recommendations based on the supply chain analysis. Draw out key findings from documents you have analyzed so that the client reads these first. Again, you do not want to force the client to find out about a company's criminal history ten pages into your report. Very clearly itemize what is important in your summary, and what needs to be done.

- **Supply Chain Analysis**

Logistics - Inbound – Warehousing and Internal Handling of Products

What sorts of warehouse conditions apply? Be ready to define how the product is handled and stored. If refrigeration is necessary, is that addressed? Which vendors are being used to service and repair those air conditioners? If the company produces a controlled substance, a foodstuff or a potentially hazardous product, consider which oversight agency (EPA, OSHA, FDA, local labor commission, or labor union) would be on-site and writing reports about the internal logistics.

> *EPA and OSHA reported multiple violations over the course of five years. OSHA deemed the equipment "hazardous" in light of an employee accident that was caused by a faulty processing belt in shipping. Additionally, the EPA has cited the company two years in a row for health-code violations related to mouse feces.*

Logistics – Outbound – Distribution

How are the products shipped? Find out if the company itself ships the products or if it uses an outside contractor to haul the products to stores or the final location.

> *From all accounts, it appears that the company is using a third-party vendor, Johnson Trucking Co., to deliver its product to market. No violations or disparaging information was located in a brief search on Johnson.*

Operations – Product Development and Manufacturing

Who is making the product? Is there special machinery involved in the creation of the manufactured goods?

> *According to interviews with local union members, the products are made completely on-site; however, twice a year, when the plant shuts down for maintenance, the company subcontracts its product development to Temporary Product Developers located in (Location).*

Support Teams – Research & Development, Manufacturing Groups, and Unions

The workforce for the product could be spread out among disparate groups throughout the country and the world.

> *The subject company **appears to be** a local small mom-and-pop operation, based on the size of office space they lease and the number of employees in the United States mentioned in their business report. This was verified as well through an interview with the chairman of another company, when he mentioned he thought too that they were a "local company." He referred to a conversation he had with the subject company's CEO. During that conversation the CEO revealed the US location was only for marketing team, and their research and development lab was located in Tel Aviv, Israel.*

Human Resources – Support for Support Teams and Management

This is management analysis.

> *No mention of union problems was located in the media. When interviewing several members of the union, they expressed overall satisfaction with the employers. However, they did mention a formal complaint about the aging equipment, as cited in an OSHA report. They said the equipment was a concern and that they were lobbying management to make the necessary upgrades.*

> *No legal filings were located against the company management.*

Infrastructure – Location, Security, and Risk Management

What contingency plans are in place to get the business back into manufacturing?

The company did not have a disaster-recovery plan in place. To date, it has not suffered any unscheduled closings, but it does close twice a year for maintenance. In a discrete interview with the COO, he stated that the company was developing a disaster-recovery plan to meet the risk-assessment requirements of its insurance policy.

Technology – Tracking of Products, Customer Intelligence, and Market Basket Analysis

Customer relationship management (CRM) tools are standard for companies selling products.

The company does not have a standard CRM program in place. Orders are currently generated through phone and on-site sales.

Body of Report

- **Corporate Information**

  The company headquarters and manufacturing plant are located at 170 Dryer Road, Swisstown, in Morris County, New Jersey 07524. The phone number is (908) 555-4567 and its Web site is www.company.com. The company's research and development division is based in Tel Aviv, Israel, the original location of the company before it established its headquarters in the U.S. The company also has a small sales division based in New York, New York.

- **Company History and Current Standing**

  Written in paragraph form, discuss the history of the company, which is usually found on its Web site or in the annual report. In this section, detail the financial health of the company and add any other details that seem appropriate.

- **Management**

  List the management-team members, their positions, if they sit on any boards, and any biographies that can be located. Write any affiliations they may have outside of their particular company. If necessary, a principal report for each of the top managers should be conducted.

- **Board Positions**

  List the board members, their positions on the board, if they sit on any other boards and any short biographies that can be located about them.

- **Political Affiliations and Charitable Works**

  Companies also can have political affiliations. Be sure to mention if a company is sponsoring any fundraisers for one political party or the other. Note that companies will often play both sides and will not automatically discount any future powers.

  Companies often sponsor charitable events as well. Find out what is the cause or mission of the event. It might be connected to a personal matter for one of the company's chief officers. For example, if the chairman of the board's son has autism, there is a good chance that his company will be sponsoring a fundraiser to help raise autism awareness.

- **Certifications, Credentials, and Special Licenses**

  If your company holds a business license or has received special certifications in ISO[40] or other regulatory organizations, list each independently.

  - Certification
  - Expiration
  - Issuing Agency
  - Disciplinary actions, if any

- **Identified Assets**

  If you were conducting an asset investigation, this section would become voluminous, as you outlined the company's physical assets, such as property, automobiles, vessels, and possibly airplanes. However, standard reports should include subsidiaries, UCC filings, intellectual properties, and any low-hung assets worth mentioning.

- **Financial Assets**

  Financial assets to investigate and include are:

  - Subsidiaries
  - Stock ownership
  - UCCs
  - Vessels, Airplanes, and Automobiles
  - Intellectual Property F

- **Property**

  Following the APA Style Manual in citing works for papers, I use the same style guide for professional reports. See the following examples.

  Sample text using fonts from APA Style Manual:

  - Copyrights
    - Smith, J. (1999). *Fuel: Processing Methods*. Chicago, IL: CCR Publishing.
  - Patents
    - Smith, J. (1995). U.S. Patent No. 123,434. Washington, D.C.: U.S. Patent and Trademark Office.
  - Trademarks
    - Smith, J. (1995). Fuel Methods. Washington, D.C.: U.S. Patent and Trademark Office.

- **Legal Findings**

  Civil and criminal matters should be cited clearly and separately in this portion, just as in the principal report. Report criminal matters first. Make sure you know the search variables of the sources you used so that you can accurately report what was and was not searched. For example, many states only offer convictions history and do not indicate arrests without dispositions.

---

[40] International Organization for Standardization, see www.iso.com.

Example:

For the last seven years in (STATE), there were no convictions, misdemeanors, or felonies located.

A domestic dispute charge was filed in (COUNTY) on 12/24/1999.

Then list the details.

There are two format methods to use to report civil cases. The first example is reported as follows:

> *Case name*
> *Date filed*
> *Date terminated*
> *Office*
> *Nature of suit*
> *Cause*
> *Plaintiff*
> *Defendant*

If you notice names or further content in the dockets or summary, continue your listing with a short narrative. The second example is:

On January 15, 1999, ABC Company filed a breach-of-contract claim against the Smith Group in New York County Supreme Court. Defendants named, in addition to the Smith Group, were Kathy and John Smith. The case was voluntarily dismissed on June 9, 1999.

- **Regulatory, Sanction, and Disciplinary Issues**

  Reporting Regulatory Issues

  Online searches, through various U.S. regulatory agencies like the Office of Foreign Asset Control, the Central Contractors Registry, and the Excluded Parties Database, did not reveal any matches to the subject.

  Reporting Disciplinary Issues

  A search in the Health and Human Services Office of Inspector General did not reveal any matches to the subject. Nor were there any matches located in the State of Florida Disciplinary Actions database for physicians.

- **Financial Troubles**

  Liens and debts, caused by lawsuits or bankruptcies, are reported straightforward.

  Tax Liens – Judgments

  Company is seen to have an unsatisfied federal tax lien of $10,000 from 1998, registered in the state of Montana.

  Company has an unsatisfied judgment/lien for $5,000, resulting from a lawsuit filed in 1999 by the ABC Company.

Bankruptcies

Company filed for Chapter 11 bankruptcy protection on August 2, 1998. Bankruptcy was granted and a list of the debts and creditors can be provided, if requested.

You can list the creditors and the money owed, but appending or offering for further information later is better, unless you see something significant in the creditor's report.

* **Media**

The media findings should be reported in descending order. There are two schools of thought on how to report media issues and both are certainly acceptable.

You can summarize the story for brevity sake, which is a more professional approach to report writing. Sample:

    −   *Date – Source – Title*

        •   *Truncated article, italicized, justified, and indented .5 on each side.*

Or you can include key portions of the article, quoting it entirely, or paraphrasing the report. In some cases, this is necessary because the subject material may be beyond your comprehension of the topic, and the paraphrasing could turn out to be inaccurate. Sample:

    −   *Summary of article as follows.*

        •   *On June 2, 1996, the* New York Times *reported that Bob Smith was found guilty of racketeering.*

Disclaimer for Database Errors

Sometimes databases and online sources make mistakes, or the details cannot be verified. In the footer, on the last page of all my reports, I add the following statement to protect myself against errors and omissions that occur from badly obtained data:

> Information is obtained from a multitude of databases, records-keeping systems, and other sources, of which [Company Name] and/or its suppliers have no control. These are fallible, electronic and human sources. There can be absolutely no warranty expressed or implied as to the accuracy, completeness, timeliness, or availability of the records listed, nor to the fitness for the purpose of the recipient of such records or reports.

> Information provided may be limited or not totally current. There is absolutely no guarantee that the information exclusively pertains to the search criteria information, which was submitted by the requesting party.

Your reports have serious implications in the business world and the personal lives of people you investigate. Yet, as investigators we rely heavily on the database services we use, and albeit we try to discern and verify every last detail, no system, database or analysis is ever 100%

perfect. Take the time to consult with a business attorney or a veteran investigator to understand the implications of the information you are selling as a report. Also, consider talking with a business insurance specialist who sells Errors and Omissions Liability insurance, and make sure you understand what the policy will cover and what it will not.

In closing, be sure to conduct your own research on your exposure to the liabilities and risks within your individual industry.

Chapter 13

Establishing Your Costs and Client Invoicing

Establishing the Cost of the Report

Often for many investigators two of the more difficult tasks is recognizing their costs and mastering how to bill the client. With experience you can gauge and anticipate your costs; however, even seasoned investigators have been surprised by greater than anticipated expenses. For example, if a court document needs to be pulled, copied and sent to a client, what if it contained dozens of pages more than anticipated. If the copy fee is $1.00 page, and you quoted $5.00 instead of $55.00, you are in trouble. Between managing subcontractors, database costs, as well as any other reports purchased, the cost of conducting the investigation can skyrocket quickly.

Use a Tracking System

The best way to monitor these is to create a **tracking system** and **checklist**. There are Case Management Software Programs that provide this type of service. They can be quite helpful if you have large caseloads and even if you have many investigators working for you. However, a simple system where you write down each report that you pull and each database you use also works well. Create a checklist or file for each case, and list all the costs you encounter. Even generic check-book programs like *QuickBooks* or *Quicken* can be used for cost accounting purposes.

Another key point is to take advantage of cost tracking features that database and online vendors offer. For example, when you log into systems for ChoicePoint, Accurint, LexisNexis, Dun & Bradstreet, etc., use the place they provide to record a project name or number. Then, when invoices come in at the end of the month, just separate the costs by the respective names or numbers and record the figures as you would any other project cost. Be prepared for some slow-coming invoices, such as PACER which send bills quarterly.

Other costs in a case may involve hiring outside record retrievers, ordering unusual reports specific to the case, office expenses such as printing, binding and mailing the report, and the traditional expenses such as mileage, film (surveillance), meals, etc.

> **Author Tip** ➡ Make sure when you hire a public record retriever or sub-contractor in a foreign country, you clarify all the costs up front. In instances when costs are unsure (i.e. record retriever doesn't know how many pages until file is found), ask to be contacted to verify the final cost or set a limit of a dollar amount not to exceed with approval from you.

Tracking Database Costs

Database costs should be somewhat predictable if you pay by the report. The following is an example of an investigator's "hard" or true costs on a basic due diligence of one small US company with three executives—

- 3 comprehensive reports $60.00 @ $20 per report.
- 1 D&B Business Report $75.00
- 1 Experian Business Report $30.00
- 20 News Media articles - $60 @ $3.00 per story.

The investigator's hard cost for this case, for this particular set of searches, is $225.00.

However, if you pay a vendor by subscription or on an "all you can eat" program, then you have two choices.

1. If you know how many persons or companies you are investigating for the subscription's billing period, you can devise a simple matrix that will calculate the cost. And for goodness sake round up to make it easier.

2. Standardize your costs. Say you figure you average X cases a month that use a particular service, simply divide the subscription cost by X. If you have a busy month, then the better for you.

Tracking Your Time

There is one cost you do not want to forget. **Yourself!** Investigators often discount their own hours in order to keep the price down. Remember your client is hiring you for your skill set, not the fancy databases and marketing expertise you have. Do not ever discount your own fee; otherwise your client will expect a reduced fee every time and will not understand your value and your worth. If you want to impress a client, then slice a percentage off the bill, but explain that this is a special situation.

Billing the Client

After a few years of conducting the same types of investigations over and over again, you develop a sense of how much a case will cost. Nonetheless, if your normal procedure is to create invoices on the fly and by the seat of your pants, you are inviting trouble and establishing poor precedent. Using an established pricing method goes a long way to insure that you will not be losing money or overcharging when sending an invoice. It also sends a message to your clients that you are a professional service firm and have checks and balances in place for your own financial affairs. However, the invoice to the client should come out to them within 30 days of closing the case and sending the final report.

Marking Up your Hard Costs

A rule of thumb is to mark up or write up your hard costs for research work and database expenses for U.S. company searches by 15%. Increase the mark up for foreign searches, depending on the time it takes you to find and hire someone overseas to pull documents, research legal and business filings by hand.

Billing Models

The four most popular and efficient billing models are—

1. **By the Investigation**

2. **By the Hour**

3. **Time and Expense**

4. **Hybrid**

Charge by the investigation

This is a good method for repeat clients who regularly order the same types of investigations. They can anticipate cost and budget for it. However, you have to be careful when taking in the new project. A standard U.S. company due diligence may run a few thousand dollars, which is enough to do your job and make a profit. However, if a client orders a due diligence report on a much larger company, perhaps even foreign, with dozens of subsidiaries, you must realize that the case will need a larger budget. The trick is to always do a little pre-search on the company or person you are investigating first to get a sense of how large they are and how involved your investigation may be.

Charge by the Hour

Analyze your database costs in relation to the type of investigation and compare that hourly rate to your own hourly rate. For example, if you know your database costs always come in at about 20% of your hourly rate, then you can bump your hourly costs up by 20 to 25%. This enables you to give your client a flat hourly rate. Clients like to know they can anticipate costs by the hours you work and are not surprised with extra database costs on the invoice.

However, you have to be able to pre-assess which databases you will need to conduct your work and quote your client in hourly increments. If you believe you are going to need $1,000 dollars worth of reports and database costs before you even start, then use the next method by all means.

Time and Expense

This method combines a flat hourly rate for your time, plus the databases fees and reports that you provide. This is the fairest of billing methods, because it is the most detailed. However, the downside is that you will have to wait to bill the client until you to get all of your monthly invoices from all the vendors used. The client also might ask for a breakdown by database vendor on the invoice.

Hybrid

Hybrid is a combination of the above three billing styles. During the course of a "By the Investigation" billable case, you may come across information the client never anticipated and wants you to pursue. This is out of the scope of your original flat rate billable time, so now you have to charge additional fees. For example, four subsidiaries appear when the client thought it was only one. Now that you have to investigate the other three, calculate what it will cost including time involved and project a new budget to the client.

If your hourly rate is stated in the agreed upon Letter of Agreement, you must first clear the extra charges before proceeding. If you do not know how costly the additional direction of the investigation will be and if that doubt concerns your client, offer a few stopping points. Give yourself enough room in the budget to obtain what is needed initially and tell the client you will check in when you hit that budget amount.

Overall

Any one of these billable methods is acceptable, so long as you can remain consistent with your clients and they are fine with your billing methods.

If you have a fully staffed office, the third option might be best because an administrator can calculate the invoices by project numbers and database costs per the firms work. The first and second invoicing methods are easiest, but you should be able to produce your vendor invoices for specific database usage if necessary.

No matter which billing method you utilize **clear it with the customer before you start!** Have them agree to the price per job or price per hour in an email, fax or signed contract. A verbal agreement is not enough.

Occasionally a client may be unhappy about the amount of the invoice. If you met your obligations, did a terrific job, but the answer you returned was not what the client wanted to hear, stick by your guns. I have handed over pretty empty reports on occasion because there was nothing to be found. The report essentially highlighted all the places I looked and all the basic information discovered, but there was no fraud, as client claimed, and the company examined was on the up and up. I did my investigation, reported in as stated and invoiced the client. The client was upset because "you did not find anything." I clearly pointed out all the details of the investigation and that there was nothing to find and firmly told the client that the invoice would stay put.[41]

However, if you missed something in the report of if your work was sub par and there you are handing over a big invoice at the end, you will not see that client again.

Customer Satisfaction Pointers

When a client calls you to conduct an investigation, your purpose is to conduct the best investigation possible without compromising your ethics or your client's reputation when gathering information. You must pool that information, present a reasonably intelligent and smart looking report to the client and follow up after the client has had a chance to review the findings. The client's opinion of you and your work is based on bringing the client information that is accurate, timely and helpful to the decision making process.

The Follow-up Process

A week later, make sure to pick up the phone or send an email to the client, asking if there are any questions about the report. Surely there may be something in the document that might be very clear to you as the author; however, the client may not fully understand. This interaction will also give the client a chance to say what a great job you did or give the client a chance to comment on an aspect of the case you might have missed.

On the follow-up, there are **four questions** to remember to always ask–

1. Do you have any questions or concerns on the report I sent to you last week?

2. Was the report style to your liking? Or do you have a preference to layout or analysis methodology?

3. Is there anything you would like me to follow up on? (Refer the client to any recommendations you made.)

4. Is there any other investigation I may be of assistance with at this time? Or is there someone else in your practice or office that also may require an investigator.

Never be afraid to ask for additional work! The client knows you are in business. Just be professional about it and not annoying. If the client has nothing for you at the time and seems satisfied with what you sent, then ask a **final fifth question**—

5. Would you mind if I followed up in a few weeks to make sure there are no remaining issues on this case or solicit you for more work?

---

[41] A year later the other company sued my client for fraud. My client tried to establish a smear campaign using investigators to insinuate fraudulent activity, when the client was actually the suspicious party. I am SO GLAD I stuck to my findings!

One Last Comment

In the beginning of my practice I would never send work away. One month I was overwhelmed, but still accepted a rush case. Bad mistake. I missed key information which the client already knew about. The client pointed this out in the report and sent it back to me. My entire practice grounded to a halt and my credibility was on the line.

I threw myself on the sword, called the client and told him I would move all my other work out of the way, make him my number one priority. I promised to rebuild the entire report from scratch and would not charge a fee for the work. After sending the revised report, a week later I followed up with the client. He was still a bit hot about the issue, because my tardiness made him tardy. I offered to do the next report for free. He agreed and when the next case came through, I made sure it was stellar going out to him.

By that point, all was forgiven and I had saved what turned out to be a very valuable client and learned a very valuable lesson – never let quantity sacrifice quality.

In closing, I hope I have given you insight and education on how to perform quality business investigations. And I wish you the very best in your investigative endeavors.

Section 4

Appendix

Appendix 1   Sample Agreements

Agreement to Provide Investigative Services

Non-Disclosure Agreement

Appendix 2   Resource Lists – U.S.

Trade Journals and Industry Magazines

National Trade Associations with Investigation Interests

EPLS Contributing Agency List

State Web Sites with Free Access to Corporation and UCC Records

Appendix 3   Resource Lists – International

Foreign Security Identifiers

Company Extensions by Country

Patent and Trademarks Agencies

Enforcement Bodies

Appendix 4   Cynthia's Recommend Reading

Appendix 1

Sample Agreements

There are two sample agreements presented that business investigators will find useful—

- Agreement to Provide Investigative Services
- Non-Disclosure Agreement

Agreement to Provide Investigative Services

As an investigator, you should carry a standard form document that allows you to enter the specifics about the case and with the client. You can simply place this as a letter on company stationary. The information could include the following—

- Your company name, address and contact information
- Your client's name, address and contact information
- Date and time order placed
- Client instructions
- Any agreed upon specifics, like turnaround time or pricing
- Anticipated results, if applicable

Non-Disclosure Agreement

A Non-Disclosure Agreement (NDA) should be a standard item signed by both parties when an investigator takes on a new client. Every new client should ask you to sign their own NDA. If the client does do not suggest this, offer one of your own. The NDR can be part a package with the Letter of Agreement or the Contract for new clients. An NDA is especially important for compliance with federal regulations mentioned previously, such as SOX and HIPPA, but should be an expected requirement from all clients due to the sensitive nature of investigative work.

An NDA is especially important for compliance with federal regulations mentioned previously, such as SOX and HIPPA, but should be an expected requirement from all clients due to the sensitive nature of investigative work.

AGREEMENT TO PROVIDE INVESTIGATIVE SERVICES

THIS AGREEMENT, dated _____, is made **BETWEEN** the Client,

\<CLIENT NAME\>

whose address is _____

AND   **\<YOUR INVESTIGATIVE AGENCY\>**

whose address is _____

1. **Investigative Services to be Provided**

    Research of given parties such as companies and individuals to include public record, open source information and databases. Discreet inquires may also include interviews and site visits with client pre-approval.

2. **Legal Fees**

    A. Initial Payment. You agree to pay the INVESTIGATIVE AGENCY $x,xxx for fees and expenses in connection with services under this Agreement.

    B. Hourly Rate. You agree to pay the INVESTIGATIVE AGENCY for investigative services at the hourly rate of $xxx.xx per hour.

    C. Expenses. In addition to hourly rate, any expenses incurred such as database costs, report fees, any travel related costs, will be the responsibility of the Company.

    The INVESTIGATIVE AGENCY reserves the right to increase the above hourly rates after one year from the date hereof.

3. **Your Responsibility**

    You must fully cooperate with the INVESTIGATIVE AGENCY and provide all information relevant to the issues involved in this matter.

4. **Bills**

    The INVESTIGATIVE AGENCY will send you itemized bills from time to time.

5. Signatures

You and the INVESTIGATIVE AGENCY have read and agreed to this Agreement. The INVESTIGATIVE AGENCY has answered all of your questions and fully explained this Agreement to your complete satisfaction. You have been given a copy of this Agreement.

BY: INVESTIGATIVE AGENCY

_____

NAME

_____

POSITION

_____

DATE

BY: CLIENT

_____

CLIENT NAME

_____

POSITION

_____

DATE

MUTUAL NON-DISCLOSURE AGREEMENT

This Mutual Non-disclosure Agreement (this "Agreement") is entered into by CLIENT COMPANY ("CLIENT COMPANY"), and _____, a YOUR COMPANY ("Company"), effective as of _____, 200_.

BACKGROUND

CLIENT COMPANY and Company (each, a "Party", and collectively, the "Parties") intend to enter into discussions concerning a possible business transaction (the "Transaction").   In connection with those discussions, each Party will need to disclose certain of its confidential and proprietary information and materials to the other Party. The Parties wish to enter into this Agreement to provide for the disclosure of that confidential and proprietary information and to restrict the use and disclosure of that information and materials by the receiving Party.

The Parties agree as follows:

1. Definition of Confidential Information. "Confidential Information" means (a) information and materials that are identified in writing as CONFIDENTIAL at the time of disclosure, (b) information disclosed orally and subsequently identified in writing as CONFIDENTIAL within thirty days following the initial disclosure of such information, (c) information or materials that the disclosing Party treats as confidential and does not disclose publicly, or (d) the information and materials identified on Exhibit A to this Agreement.   The Party disclosing Confidential Information is referred to in this Agreement as the "Disclosing Party," and the Party receiving such Confidential Information is referred to as the "Receiving Party." The term "Confidential Information" includes any modifications or derivatives prepared by the Receiving Party that contain or are based upon Confidential Information disclosed by the Disclosing Party, including analysis, reports or summaries of that information. Notwithstanding anything to the contrary set forth herein, no provision in this Agreement is, or is intended to be construed as, a condition of confidentiality within the meaning of Sections 6011, 6111 or 6112 of the Internal Revenue Code of 1986, as amended, or the regulations thereunder, or any similar state legislation. The CLIENT COMPANY, Inc., and its subsidiaries and affiliates ("CLIENT COMPANY"), and each employee representative, or other agent of CLIENT COMPANY, may disclose to any and all persons, without limitation of any kind, the tax treatment and tax structure of any transaction within the scope of this Agreement that reduces or defers federal tax or state income or franchise taxes and all materials of any kind (including opinions or other tax analyses) that are provided to CLIENT COMPANY relating to such tax treatment or tax structure.

2. Limitations on Use. Confidential Information must be used by the Receiving Party only in connection with analysis of, and discussions concerning a proposed Transaction with the Disclosing Party as contemplated in the Background or as directed in writing by the Disclosing Party. Receiving Party must not use Confidential Information at any time, in any fashion, form or manner, for any other purpose.

3. Limitations on Disclosure. Receiving Party will use the same measures to protect the confidentiality of the Confidential Information that it uses to protect the confidentiality of its own proprietary and confidential information and materials of like kind, but in no event less than a reasonable standard of care. Receiving Party will take (and will cause its employees and agents to take) any steps required to avoid inadvertent disclosure of materials in Receiving Party's possession.

4. Access to the Confidential Information. Access to the Confidential Information must be restricted to personnel of Receiving Party engaged in the analysis and discussions concerning a possible Transaction with the Disclosing Party as contemplated in the Background Statement. Receiving Party will furnish access to the Confidential Information to its employees and third party contractors solely on a need-to-know basis. Each Party will furnish the other with a complete list of its employees and agents who have been furnished access to the Confidential Information of the other Party.

5. Ownership of Confidential Information. No Licenses. Confidential Information disclosed by the Disclosing Party to the Receiving Party will at all times remain the property of the Disclosing Party. No license under any trade secrets, copyrights, or other rights is granted under this Agreement or by any disclosure of Confidential Information under this Agreement.

6. Copies of Confidential Information. Confidential Information must not be copied or reproduced by Receiving Party without the Disclosing Party's prior written approval.

7. Return of Confidential Information. All Confidential Information made available under this Agreement, including copies of Confidential Information, must be returned to the Disclosing Party upon the termination of discussions concerning a possible Transaction between the Parties, or, if earlier, upon the request by the Disclosing Party. Any materials prepared by the Receiving Party which include any Confidential Information of the Disclosing Party, including summaries or extracts thereof, must be destroyed, and written certification of such destruction provided to the Disclosing Party.

8. Exceptions. Nothing in this Agreement will prohibit or limit Receiving Party's use of information (a) known to Receiving Party prior to disclosure by the Disclosing Party, (b) that is independently developed by the Receiving Party, without reference to the Confidential Information, or (c) that is or becomes publicly available through no breach of this Agreement by the Receiving Party.

9. Binding Agreement. This Agreement is and will be binding upon the Parties and each of their respective affiliates, and upon their respective heirs, successors, representatives and assigns.

10. Governing Law. The validity, performance, construction and effect of this Agreement will be governed by the laws of the State of <CLIENT COMPANY'S STATE>, without regard to that state's conflict of laws provisions.

11. Equitable Remedies. The Parties recognize that serious injury could result to the Disclosing Party and its business if the Receiving Party breaches its obligations under this Agreement. Therefore, Receiving Party agrees that the Disclosing Party will be entitled to a restraining order, injunction or other equitable relief if Receiving Party breaches its obligations under this Agreement, in addition to any other remedies and damages that would be available at law or equity.

12. Compelled Disclosures. If Receiving Party receives a subpoena or other validly issued administrative or judicial process demanding Confidential Information, Receiving Party must promptly notify Disclosing Party and tender to it the defense of that demand. Unless the demand has been timely limited, quashed or extended, Receiving Party will thereafter be entitled to comply with such demand to the extent permitted by law. If requested by the Disclosing Party, Receiving Party will cooperate (at the expense of the Disclosing Party) in the defense of a demand.

13. No Use of Names. Receiving Party may not use the name or logo of CLIENT COMPANY or any of its affiliates, or any abbreviation or adaptation thereof, in any advertising, trade display, or published statement or press release, or for any other commercial purpose, without the prior written consent of CLIENT COMPANY(in its sole discretion). The fact that the Parties are engaged in discussions concerning a Possible Business Arrangement, and the terms of those discussions, is Confidential Information and may not be disclosed for any purpose.

14. Non-Solicitation of Employees. During the tendency of discussions concerning a possible Transaction between the Parties, and for a period of one year following termination of such discussions, (a) neither Party will solicit the employment of any employee of the other Party, and (b) if a Party is approached by an employee of the other Party concerning employment, that Party will notify (or cause the employee to notify) the other Party before making an offer of employment.

15. Term; Survival of Obligations. This Agreement will terminate upon the first to occur of (1) termination of discussions between the Parties concerning the Transaction (or if a Transaction is entered into, upon termination of the Transaction), or (2) delivery of written notice of termination by either Party to the other Party. Following termination, the obligations of Receiving Party under this Agreement with respect to the Confidential Information of Disclosing Party will continue in full force and effect as follows: (a) in the case of any information or materials that constitute a trade secret within the meaning of applicable law, for as long as such information and materials remain as a trade secret, or (b) in the case of any other information or materials, for a term of two (2) years from the date of disclosures.

16. Interpretation. The following rules of interpretation must be applied in interpreting this Agreement: (1) the headings used in this Agreement are for reference and convenience only and will not enter into the interpretation of this Agreement, (2) the provisions of the Exhibits to this Agreement are incorporated into this Agreement, (3) as used in this Agreement, the term "including" will always be deemed to mean "including, without limitation," and (4) this Agreement shall not be construed against either Party as the drafter of this Agreement.

17. No Commitment. Nothing in this Agreement will constitute a commitment by either Party to develop or disclose any information or materials, including any Confidential Information, or to acquire or recommend any product, service or asset of the other Party. The provision of Confidential Information to Receiving Party as contemplated under this Agreement and discussions held in connection with the proposed business arrangement between the Parties will not prevent either Party from pursuing similar discussions with third parties or obligate either Party to continue discussions with the other Party, nor will either Party otherwise be obligated to take, continue or forego any action with respect to the proposed business arrangement.

Disclosing Party makes no warranty as to the accuracy or completeness of any information or materials provided in connection with this Agreement.

18. Entire Agreement. This Agreement constitutes the entire agreement and understanding of the Parties with respect to the subject matter of this Agreement and supersedes all prior discussions and agreements, either oral or written, relating to the subject matter of this Agreement.

Agreed and Accepted: Agreed and Accepted:

CLIENT COMPANY   *[COMPANY]*

By:_____   By:_____
        [Signature]   *[Signature]*

_____   _____
        [Title]   *[Title]*

_____   _____
        [Date]   *[Date]*

EXHIBIT A

CONFIDENTIAL INFORMATION

Confidential Information will include:

1. All application, operating system, database, communications and other computer software, whether now or hereafter existing, and all modifications, enhancements, and versions thereof and all options with respect thereto, and all future products developed or derived there from;

2. All source and object codes, flowcharts, algorithms, coding sheets, routines, sub-routines, compilers, assemblers, design concepts and related documentation and manuals, and methodologies used in the design, development and implementation of software products;

3. Marketing and product plans, customer lists, prospect lists, and pricing information (other than published price lists);

4. Financial information and reports;

5. Employee and contractor data; and

6. Research and development plans and results.

EXHIBIT B

FORM OF EMPLOYEE ACKNOWLEDGMENT

The undersigned is an employee of _____ ("Receiving Party"), and, in connection with such employment, is being furnished access to confidential and proprietary materials of _____. ("Disclosing Party"). The undersigned has been advised and acknowledges that such materials are the confidential and proprietary materials of Disclosing Party, the use and disclosure of which is subject to the terms and conditions of a Non-Disclosure Agreement between Disclosing Party and Receiving Party effective as of _____, 200_, and the undersigned agrees to comply with the terms and conditions of such nondisclosure agreement.

_____
[Name]

_____
[Date]

Appendix 2

Resource Lists – U.S.

Appendix 2 provides five useful resource lists to investigators—

- Trade Journals and Industry Magazines
- National Trade Associations with Investigation Interests
- The Excluded Parties List System (EPLS) Contributors
- State Links with Free Web Access to Corporation & Business Entity Records
- State Links with Free Web Access to UCC Filing Index or Records

Trade Journals and Industry Magazines

American Painting Contractor	www.paintmag.com
Appliance Design Magazine	www.appliancedesign.com
Architectural Record	www.archrecord.construction.com
Architecture Magazine	www.architecturemagazine.com
Architecture Week	www.architectureweek.com
Ask Chemical Engineering	www.AskaChE.com
Builder Online	www.builderonline.com
BUILDERnews	http://bnmag.com
Building Operating Management Magazine	www.facilitiesnet.com/bom
Building Operations and Management Magazines	www.facilitiesnet.com
Buildings Magazine Online	www.buildings.com
Commercial Construction Magazine	www.cc-mag.net
Construction News	www.constructionnews.net

Contracting Business Magazine -	www.contractingbusiness.com
EC&M News – for Electrical Professionals	http://ecmweb.com
EE Times (for technology engineers)	www.eetimes.com
Electrical Business Online	www.ebmag.com
Electrical Contractor Magazine	www.ecmag.com
Electrical Wholesaling	www.ewweb.com
Electronic Product News Online	www.epn-online.com
Electronic Products	www2.electronicproducts.com
Elevator World	www.elevator-world.com
Engineer Supply	www.engineersupply.com
Engineered Systems	www.esmagazine.com
ENREngineeringNew-Record	http://enr.construction.com/Default.asp
Environmental News Network	www.enn.com
Evaluation Engineering	www.evaluationengineering.com
Facility Care	www.facilitycare.com
Flooring Magazine	www.flooringmagazine.com
Glass Magazine	www.glassmsgazine.com
Heavy Equipment	www.mylittlesalesman.com
Home Appliance Magazine	www.appliance.com
HPAC Interactive	http://hpac.com
HVACR Business News	www.hvacrbusiness.com
Industrial Maintenance & Plant Operation Magazine	www.impomag.com
Industry Week	www.industryweek.com
International Risk Management Institute (IRMI)	www.irmi.com
International Water Power & Dam Construction	www.waterpowermagazine.com
Land Development Today	www.sldtonline.com
Maintenance Solutions Magazine	www.facilitiesnet.com/ms
METALmag	www.metalmag.com
Modern Power Systems	www.modernpowersystems.com
National Work Zone Safety Information	www.workzonesafety.org
Nuclear Engineering International	www.neimagazine.com
Painters Chat Room	www.painterschatroom.com
Pavement Magazine	www.forconstructionpros.com
Planning Commissioners Journal	http://pcj.typepad.com

Plant Services Online Magazine	www.plantservices.com
Portable Restroom Operator	www.1promag.com
Power Magazine	www.powermag.com
R.S. Means (construction costs)	www.rsmeans.com
Remodeling Online Magazine	www.remodeling.hw.net
Roofing Contractor Online Magazine	www.roofingcontractor.com
SCRAP Magazine	www.scrap.org
Stone World	www.stoneworld.com
The Metal Building Network	www.metalbuilding.net
The Newsmagazine of Mechanical Contracting	www.contractormag.com
Today's Facility Manager -	www.todaysfacilitymanager.com
Transmission & Distribution World (TD World)	http://tdworld.com
Trenchless Technology Online Magazine	www.trenchlessonline.com
Underspace	www.underspace.com
Window & Door Magazine	www.windowanddoor.com
Workplace HR & Safety	www.workplacemagazine.com

Links Lists to Multiple Magazines

www.acbj.com	42 links to city business journals
www.forconstructionpros.com	5 magazines focused on concrete and paving
www.freeconstructionmagazines.com	Free Construction Magazines
www.govcon.com	12+ government magazines plus other features
www.HVACPortal.com	Links to 14 online magazines

National Trade Associations With Investigation Interests

NALA	National Association of Legal Assistants	www.nala.org
NALI	National Association of Legal Investigators	www.nalionline.org
NALSC	National Association of Legal Search Consultants	www.nalsc.org
NAMSS	National Association of Medical Staff Svcs	www.namss.org
NAPBS	National Association of Professional Background Screeners	www.napbs.com
NAPPS	National Association of Professional Process Servers	www.napps.org
NAPIA	National Association of Public Insurance Adjustors	www.napia.com
NAREIT	National Association of Real Estate Investment Trusts	www.reit.org
NARPM	National Association of Residential Property Managers	www.narpm.org
NASA	National Association of Screening Agencies	www.n-a-s-a.com
NAWBO	National Association of Women Business Owners	www.nawbo.org
ESA	Electronic Security Association (was National Burglar & Fire Alarm Association)	www.alarm.org
NCISS	National Council of Investigation & Security Services	www.nciss.org
NCRA	National Court Reporters Association	www.verbatimreporters.com
NCRA	National Credit Reporting Association	www.ncrainc.org
NDIA	National Defender Investigator Association	www.ndia.net
NFIB	National Federation of Independent Businesses	www.nfib.com
NFPA	National Federation of Paralegal Associations	www.paralegals.org/
NFIP	National Flood Insurance Program	www.fema.gov/business/nfip
NGS	National Genealogical Society	www.ngsgenealogy.org
NHRA	National Human Resources Association	www.humanresources.org
NICB	National Insurance Crime Bureau	www.nicb.org
NLG	National Lawyers Guild	www.nlg.org
NPPRA	National Public Record Research Association	www.nprra.org
NSA	National Sheriffs' Association	www.sheriffs.org
PBUS	Professional Bail Agents of the United States	www.pbus.com
PIHRA	Professionals in Human Resources Association	www.pihra.org
PRRN	Public Record Retriever Network	www.brbpub.com/prrn
REIPA	Real Estate Information Providers Association	www.reipa.org
SCIP	Society of Competitive Intelligence Professionals	www.scip.org
SFSA	Society of Former Special Agents of the FBI	www.socxfbi.org
SHRM	Society of Human Resources Management	www.shrm.org
SILA	Society of Insurance License Administrators	www.sila.org
SIIA	Software & Information Industry Association	www.siia.net
SLA	Special Libraries Association	www.sla.org
W.A.D	World Association of Detectives	www.wad.net

EPLS Contributing Agency List

The Excluded Parties List System (EPLS) EPLS contains information on individuals and firms which have been excluded by over the federal government agencies listed below from receiving federal contracts or federally approved subcontracts, and certain types of federal financial and non-financial assistance and benefits.

- Agency for International Development
- Appalachian Regional Commission
- Broadcasting Board of Governors
- Bureau of Industry and Security
- Commission on Civil Rights
- Consumer Product Safety Commission
- Corporation for National Service
- Customs and Border Protection
- Defense Information Systems Agency
- Defense Logistics Agency
- Defense Logistics Agency DLA-DG
- Defense Threat Reduction Agency
- Department of Agriculture
- Department of Agriculture USDA
- Department of Commerce
- Department of Defense
- Department of Education
- Department of Energy
- Department of Energy DOE-MAS
- Department of Health and Human Services
- Department of Homeland Security
- Department of Housing and Urban Development
- Department of Interior
- Department of Justice
- Department of Labor
- Department of Navy
- Department of State
- Department of State STATE-AOPE
- Department of the Air Force
- Department of the Army
- Department of Transportation
- Department of Treasury
- Department of Treasury TREAS-DO
- Department of Veterans Affairs

- Environmental Protection Agency
- Equal Employment Opportunity Commission
- Export-Import Bank of the United States
- Farm Credit Administration
- Federal Aviation Administration
- Federal Communications Commission
- Federal Deposit Insurance Corporation
- Federal Election Commission
- Federal Emergency Management Agency
- Federal Highway Administration
- Federal Labor Relations Authority
- Federal Law Enforcement Training Center
- Federal Mediation and Concilation Service
- Federal Motor Carrier Safety Administration
- Federal Railroad Administration
- Federal Trade Commission
- Federal Transit Administration
- General Services Administration
- Government Accountability Office
- Government Printing Office
- Headquarters Procurement Operations
- Immigration and Customs Enforcement
- Institute of Museum and Library Services
- Maritime Administration
- Missile Defense Agency
- National Aeronautics and Space Administration
- National Archives and Records Administration
- National Endowment for the Arts
- National Endowment for the Humanities
- National Geospatial-Intelligency Agency
- National Highway Traffic Safety Administration
- National Imagery Mapping Agency
- National Labor Relations Board
- National Nuclear Security Administration
- National Science Foundation
- Nuclear Regulatory Commission
- Office of Foreign Assets Control
- Office of Management and Budget
- Office of Personnel Management
- Office of the Secretary/Department of Transportation
- Overseas Private Investment Corporation

- Panama Canal Commission
- Peace Corps
- Pipeline and Hazardous Materials Administration
- Postal Service
- Railroad Retirement Board
- Research and Innovative Technology Administration
- Research and Special Programs Administration
- Small Business Administration
- Social Security Administration
- Transportation Security Administration
- U.S. Coast Guard
- U.S. International Trade Commission
- U.S. Secret Service
- U.S. Trade and Development

State Links with Free Web Access to Corporation & Business Entity Records

Alabama	http://www.sos.alabama.gov/BusinessServices/Default.aspx
Alaska	https://myalaska.state.ak.us/business/
Arizona – eFilings Search	https://edocket.azcc.gov/
Arizona - Registered Name Search	http://starpas.azcc.gov/scripts/cgiip.exe/WService=wsbroker1/main.p
Arkansas,	http://www.sos.arkansas.gov/corps/
California	http://kepler.ss.ca.gov/
Colorado	http://www.sos.state.co.us/pubs/business/main.htm
Connecticut	http://www.concord-sots.ct.gov/CONCORD/index.jsp
Delaware	https://delecorp.delaware.gov/tin/GINameSearch.jsp
Florida	http://www.sunbiz.org
Georgia - Site 1	https://corp.sos.state.ga.us/corp/soskb/login.asp
Georgia - Site 2	http://www.ganet.org/services/corp/individual.html
Hawaii	http://hawaii.gov/dcca/breg/online/
Idaho	http://www.accessidaho.org/public/sos/corp/search.html?SearchFormstep=crit
Illinois	http://www.ilsos.gov/corporatellc/
Indiana	http://www.in.gov/sos/business/index.htm
Iowa	http://www.sos.state.ia.us/corp/corp_search.asp
Kansas	http://www.accesskansas.org/srv-corporations/index.do
Kentucky	http://sos.ky.gov/business/filings/online/
Louisiana	http://www.sos.louisiana.gov/
Maine	https://icrs.informe.org/nei-sos-icrs/ICRS
Maryland	http://www.dat.state.md.us/sdatweb/charter.html
Massachusetts	http://corp.sec.state.ma.us/corp/corpsearch/corpsearchinput.asp
Michigan	http://www.cis.state.mi.us/bcs_corp/sr_corp.asp
Minnesota	http://da.sos.state.mn.us/minnesota/corp_inquiry-find.asp?:Norder_item_type_id=10&sm=7
Mississippi	http://www.sos.state.ms.us/busserv/corp/soskb/csearch.asp
Missouri	https://www.sos.mo.gov/BusinessEntity/soskb/csearch.asp
Montana	https://app.mt.gov/bes/
Nebraska	https://www.nebraska.gov/sos/corp/corpsearch.cgi?nav=search
Nevada	https://esos.state.nv.us/SOSServices/AnonymousAccess/CorpSearch/CorpSearch.aspx
New Hampshire	https://www.sos.nh.gov/corporate/soskb/csearch.asp
New Jersey	https://accessnet.state.nj.us/home.asp

New Mexico	http://www.nmprc.state.nm.us/cii.htm
New York	http://appsext8.dos.state.ny.us/corp_public/CORPSEARCH.ENTITY_SEARCH_ENTRY
North Carolina	http://www.secretary.state.nc.us/Corporations/
North Dakota	https://secure.apps.state.nd.us/sc/busnsrch/busnSearch.htm
Ohio	http://www.sos.state.oh.us/SOS/Uniform%20Commercial%20Code.aspx
Oklahoma	https://www.sos.ok.gov/corp/corpInquiryFind.aspx
Oregon	http://egov.sos.state.or.us/br/pkg_web_name_srch_inq.login
Pennsylvania	https://www.corporations.state.pa.us/corp/soskb/csearch.asp?corpsNav=|
Rhode Island	http://ucc.state.ri.us/CorpSearch/CorpSearchInput.asp
South Carolina	http://www.scsos.com/corp_search.htm
South Dakota	http://apps.sd.gov/applications/st32cprs/soscorplookup.aspx
Tennessee	http://tnbear.tn.gov/ECommerce/FilingSearch.aspx
Texas	www.sos.state.tx.us/corp/sosda/index.shtml
Texas	https://ourcpa.cpa.state.tx.us/coa/Index.html
Utah	http://www.utah.gov/services/business.html?type=citizen
Vermont	http://www.sec.state.vt.us/seek/corpseek.htm
Virginia	http://docket.scc.virginia.gov:8080/vaprod/main.asp
Virginia	http://www.scc.virginia.gov/clk/bussrch.aspx
Washington	http://www.sos.wa.gov/corps/search.aspx
West Virginia	http://apps.sos.wv.gov/wvcorporations/
Wisconsin	https://www.wdfi.org/apps/CorpSearch/Search.aspx?
Wyoming	https://wyobiz.wy.gov/

State Links with Free Web Access to UCC Filing Index or Records

Note: If a state is not listed, then the record access requires a subscription. Below is a Free List only.

Alabama	http://www.sos.alabama.gov/BusinessServices/Default.aspx
Alaska	http://dnr.alaska.gov/ssd/ucc/search.cfm
Arizona	www.azsos.gov/scripts/ucc_search.dll
California	https://uccconnect.ss.ca.gov/acct/acct-login.asp
Colorado	www.sos.state.co.us/pubs/business/search_records.htm
Connecticut	http://www.concord-sots.ct.gov/CONCORD/online?sn=InquiryServlet&eid=199
District of Columbia	www.washington.dc.us.landata.com
Florida	www.floridaucc.com/pls/ucc/searchoptions
Georgia	www.gsccca.org/search/
Hawaii	http://hawaii.gov/dlnr/boc
Idaho	https://www.accessidaho.org/secure/sos/liens/search.html
Illinois	www.ilsos.gov/UCC/
Indiana	https://secure.in.gov/sos/bus_service/online_ucc/browse/default.asp
Iowa	http://iowalandrecords.org/portal/
Iowa	www.sos.state.ia.us/Search/UCC/search.aspx?ucc
Iowa (Non-RA-9)	www.sos.state.ia.us/Search/UCCAlternative/search.aspx
Kansas	www.accesskansas.org/srv-corporations/index.do
Kentucky	http://apps.sos.ky.gov/business/ucc/(brfzfm55yycrzh450ow2ml55)/search.aspx
Maine	www.maine.gov/sos/cec/corp/debtor_index.shtml
Maryland	http://sdatcert3.resiusa.org/ucc-charter/
Massachusetts	http://corp.sec.state.ma.us/uccFiling/uccSearch/Default.aspx
Michigan	http://apps.michigan.gov/UCC/Home.aspx
Minnesota	http://da.sos.state.mn.us/minnesota/ucc_order/ucc_filing_search.asp?sm=10
Mississippi	http://www.sos.ms.gov/business_services_ucc2.aspx
Missouri	www.sos.mo.gov/ucc/soskb/searchstandardRA9.asp
Montana	https://esos.state.nv.us/NVUCC/user/login.asp
Nevada	https://esos.state.nv.us/NVUCC/user/login.asp
New Jersey	https://www.state.nj.us/treasury/revenue/dcr/filing/ucc_lead.htm
New Mexico	https://secure.sos.state.nm.us/ucc/soskb/SearchStandardRA9.asp
New York	http://appsext8.dos.state.ny.us/pls/ucc_public/web_search.main_frame
North Carolina	www.secretary.state.nc.us/ucc/
North Dakota	www.nd.gov/sos/businessserv/centralindex/direct-access-searches.html
Ohio	www.sos.state.oh.us/sos/ucc/UCC.aspx?Section=101
Oklahoma	http://countyclerk.oklahomacounty.org/UCC-SearchSite.html

Oregon	http://ucc.sos.state.or.us/ucc/soskb/SearchStandardRA9.asp
Pennsylvania	https://www.corporations.state.pa.us/ucc/soskb/SearchStandardRA9.asp
Rhode Island	http://ucc.state.ri.us/psearch/
South Carolina	www.scsos.com/uccsearch.htm
Tennessee	www.ja.state.tn.us/sos/iets3/ieuc/PgUCCSearch.jsp
Utah	https://secure.utah.gov/uccsearch/uccs
Vermont	www.sec.state.vt.us/seek/ucc_seek.htm
Virginia	www.scc.virginia.gov/division/clk/diracc.htm
Washington	https://fortress.wa.gov/dol/ucc/
West Virginia	www.wvsos.com/UccSearch/index-noecomm.aspx
Wisconsin	www.wdfi.org/ucc/search/

Appendix 3

Resource Lists - International

Appendix 3 contains four very useful lists.

- Foreign Security Identifiers
- Company Extensions by Country
- Foreign Government Agencies for Trademarks and Patents
- Foreign Enforcement Bodies

The first two lists come from the **Winthrop Corporation**. The author and the publisher both wish to thank the Winthrop Corporation for giving us permission to include this excellent material herein. Please visit www.CorporateInformation.com for details on the competitive analysis and research that the Winthrop Corporation provides to clients.

Foreign Security Identifiers

Bonds and Stocks usually have one or more identifier codes, issued by various clearing houses or other agencies. The purpose of these identifiers is to prevent confusion when discussing a particular security, particularly a bond. While a company will usually only have one class of stock, it can have many different bond issues. The following is a list of various security identifiers along with information about their structure and issuers.

ID	Description
Cedel	No longer used; replaced by the Common Code on January 1, 1991.
CIN	CUSIP International Number. Used for non-U.S. and non-Canadian securities. Nine characters. The first character is always a letter, which represents the country of issue. The country codes are as follows: A=Austria, B=Belgium, C=China, D=Germany, E=Spain, F=France, G=Great Britain, H=Switzerland, J=Japan, K=Denmark, L=Luxembourg, M= MiddleEast, N=Netherlands P= South America, Q=Australia, R=Norway, S=South Africa, T= Italy, U= United States, V =Africa(Other), W= Sweden, X=Europe (Other), Y=Asia. The next five characters are numbers which represent the issuer, followed by two digits representing the security. The final digit is the check digit.

Common Code	Issued in Luxembourg, replaces CEDEL and Euroclear codes. Nine digits. Final digit is a check digit, computed on a multiplicative system.
CUSIP	Committee on Uniform Securities Identification Procedures. Standard & Poor's assigns a nine character code to stocks and bonds. The first six characters identify the issuer. The next two characters represent the security that was issued, and the ninth character is a check digit, which is computed using a modulus 10 double add double calculation. For Canadian and U.S. securities, the first character is always a digit. Other countries use an alphabetic first character. See CIN number, above.
Euroclear	Not used anymore; replaced by the Common Code on January 1, 1991.
ISIN	International Securities Identification Number. This is a twelve character code developed by the International Standards Organization (ISO) that represents a security. The first two letters always represent the country code, and the ISO standards are used. Basically, these are the same two letters as used in Internet addresses (however GB, not UK, is used for the United Kingdom of Great Britain and Northern Ireland). The next nine characters usually use some other code, such as CUSIP in the United States, SEDOL in Great Britain, etc. Leading spaces are padded with 0. The final digit is the check digit, also computed with modulus 10 double add double, but it is different from the method used in CUSIP's.
RIC	Reuter Identification Code. Used on the Reuters Terminal to pull up a particular security. When an equal sign is the last character, that symbol is a master RIC. An RIC that has an equal sign followed by some additional letters means that this string contains the price quoted by some entity. That entity is denoted by those letters following the equal sign.
SEDOL	Stock Exchange Daily Official List. Securities identification code issued by the London Stock Exchange. Has a built in check digit system.
SIC	Standard Industrial Code. Denotes the company's line of business. Does not symbolize a security.
SICC	Security Identification Code Conference. Used in Japan instead of ticker symbols, usually four digits.
Sicovam	Société Interprofessional Pour La Compensation des Valeurs Mobiliers. Used in France.
SVM	Used in Belgium.
Valoren	Identifier for Swiss securities. No check digit system.
Wertpapier Kenn-nummer	Issued in Germany by the Wertpapier Mitteilungen. Six digits, no check digit. Different ranges of numbers represent different classes of securities. Sometimes called WPK. Note that this number has widespread use in Germany: much more so than the CUSIP in the United States, for instance.
WKN	See Wertpapier Kenn-Nummer.
WPK	See Wertpapier Kenn-Nummer.

Company Extensions by Country

This page provides definitions of company "extensions" and security identifiers. While U.S. companies are usually followed by "Inc.", many foreign companies have different endings. This section tells what these terms mean, and where they are used. If you don't know what country a company is based in, this list of identifiers might help narrow your search.

Ext.	Country	Description
A. en P.	Mexico	*Asociación en Participación.* Joint venture
AB	Sweden	*Aktiebolag.* Stock company -- can be publicly-traded or privately-held. In Sweden, privately-held AB's must have capital of at least SEK 100,000 upon incorporation. AB's are also required to allocate at least 10% of the profits for reserves per year until reserves are at least 20% of the start-up capital. Publicly-traded AB's in Sweden must have capital of at least SEK 500,000. There must be at least three board members for Swedish AB's. An Annual General Meeting is required. AB's are registered with the Swedish Patent and Registration Office (*Patent- och Registreringsverket* or PRV). The Swedish automobile and aircraft manufacturer SAAB is actually an acronym -- Svenska Aeroplan Aktiebolaget. Aktiebolaget is sometimes used instead of Aktiebolag, since the definite article is appended to the end of the word in Swedish (Aktiebolaget means THE stock company whereas Aktiebolag means just Stock Company).
AB	Finland	*Aktiebolag.* In Finland, many companies use both this Swedish abbreviation and the Finnish language Oy designation, since Finland is a bilingual country. In Finland, an AB is only private (Apb is the public equivalent).
A.C.	Mexico	*Asociación Civil.* Civil Association of a non-commercial nature.
ACE	Portugal	*Agrupamento Complementar de Empresas.* Association of businesses
AD	Bulgaria	*Aktzionerno Druzhestvo.* Limited Liability company, can be publicly-traded.
AE	Greece	*Anonymos Etairia.* Limited company. Must have a board of three to nine members.
AG	Austria	*Aktiengesellschaft.* Translates to "stock corporation". Minimum share capital is ATS 1 million. Par value of each share must be ATS 100, ATS 500, or a multiple of ATS 1,000. As in Germany, an Austrian AG must have both a *Vorstand* and an *Aufsichtsrat*.
AG	Germany	*Aktiengesellschaft.* Translates to "stock corporation." In Germany, all publicly traded companies are AG's, but not all AG's are publicly traded. AG's have two sets of boards -- the *Vorstand*, which usually consists of the CEO, CFO and other top management, and an *Aufsichtsrat*, which translates to "supervisory board," which has the function of overseeing management and representing the shareholders. German law prohibits individuals from being members of both boards at the same time. AG's in Germany require a minimum of DM 100,000 share capital and at least five shareholders at incorporation. Minimum par value for shares is DM 50.

AG	Switzerland	*Aktiengesellschaft.* Translates to "stock corporation." In Switzerland, AG's must have at least CHF 100,000 share capital, and each share must be at least CHF 0.01 par value. When a Swiss entity registers as an AG, 3% of the capital must be paid to the authorities as a Tax if the share capital is equal to or more than CHF 250,000. There must be three shareholders (although they can be nominees). An annual audit is required, and an annual directors meeting and shareholders meetings must be held in Switzerland.
AL	Norway	*Andelslag.* Co-operative society.
		Note: this was formerly written as A.L. and A/L, but financial law reform has dictated that periods and slashes should no longer be used.
AmbA	Denmark	*Andelsselskab.*
ANS	Norway	*Ansvarlig selskap.* Trading partnership.
Apb	Finland	*Publikt Aktiebolag.* Public limited company. This is the Swedish language equivalent to the more commonly used Oyj in Finland. Finland is technically bilingual, so this could be used, but it is not likely.
ApS	Denmark	*Anpartsselskab.* Limited liability corporation, required minimum share capital of DKK 200,000.
ApS & Co. K/S	Denmark	Similar to a K/S, but the entity with unlimited liability is a company (ApS) instead of an individual.
AS	Norway	*Aksjeselskap,* translates to "stock company," and gives owners limited liability. In Norway, publicly traded companies now use the ASA notation, and no longer use this notation. Private companies still use this AS notation. An AS requires minimum share capital of NOK 100,000, of which at least 50% must be paid up at incorporation.
		Note: this was formerly written as A.S. and A/S, but financial law reform has dictated that periods and slashes should no longer be used.
A/S	Denmark	*Aktieselskap,* translates to "stock company", and gives the owners limited liability. Danish companies require minimum share capital of DKK 500,000.
A.S.	Czech Republic	*Akciova spolecnost.* Joint stock company. Owners have limited liability. Share capital must be at least CZK 1 million. The company must put at least 20% of the capital into a reserve fund, which is funded by after-tax profits. The accounts must be audited annually. There must be at least three members on the board of directors, and each member must be a Czech citizen or resident.
A.S.	Estonia	*Aktsiaselts,* Joint Stock company.
A.S.	Slovakia	*Akciova Spolocnost,* Joint stock company
A.S.	Turkey	*Anonim Sirket,* a limited liability company
ASA	Norway	*Allmennaksjeselskap.* Stock company. This acronym was chosen because Aas is a very common surname in Norway, which might have created some confusion. Since 1996, all publicly traded Norwegian companies are now incorporated in this legal structure, but not all ASA's are publicly traded.
		Note: this was formerly written as A.S.A. and A/S/A, but financial law reform has dictated that periods and slashes should no longer be used.

AVV	Aruba	*Aruba Vrijgestelde Vennootschap.* Aruba Exempt Company. This type of company is intended for non-residents of Aruba: and such a company pays no taxes (but must instead pay an annual registration fee of AFl 500, or about US$280). Registered or bearer shares may be issued, and preference shares are also allowed. Minimum share capital is AFl 10,000. There are no financial statements that are required to be filed, but there must be representation by a local Aruban company (usually a Trust Agent).
Bpk	South Africa	*Beperk*
Bt	Hungary	*Beteti társaság.* Limited liability partnership.
B.V.	Belgium	*Besloten Vennootschap.* Limited liability company.
B.V.	Netherlands	*Besloten Vennootschap..* Limited liability company. Capital of at least 40,000 NLG is required to start a BV.
B.V.	Netherlands Antilles	*Besloten Vennootschap.* Limited liability company. Many companies incorporated in the Netherlands Antilles are merely shells created for tax purposes.
BVBA	Belgium	*Besloten Vennootschap met Beperkte Aansprakelijkheid.* Flemish language equivalent of the SPRL. It means that the company is a private limited company. Capital must be at least BEF 750,000, with at least BEF 250,000 paid up.
CA	Ecuador	*Compania anonima.*
Corp.	USA	*Corporation.* Same meaning as Incorporated.
C.V.	Netherlands	*Commanditaire Vennootschap.* Limited Partnership. One partner must have unlimited liability, and the others can have limited liability.
CVA	Belgium	*Commanditaire Vennootschap op Aandelen. Limited partnership with shares. Flemish language equivalent to the French language SCA*
CVoA	Netherlands	*Commanditaire Vennootschap op Andelen.* Limited Partnership, with shares
DA	Norway	*Selskap med delt ansar.* Limited Partnership
		Note: this was formerly written as D.A. and D/A, but financial law reform has dictated that periods and slashes should no longer be used.
d/b/a	USA	*Doing Business As.* Used often by individuals who want to have a business name, but don't want to incorporate. Companies also use this designation when they operate under a name other than the owner's personal name or the name of a filed corporation/LLC.
d.d.	Croatia	*Dionicko drustvo.* Joint stock company.
d.d.	Slovenia	*Delniska druzba.* Stock company -- all publicly traded companies must have this structure. Must have capital of SIT 3 million, and each share must have par value of SIT 1,000. Minimum of five shareholders.
d.n.o.	Slovenia	*Druzba z neomejeno odgovornostjo.* Partnership -- all partners have unlimited liability.
d.o.o.	Croatia	*Drustvo s ogranicenom odgovornoscu..* Limited Liability company.
d.o.o.	Slovenia	*Druzba z omejeno odgovornostjo.* Limited Liability company. Must have a share capital of at least SIT 1.5 million, and each partner must invest at least SIT 10,000.
EE	Greece	*Eterrorrythmos.* Limited liability partnership.

EEG	Austria	*Eingetragene Erwerbsgesellschaft.* Professional Partnership.
EIRL	Peru	*Empresa Individual de Responsabilidad Limitada.* Personal business with limited liability.
ELP	Bahamas	*Exempted Limited Partnership.* Has one or more limited partners, and one general partner, which must be a resident of the Bahamas or a company incorporated in the Bahamas. Cannot conduct business in the Bahamas, but may conduct business elsewhere. Usually set up for tax purposes.
EOOD	Bulgaria	*Ednolichno Druzhestvo s Ogranichena Otgovornost.* Limited liability company. Requires only one shareholder.
EPE	Greece	*Etairia periorismenis evthinis.* Limited liability company.
EURL	France	*Enterprise Unipersonnelle à Responsabilité Limitée.* Sole proprietorship with limited liability.
e.V.	Germany	*Eingetragener Verein.* Non profit society/association.
GbR	Germany	*Gesellschaft burgerlichen Rechts.* Partnership without a legal name. Mainly used for non-commercial purposes. Partners have full liability.
GCV	Belgium	*Gewone Commanditaire Vennootschap.* Limited Partnership. The Flemish language equivalent to the French language SCS.
GesmbH	Austria	See GmbH. This abbreviation is only used in Austria (not Germany or Switzerland).
GIE	France	*Groupement d'intéret économique.* Economic Grouping of Interest. Two or more persons or entities form an alliance with the goal of facilitating or developing economic activity of the members.
GmbH & Co. KG	Germany	Like a KG, but the entity with unlimited liability is a GmbH instead of a person. (See the KG entry for more information).
GmbH	Austria	*Gesellschaft mit beschränkter Haftung.* Translates to "Company with limited liability." In Austria, this is often GesmbH, although this abbreviation is not used in Germany or Switzerland. In Austria, there must be at least two founding shareholders of a GmbH. Insurance companies and mortgage banking companies are not permitted to exist in this form. Minimum share capital is ATS 500,000, and at least half of this must be raised in cash. Minimum par value is ATS 1,000 per share. No citizenship or residence requirement for shareholders exists, and shareholders can be other companies. A general meeting must be held at least annually. If an Austrian GmbH controls companies with 300 or more employees, or if the company has more than 300 employees itself, there must be a supervisory board, which must have at least three members, one of whom represents the workers. The supervisory board must meet at least three times annually.
GmbH	Germany	*Gesellschaft mit beschränkter Haftung.* Translates to "Company with limited liability." In Germany, a GmbH means that the company is incorporated, but it is not publicly traded (as public companies must be AG's). GmbH's are essentially partnerships without a legal name, and there must be at least two partners. There must be nominal capital of at least DM 50,000. Subsidiaries of AG's can be GmbH's.

GmbH	Switzerland	*Gesellschaft mit beschränkter Haftung*. Translates to "Company with limited liability." In Switzerland, a GmbH cannot have shares, and the owners of the company are entered into the commercial registry. Nominees can be used for anonymity.
HB	Sweden	*Handelsbolag*. Trading Partnership
hf	Iceland	*Hlutafelag*. Limited liability company.
IBC	Various	*International Business Company*. Used for offshore companies, in places such as Bahamas, Turks & Caicos Islands, etc.
Inc.	USA	Means a company is Incorporated, and the owners have limited liability. In the United States, companies can be registered in any of the 50 states -- many of the bigger corporations are registered in Delaware due to various regulations. Incorporation in the United States is very easy, and can be done for minimal fees.
Inc	Canada	Incorporated. Limited liability
I/S	Denmark	*Interessentskab*. Used in Denmark. General partnership; all partners have unlimited liability.
j.t.d.	Croatia	*Javno trgovacko drustvo*. Unlimited liability company.
KA/S	Denmark	*Kommanditaktieselskab*. Limited partnership with share capital
Kb	Sweden	*Kommanditbolag*. Limited partnership. There must be at least one partner with unlimited liability, although some partners can have limited liability. In Sweden, all Kommanditbolags must be registered with the Patent and Registration Office. Annual reports must be filed annually. If there are more than 10 employees, then the annual accounts must be audited. If there are more than 200 employees, the annual reports must be filed with the Patent and Registration Office.
Kb	Finland	*Kommanditbolag*. Limited partnership. This is a Swedish term, and since Finland is technically bilingual, this abbreviation can be used there, although the Ky designation is more common.
KD	Bulgaria	*Komanditno drushestwo*. Partnership
k.d.	Croatia	*komanditno drustvo*. Limited Partnership.
k.d.	Slovenia	*Komanditna druzba*. Limited Partnership -- there must be at least one limited partner and one unlimited partner.
KDA	Bulgaria	*Komanditno drushestwo s akzii*. Partnership with shares.
k.d.d.	Slovenia	*Komanditna delniska druzba*. Limited Partnership with shares.
Kft	Hungary	*korlátolt felelösségû társaság*. Limited liability company. Similar to the German GmbH, this type of company offers limited liability, although the shares cannot trade publicly. Requires only one shareholder. Minimum share capital is HUF 1 million.
KG	Austria	*Kommanditgesellschaft*. A partnership under a legal name. There must be two partners, at least one limited and at least one unlimited partner. The limited partner's liability is listed in the commercial register.
KG	Germany	*Kommanditgesellschaft*. A partnership under a legal name. There must be a minimum of two partners, at least one limited and at least one unlimited.
KGaA	Germany	*Kommanditgesellschaft auf Aktien*. A Limited Partnership that has shares.

KK	Japan	*Kabushiki Kaishi.* Joint Stock Company
Kkt	Hungary	*közkereseti társaság*, General Partnership. All partners have unlimited liability.
Kol. SrK	Turkey	*Kollektiv Sirket.* Unlimited liability partnership.
Kom. SrK	Turkey	*Komandit Sirket.* Limited liability partnership.
k.s.	Czech Republic	*komanditni spolecnost.* Limited partnership. One partner must have unlimited liability, although other partners can carry limited liability.
K/S	Denmark	*Kommanditselskab.* Limited partnership: at least one partner has unlimited liability and at least one partner has limited liability.
KS	Norway	*Kommandittselskap.* Limited partnership: at least one partner has unlimited liability and at least one partner has limited liability. Note: this was formerly written as K.S. and K/S, but financial law reform has dictated that periods and slashes should no longer be used.
Kv	Hungary	*Közös vállalat.* Joint Venture
Ky	Finland	*Kommandiittiyhtiö.* Limited Partnership.
Lda	Portugal	*Sociedade por Quotas Limitada.* Must have at least two shareholders, and paid in capital of at least 400,000 Escudos (800 Euros)
LDC	Bahamas	*Limited Duration Company.* A company, but it has a life of 30 years or less. Sometimes, these companies can be classified as partnerships in the United States.
LLC	USA	*Limited Liability Company.* Not really a corporation, and not really a partnership; it's something different altogether. Most states require at least two people to form an LLC, but some states require only one. An LLC has limited liability (hence the name), and unlimited life (i.e., the charter does not expire). In the United States, Corporations typically pay taxes, then distribute the profits via dividends, and the recipients must pay taxes on the dividends. An LLC allows for *pass through taxation*, which means that the income a company makes goes directly to the owners on their tax forms (even if the profits were not distributed). LLC's may have several different classes of stock.
LLP	USA	*Limited Liability Partnership.*
Ltd.	Various	*Limited.* Used in the UK and many former British colonies, as well as in other countries such as Japan. Indicates that a company is incorporated and that the owners have limited liability. This can also be used in the United States, and has the same meaning as Inc.
Ltda	Brazil	*Sociedade por Quotas de Responsabiliadade Limitada.* Means the owners have limited liability.
Ltée.	Canada	*Limitée.* French language equivalant of Ltd. (Limited). Indicates that a company is incorporated and that the owners have limited liability.
N.A.	USA	*National Association.* Used by Banks in the United States as a way of getting the word national into their name, which is a legal requirement under certain banking regulations.
NT	Canada	*iNTermediary.* Indicates that a company is a financial intermediary. However, companies are not required to use this abbreviation in their name if they are a financial intermediary -- it's merely a description.

NV	Netherlands	*Naamloze Vennootschap*. All publicly traded Dutch companies are NV's, but not all NV's are publicly traded. Dutch NV's require 100,000 NLG share capital or more.
NV	Belgium	*Naamloze Vennootschap*. This is Flemish (Dutch): In Belgium, many companies use both NV and SA (the French language equivalent).
NV	Netherlands Antilles	*Naamloze Vennootschap*. In the Netherlands Antilles, many foreign companies establish subsidiaries to shelter taxes.
NV	Suriname	*Naamloze Vennootschap*. All publicly traded companies are NV's, but not all NV's are publicly traded. NV's require SRD 5000 (USD 1850) share capital or more.
OE	Greece	*Omorrythmos*. Partnership. All partners have unlimited liability.
OHG	Austria	*Offene Handelsgesellschaft*. Partnership, with at least two partners. Partners have unlimited liability.
OHG	Germany	*Offene Handelsgesellschaft*. Partnership with a legal name, and must have at least two partners. Partners have unlimited liability.
OOD	Bulgaria	*Druzhestvo s Ogranichena Otgovornost*. Limited liability company. Requires at least two shareholders. Minimum share capital is 5000 leva (2550 Euro).
OÜ	Estonia	*Osaühing*. Private limited liability company. Minimum capital of EEK 40,000. This type of company doesn't trade on the stock exchange (as those are of the AS variety).
Oy	Finland	*Osakeyhtiö*. All corporations in Finland used to have this legal structure, although now, publicly traded companies will be OYJ (julkinen osakeyhtiö).
OYJ	Finland	*Julkinen osakeyhtiö*. Used by publicly-traded companies in Finland.
P/L	Australia	*Pty. Ltd.* Proprietary Limited Company.
PC Ltd	Australia	*Public Company Limited by Shares*
PLC	Various	*Public Limited Company* A publicly traded company and the owners have limited liability. Used in the UK, Ireland, and elsewhere. In the UK, a PLC must have at least UKP 50,000 in authorized capital, with UKP 12,500 paid up.
PMA	Indonesia	*Penenaman Modal Asing*. Foreign joint venture company.
PMDN	Indonesia	*Penanaman Modal Dalam Negeri*. Domestic Capital investment company
PrC	Ireland	*Private Company limited by shares.*
Prp. Ltd.	Botswana	Private company limited by shares.
PT	Indonesia	*Perseroan Terbuka*. Limited liability company.
Pty.	Various	Stands for Proprietary. Used in South Africa, Australia and elsewhere.
RAS	Estonia	*Riiklik Aktsiaselts*. State (owned) Joint Stock company.
Rt	Hungary	*Részvénytársaság*. Stock Company. All Hungarian publicly-traded companies are incorporated via this structure. However, an Rt doesn't necessarily mean that a company is publicly traded, and Rt companies may have as few as one shareholder. However, there are three board members required. Minimum share capital is HUF 10 million.
S. de R.L.	Mexico	*Sociedad de Responsabilidad Limitada*. Limited Partnership

List of Company Extensions appears at www.CorporateInformation.com.

S. en C. ´	Colombia & Peru	*Sociedad en Comandita.* Limited Partnership
S. en N.C.	Mexico	*Sociedad en Nombre Colectivo.* General Partnership
S/A	Brazil	*Sociedades Anônimas.* In Brazil, there must be at least two shareholders of an S/A, and they must have paid in cash at least 10% of the subscribed capital. The Capital must be deposited with the Bank of Brazil or other approved entity of the Brazilian Securities and Exchange Commission. Annual accounts must be published.
SA	Belgium	*Société Anonyme*, the Dutch language equivalent is NV. Initial capital must be BEF 2.5 million, and must be fully paid up upon incorporation.
SA	France	*Société Anonyme.*
SA	Greece	*Société Anonyme.* A Greek SA must have share capital of GRD 10 million.
sa	Italy	*Societá in accomandita per azioni.* Limited partnership with shares.
SA	Ivory Coast	*Société Anonyme.* Requires a minimum of seven shareholders. Each share must have a par value of at least 5000 CFA Francs,
SA	Luxembourg	*Société Anonyme.* There is a minimum of two shareholders, and a minimum share capital of LUF 1.25 million.
SA	Mexico	*Sociedad anónima.* Mexican SA's require a minimum capital of N$50,000. At least 20% of this must be paid-in at the time of incorporation. There is a minimum of two shareholders, but no maximum. Ordinary shareholder meetings can be called with 1/2 of the shares voting, and extraordinary meetings require a 3/4 vote. Shareholder meetings must take place in the city where the company is located, but board meetings can be abroad. 5% of annual profits must be allocated to a reserve until the reserve totals 20% of the capital.
SA	Morocco	*Société Anonyme.* SA's must have at least seven shareholders and a share capital of at least 10,000 dirhams, with each share having a minimum par value of 1000 dirhams.
SA	Poland	*Spólka akcyjna.* Stock company
SA	Portugal	*Sociedad Anónima.* Share capital minimum of PTE 5 million, and a minimum par value of PTE 1000 per share. There is a minimum of 5 shareholders. Companies are registered in the Commercial Registry.
SA	Romania	*Societate pe actiuni.* Limited liability company, can be publicly-traded. Can be set up by one or more shareholders (but not more than 50) and must have a minimum capital of RL 2 million (about $100.00). At present, capital contributed by a foreign investor is converted to lei at the prevailing market exchange rate in effect at the time the capital is contributed for accounting purposes only. Companies may maintain bank accounts in foreign currency. The registered capital is divided into equal shares whose value cannot be less than RL 100,000 (about $5.00 USD) each.
S.A.	Brazil	*Sociedade por Ações.* Privately-held company
SA de CV	Mexico	*Sociedad Anónima de Capital Variable* In Mexico, SA's can have either fixed or variable capital; this abbreviation is used for those with variable capital.
SAFI	Uruguay	*Sociedad Anonima Financiera de Inversion.* Offshore company.

S.A.I.C.A.	Venezuela	*Sociedad Anónima Inscrita de Capital Abierto* . Open Capital Company
SApA	Italy	*Societa in Accomandita per Azioni.*
Sarl	France & Other	*Société à responsabilité limitée.* Used in France and other French speaking countries. Private company.
Sarl	Luxembourg	*Société à responsabilité limitée.* Private company -- must have share capital of at least LUF 500,000, and 100% must be paid up on formation. Requires a minimum of one director and two shareholders.
SAS	Italy	*Societá in Accomandita Semplice. Limited Partnership.*
SC	France	*Société civile.* Partnership with full liability.
SC	Poland	*Spólka prawa cywilnego.* Partnership with all partners having unlimited liability.
S.C.	Spain	*Sociedad en commandita.* General Partnership.
SCA	Belgium	*Societe en commandite par actions.* Limited partnership with share capital.
SCA	Romania	*Societate in cómandita pe actiuni.* Limited liability partnership with shares.
SCP	Brazil	*Sociedade em Conta de Participacão.* This is a partnership where there is one partner assumed responsible for running the business. The other partners carry liability, but they do not have to be revealed.
SCS	Belgium & France	*Societe en Commandite Simple.*
S.C.S.	Brazil	*Sociedade em Comandita Simples.* Limited Partnership
SCS	Romania	*Societate in comandita simpla..* Limited liability partnership.
Sdn Bhd	Malaysia	*Sendirian Berhad.* Limited Liability Company.
SENC	Luxembourg	*Société en Nom Collectif.* General Partnership
SGPS	Portugal	*Sociedade gestora de participações socialis.* Holding Enterprise.
SK	Poland	*Spólka komandytowa.* Limited liability partnership.
SNC	France	*Société en nom collectif.* General Partnership
SNC	Italy	*Società in Nome Collettivo.* General Partnership.
SNC	Romania	*Societate in nume colectiv.* General Partnership.
SNC	Spain	General Partnership
SOPARFI	Luxembourg	*Société de Participation Financiére.* Holding company.
sp	France	*Societe en participation..*
SpA	Italy	*Società per Azioni..* Limited share company.
spol s.r.o.	Czech Republic	*Spolecnost s rucenim omezenym.* Limited liability company. This type of company cannot trade on the stock exchange, but owners have limited liability up to their unpaid deposits. This type of company must have share capital of at least CZK 100,000, and each shareholder must contribute at least CZK 20,000. A reserve fund of at least 10% of the share capital must be created from the profits. There is a maximum of 50 shareholders. Directors must be Czech citizens or residents. An annual audit is usually not required.
SPRL	Belgium	*Société Privée à Responsabilité Limitée.* French language equivalent to BVBA -- see that definition for more information.

Sp. z.o.o.	Poland	*Spólka z ograniczona odpowiedzialnoscia.* Limited liability company, privately-held.
Srl	Chile	*Sociedad de responsabilidad limitada,* Limited Liability company
Srl	Italy	*Società a Responsabilità Limitata.* Limited liability company.
Srl	Mexico	*Sociedad de responsabilidad limitada.* This type of limited liability company is really not that common in Mexico. A minimum of N$3,000 is required.
Srl	Romania	*societate cu raspondere limitata.* Limited-liability company, privately-held. Can be set up by one or more shareholders (but not more than 50) and must have a minimum capital of RL 2 million (about $100.00). At present, capital contributed by a foreign investor is converted to lei at the prevailing market exchange rate in effect at the time the capital is contributed for accounting purposes only. Companies may maintain bank accounts in foreign currency. The registered capital is divided into equal shares whose value cannot be less than RL 100,000 (about $5.00) each.
Srl	Spain	*Sociedad Regular Colectiva.*
td	Slovenia	*Tiha druzba.* Sole proprietorship.
TLS	Turkey	*Türk Limited Sirket.* Private Limited Liability Company
VEB	East Germany	*Volkseigner Betrieb.* Term for East German companies before Reunification. They were all either shut down, or converted into AGs or GmbHs by the Privitization Agency (Treuhandanstalt).
VOF	Netherlands	*Vennootschap onder firma.* General partnership.
v.o.s.	Czech Rep	*Verejna obchodni spolecnost.* General partnership. Partners are fully liable.

Appendix 3

Resource Lists - International

Selected Patent and Trademarks Agencies

Australia	www.ipaustralia.gov.au/patents/search_index.htm
Brazil	www.inpi.gov.br/
Bulgaria	http://www.bpo.bg/
Canada	http://brevets-patents.ic.gc.ca/opic-cipo/cpd/eng/introduction.html http://www.ic.gc.ca/app/opic-cipo/trdmrks/srch/tmSrch.do?lang=eng
Chile	www.dpi.cl/dpi_web/Frm_Login_default2.htm
China	http://www.sipo.gov.cn/sipo_English/
Colombia	www.bancopatentes.gov.co/
Czech Republic	http://www.upv.cz/cs.html
European Patent Office	www.espacenet.com/index.en.htm
Finland	http://patent.prh.fi/
France	http://www.inpi.fr/?rub_id=8
Germany	http://www.dpma.de/
Hungary	http://www.hpo.hu/English/
India	http://www.ipindia.nic.in/
Ireland	http://www.patentsoffice.ie/
Japan	www.jpo.go.jp/
Mexico	http://www.impi.gob.mx/wb/impi_en/Home
Netherlands	www.octrooicentrum.nl/
New Zealand	http://www.iponz.govt.nz/cms
Romania	http://www.osim.ro/
Russia	http://www1.fips.ru/wps/wcm/connect/content_ru/ru
Singapore	www.epatents.gov.sg/PE/

Slovakia	http://www.indprop.gov.sk/?introduction
Slovenia	http://www.uil-sipo.si/sipo/office/tools/home/
Spain	http://www.oepm.es/cs/
Switzerland	https://www.ige.ch/en.html
Turkey	http://www.turkpatent.gov.tr/portal/default.jsp
United Kingdom	http://www.ipo.gov.uk/

Enforcement Bodies

These foreign regulatory bodies and law enforcement entities are organized by region.

Africa/Asia/Pacific Enforcement Bodies

Australian Prudential Regulation Authority

Australian Securities and Investments Commission

Central Bureau of Investigation, India

Financial Services Agency, Japan

Financial Services Board, South Africa

Financial Services Commission, Mauritius

Hong Kong Monetary Authority

Hong Kong Securities and Futures Commission

Indonesian Capital Market Executive Agency (Bapepam)

InvestED - Hong Kong SFC

Monetary Authority of Macao

Monetary Authority of Singapore

Reserve Bank of India

Securities and Exchange Commission of Pakistan

Securities and Exchange Commission, Republic of the Philippines

Securities and Exchange Commission, Thailand

Securities and Exchange Surveillance Commission, Japan

Securities Commission of New Zealand

Securities Commission, Malaysia

UK Enforcement Bodies

Assets Recovery Agency

Financial Services Authority (FSA)

Gibraltar Financial Services Commission

Guernsey Financial Services Commission

Investment Management Regulatory Organisation

Isle of Man Financial Supervision Commission

Jersey Financial Services Commission

Lloyd's Insurance Market

Personal Investment Authority

Securities and Futures Authority

European Enforcement Bodies

Autorité des marchés financiers, France
BaFin - Federal Financial Supervisory Authority, Germany
Banking, Finance and Insurance Commission (CBFA), Belgium
Banque de France, CECEI, France
Banque de France, Commission Bancaire, France
Capital Market Commission, Greece
Comision Nacional del Mercado de Valores, Spain
Commission de Surveillance du Secteur Financier, Luxembourg
Commissione Nazionale per le Societa e la Borsa, Italy
Cyprus Securities and Exchange Commission
Czech National Bank
Danish Financial Supervisory Authority
Financial Market Authority, Austria
Financial Market Authority, Slovakia
Financial Regulator, Ireland
Financial Supervisory Authority of Norway (Kredittilsynet)
Finnish Financial Supervision Authority
Hungarian Financial Supervisory Authority
Insurance Supervisory Commission of the Republic of Lithuania
Malta Financial Services Authority
Netherlands Authority for the Financial Markets
Polish Securities and Exchange Commission
Portuguese Securities Market Commission (CMVM)
Securities Commission of the Republic of Lithuania
Securities Market Agency, Slovenia
Swedish Financial Supervisory Authority (Finansinspektionen)
Swiss Federal Banking Commission

Latin American / Caribbean Enforcement Bodies

British Virgin Islands Financial Services Commission
Cayman Islands Monetary Authority
Central Bank of Belize
Central Bank of The Bahamas
Chilean Securities and Insurance Supervisor
International Financial Services Commission, Belize

North American Enforcement Bodies

Autorité des marchés financiers, Canada
British Columbia Securities Commission, Canada
Commodity Futures Trading Commission (CFTC)

Financial Crimes Enforcement Network (FinCEN)
Investment Dealers Association of Canada
Manitoba Securities Commission, Canada
Market Regulation Services Inc., Canada
Mutual Fund Dealers Association of Canada
Office of the Superintendent of Financial Institutions, Canada
Ontario Securities Commission, Canada
Saskatchewan Financial Services Commission, Canada
Securities Commission of Newfoundland and Labrador, Canada

Appendix 4

Cynthia's Recommended Reading List

Recommended Reading

Books

Business Information Sources
by Lorna M. Daniells
University of California Press; 3rd edition (October 12, 1993) 0520081803

Corporate Investigations (Hardcover)
Edited by Reginald J. Montgomery & William J. Majeski
Lawyers and Judges Publishing; 2nd edition (March 30, 2005) 1933264020

Information Anxiety 2
by Richard Saul Wurman, David Sume & Loring Leifer
Que; 2Rev Ed edition (December 14, 2000) 0789724103

International Business Information on the Web: Searcher Magazine's Guide to Sites and Strategies for Global Business Research
by Sheri R. Lanza & Barbara Gilder Quint
Cyberage Books (May 2001) 0910965463

Introduction to Reference Work, Volume I (Hardcover)
by William A Katz
McGraw-Hill Humanities/Social Sciences/Languages; 8 edition (April 27, 2001) 0072441070

The Manual to Online Public Records
by Michael L. Sankey & Cynthia Hetherington
Facts on Demand Press; 2nd edition (July, 2010) 1889150568

Public Records Research Tips Book
by Michael L. Sankey
Facts on Demand Press; 1st edition (January, 2008) 1889150509

Strategic and Competitive Analysis: Methods and Techniques for Analyzing Business Competition
by Craig S. Fleisher & Babette Bensoussan
Prentice Hall; US Ed edition (March 29, 2002) 0130888524

Strauss's Handbook of Business Information: A Guide for Librarians, Students, and Researchers
by Rita W. Moss
Libraries Unlimited; 2nd edition (November 30, 2003) 1563085208

The Extreme Searcher's Internet Handbook: A Guide for the Serious Searcher
by Randolph Hock
Information Today, Inc.; 2nd edition (April 1, 2007) 0910965765

The Investigator's Little Black Book 3
by Robert Scott
Crime Time Publishing Company; 3rd edition (January 2002) 0965236943

The Invisible Web: Uncovering Information Sources Search Engines Can't See
by Chris Sherman
Cyberage Books (September 2001) 091096551X

The Skeptical Business Searcher: The Information Advisor's Guide to Evaluating Web Data, Sites, and Sources
by Robert Berkman
Information Today, Inc. (December 1, 2005) 0910965668

The Sourcebook to Public Record Information: The Comprehensive Guide to County, State, and Federal Public Record Sources
By BRB Publications, Inc. 10th Edition (March 2009) 1879792923

Magazines

PI Magazine	www.pimagazine.com
Searcher Magazine	www.infotoday.com/searcher/default.asp
Online	www.infotoday.com/online/default.shtml
Information Advisor	www.informationadvisor.com/
Cyberskeptic's Guide	www.cyberskeptic.com/cs/

Index

Notes:

Meet the Author

The founder of the Hetherington Group, Cynthia Hetherington, has been working with private investigators, security specialists, and law enforcement professionals since 1993. Using her Masters in Library Science & Masters of Information Systems Management, combined with over 20 years of computer experience, Cynthia has found a niche in the investigative industry, assisting members of the trade in online and Internet research. A widely-published author, Cynthia authored Business Background Investigations (2007) and co-authored The Manual to Online Public Records (2008), published by Facts on Demand Press. She is the Editor-in-Chief of Data2know.com: Internet & Online Intelligence Newsletter and has co-authored articles on steganography, computer forensics, internet investigations and other security-focused monographs. She is also recognized for providing corporate security officials, military intelligence units, and federal, state and local agencies with training on online intelligence practices.

The Hetherington Group, a firm dedicated to private, corporate, and government investigation and security, is composed of three branches. First, a firm recognized for providing corporate security officials, military intelligence units, and federal, state and local law enforcement agencies with training in online intelligence practices, techniques, and insights. Second, publisher of the DATA2KNOW.COM Internet and Intelligence Newsletter, a quarterly publication for investigators and security professionals. Third, one of the industry's most trusted private investigative divisions serving the needs of the private business sector. Hetherington Group retains some of the industry's most highly regarded nationally known investigative experts.

To contact Ms. Hetherington, please email her at ch@hetheringtongroup.com.